C000125163

THE HISTORY OF

HAMPSHIRE
COUNTY
CRICKET CLUB

THE CHRISTOPHER HELM COUNTY CRICKET HISTORIES

Series Editors:
Peter Arnold and Peter Wynne-Thomas

KENT
Dudley Moore, with a personal view by
Derek Underwood

MIDDLESEX
David Lemmon, with a personal view by
Denis Compton

THE HISTORY OF

HAMPSHIRE
COUNTY
CRICKET CLUB

Peter Wynne-Thomas

With a personal view by
JOHN ARLOTT

Statistics by Victor Isaacs

CHRISTOPHER HELM
London

© 1988 Peter Wynne Thomas and John Arlott
Christopher Helm (Publishers) Ltd, Imperial House,
21–25 North Street, Bromley, Kent BR1 1SD

ISBN 0-7470-0001-8

A CIP catalogue record for this book is available from the
British Library

Typeset by Cotswold Typesetting Ltd, Gloucester
Printed and bound by Biddles Ltd, Guildford, Surrey

CONTENTS

John Arlott, Hampshire's best-known supporter. (Courtesy of Patrick Eagar)

A PERSONAL VIEW
John Arlott

THE EDITOR'S BRIEF FOR THIS SECTION of the book is to give a personal view of the County's cricket. It is happy for the writer that the demand was not for a 'hard' history for this has been, from childhood to old age, a 'felt' experience. Anything here dealing with the County's cricket until 1934 is necessarily a matter of impressions, though it shall be brief. From 1935 onwards it is the product of first-hand observation but not, obviously, so close nor so complete as that of a constantly involved player.

The first impression grew out of absolutely nothing. Hampshire cricket during the years of the First World War was as minimal – virtually non-existent – as at any time in its long history. In 1917, thanks to 'the generosity of shareholders who had refunded dividends to the amount of £80 3s 5d, the bank overdraft had been paid off.' The County Ground at Southampton was used by military teams, often for war charity matches; there was, though, not even such a skeleton County fixture list as existed during the hostilities following 1939.

For a small boy in the north of Hampshire, the whole concept of cricket was remote. In 1919, though, men – club cricketers – emerged in Basingstoke to play a game which was a revelation to the youngster. Soon, too, an immensely strong Hampshire Club and Ground side came to play Basingstoke and North Hants. In the 1919 season of two-day matches, there were many opportunities for such missionary efforts as this and Hampshire were not slow to use them. The north of the County, of course, has always been something of a desert so far as the first-class game is concerned. Thus, the coming of a side with the great names in it was quite a local event. On one of these occasions the Hon Lionel Tennyson – grandson of the Laureate and later, of course, to become Lord Tennyson – provided the entertainment of one of his big hitting innings, a most memorable performance.

Even to a boy, though, it was apparent that this was not *quite* the real thing. Following first-class cricket in those days – with no radio nor television coverage – amounted generally to reading the morning papers, which also proved a sadly infallible method of absorbing cricketing clichés. When the issue of a match became close, though, it was the habit of little boys about Basingstoke to accost people coming off the London train with the evening paper and its stop press news, to ask: 'How are Hampshire getting on, mister?'; invariably followed in those days by: 'How many did Mead get?' No doubt the people able to watch the first-class game regularly might respect the amount of runs that Mead scored, if not his style; but for schoolboys unable to watch him he was the Hampshire idol. In the early post-war years (1919–26) Hampshire generally put up a respectable performance – twice sixth and three times seventh in the Championship – but from 1927 onwards until the outbreak of the Second World War they were always in the lower half of the table.

During their years of success and even for some time afterwards the main strength lay in seven men. They were:

The Honourable Lionel (later Lord) Tennyson, who played from 1913 to 1935
Alec Bowell, 1902–27,
Philip Mead, 1905–36,
Jack Newman, 1906–30,
Alec Kennedy, 1907–36,
George Brown, 1909–33,
Walter Livsey, 1914–29.

Of them all, it is a sad thought that only one, Jack Newman, was born in Hampshire.

The first was the captain – Major The Honourable Lionel Hallam Tennyson – who held that office from 1919 to 1933, when the County Committee found itself unable to stomach his wish to forsake the captaincy on several days of the season in order to report Test Matches for the popular press. A spectacular striker of the ball and highly convivial, he genuinely captained the side, even if his tactical perception was such that he missed tricks for which the professionals found it hard to forgive him. He threw vast parties in the restaurant cars of trains on the way to or from matches; he gambled prodigiously: a misplaced Regency buck, he was perhaps the most colourful character in the game of his time.

Philip Mead, the monolithic figure of Hampshire cricket for more than a quarter of a century, was, almost deliberately, not colourful. While he regarded his captain with a certain amount of affection, he had no wish to live that kind of life. Indeed, his whole basis of craftsmanship and self-respect was based on soundness in batting. A quite monumentally secure left-hander, he scored more runs – 48,892 – for Hampshire than anyone else ever scored for any team in the history of the game; and he played more matches – 700 – for the County than any other player. Back of any reservations they might have about his rate of scoring – which, incidentally, was much higher than it often appeared – Hampshire followers regarded him with immense respect. He was not such an attractive batsman as Frank Woolley, who played in 47 more Test Matches, but it is significant that Mead's average in all cricket was seven runs an innings higher; and, in Test Matches, some 13 better. He scored 153 centuries and, with that deceptive speed of his, made 668 catches. Coming from Surrey where he was not re-engaged after the 1904 season, he played for Hampshire until 1936: scored 1,000 runs in every season, including that last one, with them. When Hampshire did not re-engage him he joined Suffolk and, in 1938 at the age of 51, was top of their averages in the Minor Counties, with a figure of 76.80, and a year later not only was their most successful batsman but finished second in the second-class averages with a figure of 71.23. It came as a shock to meet him playing in a Red Cross charity match as late as 1942 when, 55 years old and on an impossibly rough wicket, he scored 33 not out in a total of 52. The opposing side could only manage 32. When he was blind, he used to come to – and enjoy listening to and talking about – Hampshire matches at Bournemouth, where he lived with his daughter until nearly his dying day.

George Brown was a most remarkable all-round cricketer. In June 1927, when Hampshire played Northants at Southampton, he went in first, bowled, fielded and kept wicket. Indeed, he both opened the innings and kept wicket for England against Australia; took 629 first-class wickets as a fast to medium bowler; was recorded in a pre-First-World-War reference book as 'the furthest thrower in the game', and made some of the most remarkable silly mid-off and silly point catches ever seen. One of the most lovable, generous and surprising of all cricketers, some almost unbelievable stories are told about him; most of them inherently true. He did, in fact, walk all the way from Cowley to Southampton with his cricket bag on his shoulder for a county trial; and, when asked how he would have got back if he had not been engaged, he said: 'They were bound to engage me.' He did, in 1913, chest-off a fast bowler (Arthur Fielder) who was pitching short, and then went on to score 71. In 1932, he faced up similarly to another fast bowler, Gerald Hodgson, took the ball on the chest, collapsed over the stumps; but got up to make 91. He kept wicket in a Test Match wearing his motor-cycling gloves; he wore them again in a county match in preparation for the decisive final Test of 1926, broke a finger and was unable to play for England. He was a fearless left-hand bat, a fine hooker and driver, with a favourite stroke he called 'the whip', which travelled to long-leg. When he bowled, his pace could be alarming. He kept wicket with almost nonchalant ease and some of his stops in the field were too fast for the eye to follow. A mighty cricketer, he was to be relished as both player and man.

Alec Kennedy, dour, physically tough, from Edinburgh; and Jack Newman, wiry, sensitive, from Southsea, were a most redoubtable pair of all-rounders. Kennedy bowled accurate medium to fast-medium swing and was one of the first practitioners of the leg-cutter, as well as a sound orthodox batsman. Spectators used to wonder at the regularity with which he put his feet down in precisely the same place in the run-up on every occasion, so that on a damp pitch his foot prints were cut out clean and sharp on the grass. He took 100 wickets in a season 15 times; scored 1,000 runs and did the 'double' five times, and for Players v Gentlemen at The Oval in 1927 he took all ten for 37.

Jack Newman took 100 wickets in a season nine times; scored 1,000 runs six times and performed the 'double' five times. He was possibly one of the unluckiest of all cricketers never to play in a Test Match.

Alec Bowell, one of the earliest players recruited by Hampshire from the Oxford district – his son also played for the County – was a patient, right-hand batsman, orthodox and with extremely neat footwork, who occasionally bowled fast-medium, and was a brilliant cover point. In 473 matches for the County from 1902 to 1927, he scored 18,509 runs and he eight times made a thousand in a season.

Walter Livsey, who came from Todmorden, was an extremely capable wicket-keeper, who played in three Test Trials and was unlucky never to appear for England – mainly due to injuries, though, of course, he was never a first Test choice. His family moved to London and, like Philip Mead, he was at one time on the staff at The Oval. When he joined Hampshire he was put into the first team as soon as he qualified, when he created something of a nine-days' wonder by stumping Jack Hobbs off a ball that pitched wide of the leg-stump and lifted.

This group of players formed the nucleus of the Hampshire XI which, on 14, 15 and 16 June 1922, produced one of the most remarkable recoveries in the history of cricket. The other members were W. R. Shirley, an Etonian considered the product of the coaching of his father who, indeed, subsequently wrote an instructional book called 'How to Play Cricket', A. S. McIntyre and H. L. V. – Harold – Day. McIntyre was a right-hand batsman from Hartley Wintney, who played 28 games for the County between 1920 and 1923. Day was a gifted rugby player for Leicester and England, and a highly capable batsman; indeed, he was invited to join the MCC party to South Africa in 1922–23, when four other Hampshire players were also chosen. However, he was then, as so often during his peak period of performance, unable to play because of his military duties. He did, though, score a thousand runs in 1922, when he had the opportunity of sufficient matches.

To complete the XI Stuart Boyes, who had played his first match in the preceding season, provided the slow left-arm spin. He was to stay with the County until war came in 1939: took 1,472 wickets – 100 in a season three times – and developed into a distinctly useful lower-order batsman and one of the very best short-leg fieldsmen in the country.

The match was Hampshire *v* Warwickshire at Edgbaston. Gough-Calthorpe, the Warwickshire captain, won the toss and they batted. Santall made 84 and Calthorpe 70 in their total of 223. Then 'not due in any way to the condition of the ground' Hampshire were put out for 15 by Harry Howell (six for 7) and Calthorpe (four for 4). Tradition among the older players has it that, in 'inviting' Lionel Tennyson to follow-on, Calthorpe suggested that they might play golf on the Friday and that Tennyson thereupon insisted that Hampshire would be batting on Friday and offered to bet on it; and his bets were invariably heavy; we may assume, too, that the odds would be long.

In the Hampshire second innings, starting 208 behind, Bowell (45), Mead (24) and Tennyson (45) all resisted gamely but their sixth wicket fell at 186. Shirley and Brown added another 85 but, when McIntyre was out for only five, eight wickets were down and they were only 66 in front. Then, quite amazingly, Livsey, who had never scored a century in his life, had a stand of 177 with Brown; and another of 70 for the last wicket with Boyes. George Brown had made 172; Livsey was 110 not out and Warwickshire were set 314 to win. Quite understandably they were rattled by the turn of events and the old firm of Kennedy (four for 47) and Newman (five for 53) dismissed them for 158 and Hampshire, to the bewilderment of the entire cricketing world, had won by 155 runs. It was related that Lionel Tennyson threw a quite prodigious party for the team on the train – but that it was the wrong train!

Although, of course, his major cricketing career was with Sussex, C. B. Fry played 44 matches for Hampshire between 1909 and 1921. Other and often valuable performers were B. G. Melle, T. O. Jameson, A. L. Hosie and Ronny Aird. C. P. Brutton from Eastleigh batted usefully, and J. P. Parker, unorthodoxly. Lew Harfield, a useful Hampshire-born batsman, W. L. Creese, a valuable all-rounder from South Africa, and 'Lofty' Herman, that quite invaluable pace bowler who served the County so well for so many years, came into the side. Occasionally too, Giles Baring and Peter Utley bowled quite fast. With the beginning of the 1930s John Arnold – a double international who played soccer for Fulham and England – Jim Bailey, left-handed all-rounder, the humorous 'Sam' Pothecary and Neil McCorkell, a very fine wicket-keeper-batsman, began to take over from some older players.

R. H. Moore, Hampshire's highest scorer in a first-class match, made 316 against Warwickshire at Bournemouth on 28 and 29 July 1937. Batting for 380 minutes, he hit three sixes and 43 fours.

In 1935, though, when Geoffrey Lowndes, a handsome batsman who could also bowl, took over the captaincy, the side was in flux and fell to 16th position in the table.

The accession of Richard Moore from Bournemouth to the captaincy in 1936 and the addition of Cecil Paris (captain in 1938) and Howard Lawson to the side, made for a climb to tenth position, but they slumped again – to 14th in 1937 and in 1938, when 26 players appeared in the eleven. Donald 'Hooky' Walker, a gritty left-hand bat and brilliant field came in, and the Rev J. W. J. Steele, an Army chaplain and seemingly tireless fast-medium bowler. They were, though, 15th in 1939 when Cecil Paris was forced, by the claims of his legal practice, to pass on the captaincy to G. R. Taylor. Shortly before the war, Gerry Hill, off-spinner and serviceable bat; Alec MacKenzie, a leg-spinner from Kent; and George Heath, who bowled fast outswing, came in. The end of the 1939 season saw the introduction at the Bournemouth Festival of Tom Dean, a tall leg-break bowler and brilliant short-leg, and Leo Harrison, athletic outfield and talented batsman, who was to prove a stalwart of the post-1945 scene. For some years to come, though, the few gestures at county cricket were but light relief for men taking occasional rest from war.

The post-war start was far better prepared than that after the First World War: this largely due to the caretaker committee of W. K. Pearce (in addition to his war duties) the well-liked 'Spranks' – W. L. Sprankling, who handled the secretarial side – and W. F. Hodges, the treasurer. John Blake, a Marine Commando officer killed in Yugoslavia, and D. F. 'Hooky' Walker, lost on a flight over Germany in 1941, were the war sacrifices.

Len Creese, Dicky Moore, Stuart Boyes and Alec MacKenzie did not return afterwards; the first three retired, Creese and Boyes to coaching, while MacKenzie continued from his outstanding RAF career into commercial flying. 'Sam' Pothecary and Lloyd Budd played little. On the credit side, Desmond Eagar became captain-secretary, chosen by the committee in preference to F. R. Brown, and he was to become an immense asset to the County. Neville Rogers was signed from Hampshire's old reservoir of talent, Oxfordshire, while Alan Shirreff, the Wykehamist David Guard, and two players who had been outstanding in the local game, Rodney Exton from Bournemouth and Harry Downer of Southampton, all added their sparkle of promise and talent to the post-war Hampshire.

Only just over a week after VE Day, Hampshire fielded a side for a one-day game against Southampton Police – one of the strongest club sides in the County – and won, but the real business of county cricket did not begin for them until 1946.

Then off they went on the old familiar zig-zag – up one season, down the next – to such an extent that the graph on page 23 seems almost a necessity; it shows their trials, tribulations and triumphs over two periods, 1919–39 and 1946–80 – a supporter's nightmare.

The basic eleven for 1946 was:

John Arnold
Neil McCorkell
Arthur Holt
Desmond Eagar
Jim Bailey
Neville Rogers
'Lofty' Herman
Tom Dean
Gerry Hill
Charlie Knott
George Heath

while, from time to time, Leo Harrison, 'Sam' Pothecary, Alan Shirreff, David Guard, Lloyd Budd, Harry Towner and Jack Godfrey made good the gaps when, in most cases, they were free from military or other duties. The County did well to finish tenth with an unsettled side lacking the old steadying influences. Desmond Eagar was, from the first, an enthusiast for good fielding and he was well supported by the appointment of Sam Staples as coach. Money began to come in from a public long starved of cricket; the whole atmosphere was a happy one.

Season 1947 saw them drop to last but one in the Championship when, after a good start, their results – which included the first tie in the County's history – fell away. The batting was useful but the bowling, headed by that burly enthusiast, Vic Ransom (fast-medium, 54 wickets at 27.22) from Surrey was largely sustained by George Heath, with 74 at 29.48: otherwise only Jim Bailey (51) reached 50 wickets. It was a blazing summer in which the fielding stood up well to the demands of pitch and weather.

In the next year, 1948, there was another surprise and again form somersaulted. It was the year of a joint benefit for John Arnold, Jim Bailey, 'Lofty' Herman, Gerry Hill and Neil McCorkell: surely a five-man benefit is unique. Most impressively, Jim Bailey, now 40 years old, performed the double of 1,000 runs and 100 wickets in Championship matches, a feat not often to be repeated for any county. Hampshire-born, he was top of both the batting and the bowling averages. Portly, good-natured, a thoughtful, left-arm slow bowler, he was a natural cricketer of whom the County did not make the best use. On the bowling side, Heath and Ransom both fell crucially back; but the spinners Bailey (109 wickets at 17.97) and Knott, supported by Herman (65 at 29.01) more than compensated. The great portent, though few realized it at the time, was the performance of Shackleton, who in 14 matches took 17 wickets at 30.52. The fielding was first-class; Gilbert 'Dinty' Dawson, a tall strong Yorkshireman, reached a thousand runs, so, too, did Arnold, Rogers and Eagar. Leo Harrison, best of friends, made a mark as a brilliant cover field, a batsman – handicapped, though he did not know it, by failing eye-sight – and as wicketkeeper where he showed considerable natural ability when frequently taking over from McCorkell.

After such promise, 1949 was another disappointment; 16th in the Championship. Although seven batsmen scored over a thousand runs in all matches, the bowling simply disintegrated. Johnny Arnold was, to his immense mirth, top of the bowling averages with two wickets at 20. Dick Carty was next with 29, but the attack was really carried by Knott and Shackleton, who took a hundred wickets apiece, and Bailey with 82 at 29.92. This was the beginning of Shackleton's great bowling career for the County. In that, his first full season, too, he fell only 86 short of a thousand runs. It was a period of flux. Pleasant Sam Staples – never very strong – died and was replaced as coach by the redoubtable Arthur Holt, who was to become a major figure in the development of Hampshire cricket. Dawson, Heath, Dean, Taylor and Prouton were not re-engaged. The fielding continued to improve and Walker, a Yorkshireman, established himself in the team as a dogged bat. Desmond Eagar continued to urge the fielding to ever higher levels.

The erratic form continued. The County finished 12th in 1952, albeit with the youngest side in the Championship. Jim Bailey retired; Johnny Arnold, missing the last 15 matches through sickness, was nevertheless top of the batting; and Shackleton (105 at 18.61) and Cannings (75 at 26.08) set up their bowling partnership. Derek Shackleton was one of the great masters of seam bowling; quite early he developed from a slavish inswinger to one who could move the ball both ways through the air and cut it with immense effect. Steady, but not monotonous, with immense variation of movement as well as pace, with a delightfully easy action, he was an artist at medium to – at times – surprisingly fast-medium pace. He could bat a bit, too; and he was unshaken by punishment on the few occasions it was ever meted out to him. Rogers was the monumental figure of the batting with 1,706 at 35.54. He was splendidly undisturbed by opposing pace at a time when Hampshire could not reply in the same terms. He was essentially a resistant batsman, as is reflected in the number of times he carried his bat through a collapsing innings. A fine short-leg fieldsman, he was, surely, the best post-war batsman never to play for England.

For once improvement was maintained in 1951 when the County finished ninth. Even that, though, was somewhat disappointing, for they led the table in May but faded in the second half of the season. Shackleton and Cannings – in the dressing rooms 'Shack and Vic' – made a persistent, eager, attack. The batting, led in every way by Rogers, with strong support from McCorkell, and with Gray and Harrison reaching a thousand for the first time, was serviceable, and the fielding continued to improve. At the end of the season McCorkell emigrated to South Africa.

By 1952, only Hill and Knott of the pre-war side held their places in a team which finished 12th. Colin Ingleby-Mackenzie attracted attention as an attacking left-hand bat. Jim Gray, a thoughtful and diligent professional, began to open the innings and to bowl useful medium-pace seam. The spin bowling, though, lost power even as the fielding improved.

The season of 1953 saw more promise than achievement; 14th place in the Championship was relieved only by the view to the future. Roy Marshall showed, even during his qualifying period, his immense potential as a batsman; but although Walker, Gray and Rogers all reached a thousand runs, the batting constantly collapsed. Henry Horton offered immense promise; despite his ugly stance, he played very straight, his defence was sound and his temperament superb; he was to be a pillar of the batting for many years to come. Alan Rayment offered decorative stroke play and some fine cover fielding, but, once more, the major burden was shouldered by Shackleton and Cannings, with the slow left-arm of Reg Dare the main offering of spin.

The season of 1954 was a watershed; it marked the entry of Peter Sainsbury, Mervyn Burden, Malcolm Heath and Mike Barnard into the side, with Harrison taking over as regular wicket-keeper and Marshall finishing his second and final year of qualification.

Surely enough, in their Jubilee year – 1955 – Hampshire achieved the best Championship position they had known in their entire history – third. The game and cheerful Gerry Hill had gone, leaving the way completely clear to the post-war generation. At the end of the season, too, they beat Surrey, the eventual Champions, at Bournemouth. Marshall, Rogers, Horton and Gray all reached a thousand runs; Shackleton and Sainsbury took a hundred wickets apiece and Cannings 94. Harrison kept wicket well enough to be chosen for Players v Gentlemen, but sadly, while still near the height of his powers, Rogers retired. Only 14 players were used in the County matches of the season; Horton, Barnard, Sainsbury and Rayment grew into the side and Marshall became one of the 'draw cards' of the country for his attacking batting.

If sixth position in 1956 seemed disappointing after the previous year's performance, it was, nevertheless, otherwise Hampshire's best since their sixth of 1922. Marshall was not happy on the slower wickets of that summer; Cannings broke a finger, and one or two of the young players experienced the not unusual fall away of a second full season.

The 1957 season was Desmond Eagar's last as captain of the County. He had served Hampshire well as an enterprising batsman, fine short-leg, utterly enthusiastic captain, and continued as a valuable secretary. He left to Ingleby-Mackenzie what was basically the Championship-winning side of 1961. Marshall was easily top of the batting but was well supported by Gray, Horton and Ingleby-Mackenzie, all of whom reached a thousand runs for the season. Shackleton was again monumentally reliable with 144

Championship wickets at 15.69; no one else approached him, though Heath – 67 at 26.37 – provided some hostile pace and lift, and was capped. Sainsbury set a County record with 56 catches.

Colin Ingleby-Mackenzie in his first year of captaincy, 1958, took Hampshire to the highest position they had yet known – second – and they might indeed have taken the Championship if they had not fallen away in August. Marshall batted brilliantly and prolifically; Shackleton once more bowled as a master – 161 Championship wickets at 15.33; Heath came through with 119 at 16.32; Burden filled in with useful off-spin; the fielding continued brilliant, while the young captain took chances and enjoyed himself. There emerged, too, a newly promising, genuinely fast bowler in D. W. White; only 14 wickets but his pace already menacing. A major setback of the season was their dismissal for 23 – their lowest post-war total – and 55 by Derbyshire.

Ingleby-Mackenzie's willingness to gamble with declarations was never more clear than in 1959, when four of Hampshire's 11 wins were achieved in the last over. They finished eighth but played – as their captain had promised – entertaining cricket. The batting was massive – Horton, Gray and Marshall all scored more than 2,000 runs; Baldry, the newcomer from Middlesex, and Ingleby-Mackenzie, over a thousand. Almost monotonously, Shackleton was top of the bowling, with 126 wickets – nearly twice as many as the next man – at 22.43, but only Heath (68 at 35.33) gave him worthwhile assistance. The spin bowling fell tragically back with Alan Wassell, a young slow left-arm spinner from Brighton, offering the best promise.

The old tantalizing pattern was renewed in 1960; Hampshire started well but finished 12th. As had not been the case for a long time, the catching was a weakness. As usual, though, there were compensations. Sainsbury scored a thousand runs and took 67 wickets with his slow left-arm spin, while White had 114 at 18.78. Sadly, he was twice no-balled for throwing by P. A. Gibb, but few others could fault his action and he was one of the most effective fast bowlers in the country. Again the batting was massive. Horton and Marshall topped 2,000 runs; Gray and Sainsbury 1,000. Once more Shackleton's figures told their own story; 128 wickets at 16.76. It was impossible to escape a great impression of the side's promise.

Surely enough, it was redeemed in 1961 when, for the first time, Hampshire became County Champions. It would be impossible to begrudge credit to Desmond Eagar for his planning and Arthur Holt for his coaching. On the field, however, the bold and cheerful captaincy of Colin Ingleby-Mackenzie had the advantage of tremendous batting by, once again, Marshall, Horton and Gray – all of whom made more than 2,000 runs – Sainsbury, Ingleby-Mackenzie and Danny Livingstone, all with 1,000. Once again, though, the key was Derek Shackleton – 153 wickets at 19.15 – with crucial support from the high pace of David White – 117 at 24.60 – aided by the spin of Burden, Wassell and Sainsbury, and the seam of Heath and Gray. It was an all-round achievement, with some splendid fielding. Mike Barnard, a quick-witted and fast-moving inside-forward with Portsmouth, was also a brilliant slip and an intelligent batsman. Danny Livingstone from Antigua was a batsman of application, occasional brilliance and constant value. Peter Sainsbury was one of the most useful all-rounders Hampshire ever had. A determined and courageous batsman, a slow left-arm bowler who, if he had spun the ball a little more, must have been a constant Test Match player, and an unquestionably great short-leg fieldsman, he had, and has, an immense zest for the game. The celebrations on the night of 1 September, after the title was won, will never be forgotten by those fortunate enough to share in them.

Only 17 players were used in that successful season, and two of them – Bernard Harrison and Bryan Timms – were specifically reserves. The eleven in action depended upon conditions, with a choice between the pace of Malcolm Heath and the spin of Burden or Wassell. The usual eleven was:

Roy Marshall
Jimmy Gray
Henry Horton
Danny Livingstone
Peter Sainsbury
Denis Baldry or Mike Barnard
Colin Ingleby-Mackenzie
Leo Harrison
Malcolm Heath or Alan Wassell or Mervyn Burden
Derek Shackleton
David White

It was almost to be expected, on Hampshire's record, that 1962 would prove a year of anti-climax and, surely enough, they finished tenth. White broke down and, despite Wassell's 58 wickets (at 27.58) the bowling depended more than ever on Shackleton, who bowled some 300 more overs – 1,717 – and took more wickets – 172 – than anyone else in the country. Gray had an outstanding batting season; he made more runs than Marshall. Livingstone and Horton, too, batted valuably: Sainsbury, Barnard and Ingleby-Mackenzie scored more than a thousand runs, but nothing could make good Shackleton's isolation. Even the catching faltered. Probably the happiest event of the County season occurred at its end, at Southampton, against Surrey, who declared at 363 for nine. They reduced Hampshire to 128 for eight, when the young Oxford leg-spinner, Alan Castell, came in to join Danny Livingstone. Together they put on 230, a County record for the ninth wicket. Livingstone, dropped before he scored, went on to 200 – his highest first-class innings – with 3 sixes and 22 fours. Castell made 76. Surrey declared again but could not bowl Hampshire out a second time. Hampshire failed to win but the game ruined Surrey's Championship hopes.

The club's centenary year, 1963, was another disappointment. Many days were lost to the weather and a series of slow wickets sadly affected the batting. Horton, Livingstone and, above all, Marshall had a bad year. Shackleton, despite his absence in four Test Matches, was top of the bowling – 116 Championship wickets at 14.83. White took 90 and Wassell 56, but their averages were poor. There was a series of heartening performances by Alan Castell, and early appearances by the fast bowler, Robert Cottam. The fielding was generally useful and Bryan Timms succeeded Leo Harrison as wicket-keeper. In the celebratory centenary match against a powerful MCC XI at Southampton

Dean Park, Bournemouth, used by the county since 1897, and the scene of R. H. Moore's 316 in 1937. (Courtesy of Patrick Eagar)

the County were beaten by 29 runs – but that after two declarations by their opponents – in a most entertaining game.

Another unhappy season was 1964 when Hampshire finished 13th but, somewhat infuriatingly, beat both Worcestershire, the Champions, and Warwickshire, the runners-up. Shackleton, who took 138 Championship wickets at 19.98, was the first in the country to 100 wickets, which he reached just short of his 40th birthday. White took 104, but at 30.27; Cottam had a poor season but fortunately Sainsbury weighed in with 52 wickets at 24.25. Livingstone was top of the batting, followed by Horton, Marshall, Gray and Sainsbury. A newcomer from Somerset, Geoffrey Keith, gave stylish batting promise. Sainsbury bowled usefully but the rest of the attack was disappointing.

Season 1965 yielded nothing better than 12th position despite the fact that Hampshire lost only four matches; they also bowled out Yorkshire for 23 – the lowest total in that County's Championship history – when Shackleton took two for 7, White six for 10, Cottam two for 2. Shackleton was again top of the bowling, while Cottam had a good season (73 at 16.53) and White took 85 (24.56); but, apart from Sainsbury, (62 at 23.79) the spin was poor. At the end of the season Colin Ingleby-Mackenzie retired. He had captained the side with immense spirit, no little humour and with far greater shrewdness than many realized; he is still remembered with affection.

In 1966, Roy Marshall's first season as captain, the County finished 11th. Marshall himself, as new captains do not always do, batted extremely well; but the middle order fell away. It is monotonous to say that, once again, Shackleton was top of the bowling – 112 wickets at 17.11 – followed by Cottam with 61 and White with 103. The spin, however, was completely ineffective; with Castell, sadly by many standards, yet understandably, switching from leg breaks to seam-up. Barry Reed, a Wykehamist, opened with Marshall, and in his first full season made 1,000 runs and excelled as a cover field: he relished his cricket.

The 1967 season saw Hampshire 12th and, once more, the deficiency lay in spin bowling. It saw them losing far too many matches and, sadly, drawing even more (13). They simply could not get other sides out, though Cottam (102 wickets) and White (93) rendered good pace support to the tireless and infallible Shackleton (112 at 16.39). Four batsmen, too, topped a thousand runs – Sainsbury, Marshall, Livingstone and Reed – while Henry Horton though deciding to retire, still averaged 25.95. David Turner from Chippenham looked a promising left-hand bat; so did Richard Gilliat, Carthusian and Oxford Blue, who average 26 in his 13 matches; Bryan Timms again kept wicket well.

There was an immense leap forward in 1968 – to fifth – thanks largely to four players: the South African newcomer, Barry Richards, a magnificent and imperious stroke-maker, who scored 2,039 runs at 48.54, and the three seam bowlers, Cottam, Shackleton – who for once had to yield place in terms of wickets taken – and White, with just enough spin from Sainsbury to hold something near an economic balance. Marshall, though, began to lose form and the young Turner, Lewis, Wheatley and Jesty were not yet quite ready. It was, though, an immensely heartening season for the County.

1968 was Derek Shackleton's last full season. He had been an outstanding fast-medium bowler, harnessing swing, cut and nip off the pitch to an immaculate length. He set a record by taking a hundred wickets in 20 consecutive seasons; only Rhodes performed the feat more often, but he did not do so consecutively. Shackleton's 2,669 wickets (at 18.23) for Hampshire is a County record. He joined the staff in 1948, was capped in 1949, had a benefit of £5,000 in 1958 and a testimonial of about the same amount in 1967. He retired to become the coach at Canford School and a first-class umpire from 1979 to 1981. His son, Julian Shackleton, played for Gloucestershire irregularly over the period 1971–78.

The loss of 'Shack' was the major factor Hampshire had to make good in 1969. In the even, their best hopes were justified when they finished fifth once more and were second in the Sunday League despite injuries to six players. Ironically, Shackleton, recalled for a single match, finished top of the bowling averages with seven wickets at 13.57. The main attack, however, lay in the hands of White and Cottam, with some support from Sainsbury, Castell and Jesty. The fielding was again good and the lower order batsmen often made useful contributions. Jesty began to show general all-round talent, Bob Stephenson took over as wicket-keeper, and the West Indian, John Holder, looked a lively pace bowler.

The apparently inevitable disappointment came in 1970 with tenth place. Richards was away for the five matches of the Rest of the World against England: White, Gilliat, Cottam and Reed also missed a number of games. Cottam's 75 wickets was the largest haul, but Holder, White, Sainsbury and Castell all took over 40. A young Barbadian batsman, Gordon Greenidge, who had gone to school in Reading, was brought in at the age of 19 for seven matches and responded with an average of 35.10, Marshall – 1,497 in Championship matches, at an average of 39.39 – played some superb innings and captained the side thoughtfully in his last season before giving way to Richard Gilliat. Marshall was a batsman of outstanding class who was unfortunate through the qualification system of his time to be ruled out of what could otherwise have been a considerable Test career; in fact he played for West Indies on four occasions only. He continued to turn out for the County for another couple of seasons before he retired.

An improvement of a single place saw Hampshire ninth in 1971, when Sainsbury so narrowly missed performing the double. He scored 959 runs with no centuries and headed the Hampshire bowling with 101 wickets at 18.15. Cottam took 72 wickets, and a new player, Lawrence Worrell from Barbados, 44. Worrell was an all-rounder who did not maintain his undoubted early promise and left at the end of 1972, after which he played for Dorset. The younger players, Greenidge, Jesty and Stephenson, continued to improve, but White had a disappointing season through injury. In fact he never fully recovered from a cartilage operation; Cottam was released to join Northants on personal grounds, and Livingstone left the county.

At the end of 1972, Castell retired as the result of a recurrent shoulder injury, and Holder returned to the West Indies. On the credit side, Robert Herman – son of 'Lofty' – a strongly built fast-medium bowler, joined the County from Middlesex. Once again they finished ninth. Richards, Marshall and Greenidge all made 1,000 runs and Richard Lewis, a personable right-hand batsman from Winchester, began to make good the claims that had been made for him as a stylish quick scorer. David O'Sullivan, a slow left-arm bowler from New Zealand, came in for a few matches, so did Tom Mottram, a tall pace bowler from Lancashire, and John Rice, a useful-looking all-rounder, from Chandlers Ford. The bowling was not highly penetrative but the wickets were spread over seven players, three of them spinners. Richard Gilliat had extremely high fielding standards, similar to those of Desmond Eagar: a stylish left-hand bat, with the knack of drawing the best out of his players, he encouraged the younger men most effectively.

Impossible, though, not to admit that even their best friends were amazed to find Hampshire once more Champions in 1973. They started the season well and finished it strongly, with a settled side; in fact they used only 13 players and one of them, Andy Murtagh, played no more than five matches – he was a Southampton University student, a Dubliner of considerable fielding ability who sometimes proved an inspiration in that capacity. It was, in fact, an immense team effort in which six bowlers took 35 or more wickets at averages between 17.73 and 23.76. Sainsbury was top of the bowling, with Mike Taylor – an all-rounder acquired from Nottinghamshire – Jesty, O'Sullivan, Mottram and Herman hard on his heels. The catching was good and the batting sound for a long way down. Greenidge, a splendid striker of the ball, made an unusual opening partnership with the South African, Richards. Greenidge played with a straight bat, a basically correct technique and an immense power of stroke. He led Richards in the averages, with main support from Sainsbury, Gilliat, Jesty, Turner and Taylor.

The basic eleven was:
Barry Richards
Gordon Greenidge
David Turner
Richard Gilliat
Trevor Jesty
Peter Sainsbury
Richard Lewis or David O'Sullivan
Mike Taylor
Bob Stephenson
Bob Herman
Tom Mottram

Perhaps the most cruel of Hampshire's historic misfortunes was their failure to retain the Championship in 1974 when they finished second, two points behind Worcestershire. They took the lead in the Championship early in the season and led until the end, when in the last three matches five days' play were lost to rain. They had, in fact, a stronger side than in 1973. The West Indian, Anderson Roberts, had been exchanged as the overseas player for O'Sullivan, who had never really settled down. Roberts, on the other hand, was not only the fastest bowler in the country – probably in the world – but a thinking fast bowler: master not only of the bouncer, but also of the 'slow bouncer' – ask Colin Cowdrey. He was the first to a hundred wickets and finished top of the national averages, with 119 wickets at 13.62. Only one other bowler (Bedi, Northamptonshire) achieved a hundred in the season and Roberts' average was as much as 1.42 better than the next man's. In the event, Mottram was the unlucky player to be dropped: his quality was genuine but not always appreciated. Herman was second to Roberts, and Taylor third. Both had averages better than 18. Richards was again comfortably top of the batting, well supported by Gilliat, Turner, Greenidge and the quite invaluable Taylor. A fairly settled, competent and, indeed, powerful eleven was forced to sit completely inactive through the last match of the season – against Yorkshire – in which not a ball could be bowled, while Worcestershire contrived the four bowling points which gave them the title by two points.

Continuing to maintain considerable strength, Hampshire finished third, 17 points behind the Champions, Leicestershire, in 1975. It was, though, fair if not complete, satisfaction that they won the John Player League, reached the semi-final of the Benson & Hedges Cup, the quarter-final of the Gillette Cup and won the Fenner Trophy. While Roberts and Greenidge were on duty with West Indies, winning the Prudential World Cup, Hampshire lost two out of three matches; decisively, Taylor was missing for eight weeks in mid-season from injury, and Roberts missed the last three. Nevertheless, Roberts ended top of the national bowling averages. The side's ultimate weakness lay in dropped catches. This, however, was probably the most entertaining batting side the County ever fielded. Richards again played in brilliant fashion; Gilliat, Greenidge and Turner also scored a thousand runs and Sainsbury 834. Jesty, Sainsbury and Rice, and the new slow-left arm bowler, John Southern, gave Roberts most assistance, though Taylor, when fit, was intelligently useful. Sadly, though, Herman fell away.

The basic twelve was:
Barry Richards
Gordon Greenidge
David Turner
Richard Gilliat
Trevor Jesty
Mike Taylor
Peter Sainsbury
John Rice
Bob Stephenson
Anderson Roberts
John Southern
Bob Herman

Of 1976 it is tempting to say that Hampshire reverted to type. It was a season of near misses. They once stood second in the Championship but finished 12th. They bade fair to retain the John Player League; only just failed to reach the final of the Gillette Cup. Crucially, though, they were without Roberts and Greenidge, who were making major contributions to the West Indies' Test success. Richards, who averaged 49, once more stood out from all the rest as a batsman; Turner and Jesty scored a thousand runs, and Gilliat was barely short of it. There were many injuries. It must be said, though, that, on the whole, the bowling was simply not good enough. Sainsbury, gamely taking 66 wickets at 18.72, was all too substantially top of it, otherwise, only Southern (56 at 32.64) took even as many as 40 wickets.

There were those who in 1977 fancied Hampshire's chances in all four competitions. Their results, though, were poor: they were only 11th in the Championship. There were injuries to Gilliat, Greenidge, Richards and Turner. Greenidge was easily the most successful batsman, usefully backed by Jesty. Richards had, for him, a poor season and, above all, so did Roberts, who took only 40 wickets, although at 19.82. Moreover, only Southern (53 at 31.32) took over fifty wickets. Sainsbury had now retired to become the County coach and was doing his utmost with the young all-rounders, John Rice and the Shaftesbury-born Nigel Cowley. Cowley was to prove a game all-rounder; patient batsman and useful off-spinner, and Rice was a consistent trier. Herman left, but the gravest loss to the playing strength was the all-round ability and loyalty of Peter Sainsbury. Tragically, too, soon after the end of the season, Desmond Eagar died: after his enthusiastic playing days, he became, as Secretary, the architect of much of the success the County enjoyed.

The season of 1978 was not unhappy in terms of playing results; Hampshire were eighth, and won the John Player League. On the other hand, with five matches to go, Richards and Roberts, for reasons of their own, walked out of the Club for ever. It was immensely to the credit of those left behind that the services of two such fine players were made good to take the John Player title. Gordon Greenidge had another fine batting season; he was third in the national averages with 1,771 runs at 53.66. A bold, forthright batsman, he was to serve the County well for many years. Otherwise, only Turner scored a thousand runs. Roberts took 27 wickets, but Southern was again effectively the main bowler with 72 wickets at 24.80. Cowley took 52, and a young seam bowler, Keith Stevenson from Derbyshire, had 47.

The season of 1979 was bound to be hard going and few could be justifiably disappointed with the results. Their leading batsman and bowler, Barry Richards and Anderson Roberts – two of the finest players in the world – had gone, and Richard Gilliat, a sound and intelligent captain, had left to go into business. Bob Stephenson was the new captain and as a realist, he could not have been too surprised at dropping four places to 12th in the Championship. Greenidge again finished top of the batting despite losing a month to the World Cup Competition. His strongest batting support came from Rice, Turner and a newcomer, David Rock, a tall upstanding player of immense promise. The bowling suffered from the month's absence of Malcolm Marshall, the newly acquired West Indian fast bowler who, like Roberts in his time, was one of the fastest in the world. He only took 46 wickets – at 20.80 – and Keith Stevenson with 61 at 23.91 was the backbone of his support. There were experiments with a number of young players, the most promising of whom were to prove Mark Nicholas and Paul Terry. The simplest summary of the County's performances is that the bowling was useful; the batting unreliable.

The year of 1980 was an apparent nadir, yet it is difficult not to observe its promise. Hampshire could still feel their previous losses but now Greenidge and Marshall – their two best players – were absent for most of the summer on the West Indian tour. So this was a time to count new assets: Chris Smith, the South African batsman who headed the batting; Tim Tremlett, son of Maurice Tremlett of Somerset, who emerged as a most promising all-rounder; Mark Nicholas, a useful batsman who also offered occasional bowling promise; Bobby Parks, of the great cricketing family, who kept wicket; and Nick Pocock, the captain with a hard row to hoe. Hereabouts there were a number of unsuccessful recruiting experiments. No one scored a thousand runs in Championship matches and no bowler took more than 48 wickets. It would have been depressing if there had not been such clear and bright hope for the future.

There this meagre, slavish yet enthusiastic slice of 'history' must end. Since then some days have seen high success but there have still been the old familiar slumps. On the whole, though, results have been better than they ever were before. To follow the County once again at a distance and through the newspapers is oddly nostalgic. The remoteness has been eased by visits from Leo Harrison, Neville Rogers, Mike Barnard, Mark Nicholas and Paul Terry, who have brought a touch of the first-hand; like the old players' meetings at the County Ground. The young man who paid his Life Membership subscription – now seen as an absolute bargain, but which he could then ill afford – in 1946 has, indeed, had his moneysworth. It was, in truth, a happy commitment for life. May those who carry on the story have the same deep delight; and if they suffer the same disappointments, may they also enjoy the same soaring triumphs.

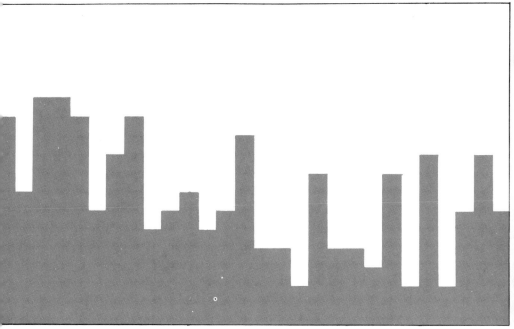

9 '20 '21 '22 '23 '24 '25 '26 '27 '28 '29 '30 '31 '32 '33 '34 '35 '36 '37 '38 '39 '46 '47 '48 '49 '50 '51 '52

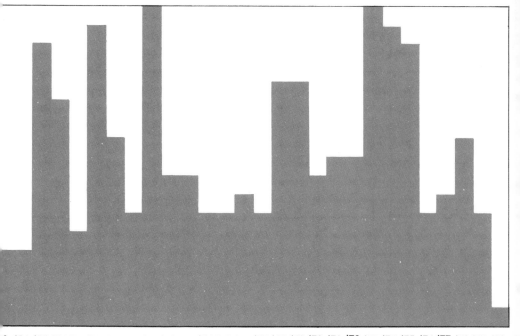

3 '54 '55 '56 '57 '58 '59 '60 '61 '62 '63 '64 '65 '66 '67 '68 '69 '70 '71 '72 '73 '74 '75 '76 '77 '78 '79 '80

BEFORE THE COUNTY CLUB

THE STORY OF HAMPSHIRE CRICKET before county matches became regimental, is dominated by the mystical Hambledon Club. Responsibility for this state of affairs rests on the shoulders of John Nyren and his amanuensis, Charles Cowden Clarke. They wrote a book, published in 1833, which has captured the imagination of successive students of the game. It chronicled the affairs of the Hambledon Club and its cricketers and possesses a literary style which evokes the atmosphere of late 18th century cricket in a way in which, much later, Neville Cardus was to bring to life Old Trafford and the Lancashire players of his youth.

John Nyren was the son of Richard Nyren, who had captained the Hambledon team at its zenith, but he was a man in his sixties when he described the Hambledon of his teens and too many historians have forgotten the way memory plays tricks with the scenes of one's childhood. The descriptions in the 1833 book have been taken too often as absolute fact, with the result that Hampshire's early cricket history has become distorted and then in more recent times modern writers, in a plausible effort to dispel the myths, have moved the other way, reducing Hambledon to a more minor role than that to which it is entitled.

Aside from John Nyren's memoirs, the factual details were further clouded by the game's first noted historian, the Reverend James Pycroft, who came on the scene in time to interview the last major surviving cricketer of the Hambledon era, William Beldham. Like Nyren, Beldham was an elderly man at the time when he described Hambledon to Pycroft and again his statements must be judged in that light.

Fortunately for history, Hambledon does not have to rely entirely on the reminiscences of Nyren and Beldham, since newspapers from the 1750s and even before carried notices, if not scores, of the principal cricket matches. Also by a stroke of luck the Minute Books and Account Books of the Hambledon Club from 1772 to 1796 survived and were published in 1923, with F. S. Ashley-Cooper acting as Editor.

Before tackling the tangled saga of the Hambledonians, it is as well to detail the few surviving facts concerning Hampshire cricket prior to the rise of the famous Club. This,

however, is something which will not occupy a great deal of
the reader's time, since such details are very sparse.

In 'School Days of Eminent Men' by John Timbs, it is
noted that Thomas Ken (afterwards Bishop Ken) 'used to
yield a cricket bat' when at Winchester – he attended that
school from 1655 to 1666.

The next Hampshire reference is as obscure:

> Thursday Sept. 5. A great cricket match was played in
> Penhurst Park, the seat of the Earl of Leicester, between
> Kent, headed by Mr Edwin Stead Esq, and Sussex, Surrey
> and Hampshire, by Sir William Gage, for 100 guineas,
> eleven on a side. (*London Journal*, 6 September 1729).

A return match was played at Lewes, but there is no note in
the brief notices to show the identity of the Hampshire
element in the combined counties eleven. Sir William Gage,
the promoter, came from the Lewes area of Sussex.

The diligent researcher Timothy McCann has discovered,
in the family papers at Goodwood, the next Hampshire
reference and this in fact leads indirectly to Hambledon. In
1741 a match was played between Portsmouth and Slindon.
The Sussex village of Slindon, being adjacent to Goodwood
House, was under the patronage of its owner, the Duke of
Richmond, and had developed a side strong enough to
challenge the leading club in England, which was the London
team based at the Artillery Ground.

Captain of the Slindon eleven in its hour of greatness was
Richard Newland, also considered the best batsman in
England. The notice of the village's most famous match
comments:

> On Monday, 6th September. Will be played in the
> Artillery Ground the greatest match at cricket that has
> been played for many years, between the famous parish of
> Slendon (*sic*) in Sussex and eleven picked gentlemen of
> London. And as 'tis expected there will be the greatest
> number of people that ever was known on a like occasion,
> it's to be hoped – nay, desired – that gentlemen will not
> crowd in, by reason of a very large sum of money which is
> laid that one of the Sussex gentlemen gets 40 notches
> himself. To begin exactly at twelve o'clock and if not
> played out that day, to be finished the Wednesday
> following. Wickets to be pitched by twelve o'clock on the
> forfeit of 100 guineas. The above parish has played 43
> matches and lost but one.

It is most probable that Richard Newland was the batsman involved in the 40 notches, but the detailed scores of this game, like so many of that era, are lost, as indeed are most of Newland's scores, though it is known that he scored 88 for England against Kent in 1745.

In the adjacent village to Slindon, Eartham, lived the Nyren family and among them was Richard Nyren, born about 1736, a nephew of Richard Newland. Nyren took a liking to cricket and received encouragement and no doubt coaching from his illustrious uncle.

Richard Nyren moved to the Hampshire village of Hambledon and became an integral part of the Hambledon cricket team. There is insufficient data to pinpoint when cricket began to be played in Hambledon, or indeed when the village side was in effect taken over by the nobility in the guise of the Hambledon Club. The earliest extant reference to cricket there is dated 1756, in which year the following notice appears in the *Reading Mercury* of 8 September: 'Lost at the Cricket Match on Broad Halfpenny on Wed Aug 18th, a dog', Broad Halfpenny being the site of the Hambledon cricket ground from the earliest recorded games at the village, though it is situated more than a mile from the village itself. The only building near it at that time was the Bat and Ball Inn, of which Richard Nyren was landlord before he moved to the George Inn in the 1760s.

In the same year as the lost dog – 1756 – Dartford played three matches against a team which is variously reported to be Hampton or Hambledon. All that is known is that Dartford won all three matches and that one of the games was played on the Artillery Ground. More definitely the reference to Hambledon playing London in 1750 is a mistake of the historian Waghorn. This side was certainly Hampton.

What makes one look twice at these 1750s references to Hambledon is the fact that the next authentic notice of the Hambledon team does not appear until 1764. This reads as follows:

On Monday September 12. A great cricket match that has been so long depending between the gentlemen of Hambledon, in Hants, called Squire Lamb's Club, and the gentlemen of Chertsey, was played at Laleham Borough. Chertsey went in first and got 48 notches; Hambledon got 76. Second innings, Chertsey headed [added] 87; John Edmonds and Thomas Baldwin turned the game by getting upwards of 40 notches. Time expired, and they postponed it till next morning, when Chertsey went in and got 12 notches; Hambledon went in, three were out for 4 notches; the next five won the game. Chertsey had three men much hurt and Hambledon had two, Mr Steward [Stewart] having a finger broke and his knee sprained. On this match great sums were depending.

In 1759, one of the England team who played against Dartford is 'Nyland' of Sussex. This is believed to be the first reference to Richard Nyren as a cricketer. He would then be about 24 – the England side does not contain any Hampshire players.

As regards the establishment of 'Hambledon Club', as opposed to a team representing the village, the historians have left a wide selection of dates for posterity to choose from. Pycroft started the trail with a quote from William Beldham:

> If you want to know, sir, the time the Hambledon Club was formed, I can tell you this; – When we [Farnham] beat them in 1780, I heard Mr Paulett say, 'Here have I been thirty years raising our club, and are we to be beaten by a mere parish?'

Taken as it stands this puts the date of the formation of Hambledon as 1750, but unless some scores were lost in the 1780s, the year of Farnham's victory was 1786, not 1780, which moves the formation to 1756. If this latter date is correct it seems most odd that matches by the Club were not printed fairly regularly in the press until 1764 – and indeed that the 1764 reference should call the Hambledon side 'Squire Lamb's Club'. Rowland Bowen suggested that Pycroft misheard 30 for 13, which fits in with the theory that Mr Paulett (actually the Reverend Charles Powlett) virtually took over the side in 1773–74 when he was made a Steward of the Club (this fact is noted in the Minutes of 1 October 1773). Powlett was no ordinary cleric, he was the illegitimate son of the 3rd Duke of Bolton and having graduated from Cambridge in the 1750s was Curate of Itchen Abbas from 1763 to 1792. The Squire Lamb of 1764 is believed to be Squire Land, who lived at Park House, Hambledon, at that time.

Whatever the speculation regarding the date of formation, there can be no arguing but that the 1770s and early 1780s

An early cricket print, depicting a match at Broadhalfpenny Down, Hambledon, in 1777. (Courtesy of the Mansell Collection)

were the great days of Hambledon and that the combination of Mr Powlett and Richard Nyren was the reason for this. During that period some leading amateur cricketers of the day joined the Club – Philip Dehaney, Thomas Ridge and the 2nd Earl of Northington among them – but it was not until the closing years of the 1780s that such names as the Earl of Winchilsea, T. A. Smith and the future 4th Duke of Richmond became members.

Another facet of Hambledon cricket which has divided historians is the nomenclature of its matches. Rowland Bowen, after much probing, announced, 'the Hambledon Club never played an eleven-a-side game in all its existence . . .' He reached this conclusion by discovering that most if not all the matches which Arthur Haygarth titled 'Hambledon Club v . . .' had other titles in newspaper notices, usually, Hampshire, sometimes Mr So-and-so's XI.

As in other cases of this sort historians have tied themselves in knots, when broadly speaking everyone is correct. The teams were promoted by the Hambledon Club and as such were rightly called the Hambledon Club Eleven; the majority of players were qualified for Hampshire by birth and/or residence and therefore Hambledon fielded a team which was either 'Hampshire' or 'Hampshire with 1 or 2 given men' and then, as in the 1764 reference, the newspaper describes the side as 'the gentlemen of Hambledon, called Squire Lamb's Club'.

The academics are creating a purely paper argument when they attempt to split the teams under two or three headings. In the case of the other counties of the 18th century exactly the same state of affairs ruled, with, for example, Dartford being also called 'Kent', and Croydon, 'Surrey' etc.

Supporters of Hampshire County Cricket are thus quite justified in calling most Hambledon teams 'Hampshire'.

Another similar argument has involved the role of the Hambledon Club as the authority on the Laws of Cricket immediately prior to MCC. The three alterations in the Laws during the supremacy of the Hambledon Club – and despite these side issues, no one doubts that the team produced by that Club was the strongest in England – were the control of the width of a bat, the addition of the third stump and the change from one bail to two.

An updated edition of the 1755 Laws, which Col Rait Kerr states were printed in 1774, was printed in Sevenoaks, but a similar edition was printed in London and dated 1774. These both list the names of the Committee which revised the Laws and the names include not only the Rev Charles Powlett, but also Philip Dehaney and Charles Coles, two other members of the Hambledon Club.

On the three points noted, there is a written extant note which proves that the Hambledon Club agreed to a limitation in the width of the bat in 1771 and this rule was inserted in the 1774 Laws as revised at the Star and Garter.

The third stump was introduced as a result of the match between Hambledon and Kent in 1775, when 'Lumpy' Stevens several times sent the ball through the wicket without disturbing the bail, when John Small was batting for Hambledon, but this inclusion of another stump did not appear in any extant version of the Laws until 1785 and the use of two bails is first noted in a version of the Laws printed about 1786 in Maidstone.

One small point on the document governing the width of the bat: it contains three signatures: Richard Nyren, Thomas Brett and John Small – three Hambledon professionals and not as one might expect the officials of the Hambledon Club.

There is no evidence to show that the Hambledon Club acted as controllers of the Laws though as the most powerful club of the time the views of their members and players obviously carried much weight when revisions were made.

All the above remarks concerning Hambledon and its affairs do not however mention their cricketing record. Taking the list of Hambledon matches printed by Ashley-Cooper in his 'Hambledon Cricket Chronicle' as a basis from which to draw some conclusions, Hambledon opposed England in 37 eleven-a-side matches between 1772 and 1788,

HAMPSHIRE *v* ENGLAND

Played on the Vine, Sevenoaks, 8 and 9 July 1774

HAMPSHIRE WON 169 RUNS

HAMPSHIRE	FIRST INNINGS		SECOND INNINGS	
J. Aylward	run out	29	c Minshull	61
R. Francis	b Bullen	4	b Wood	1
J. Small sen	b Bullen	10	run out	20
T. Sueter	c Bullen	12	b Bullen	30
G. Leer	b Frame	28	b Wood	14
*R. Nyren	b Bullen	10	c Minshull	18
P. Stewart	not out	14	b Colchin	7
'Lumpy' (E. Stevens)	c Wood of Surrey	21	b Colchin	11
E. Aburrow	b Bullen	8	b Wood	7
T. Brett	b Bullen	2	not out	4
R. Purchase	c White	0	b Colchin	0
Byes		1	Byes	9
Total		139		182

ENGLAND	FIRST INNINGS		SECOND INNINGS	
*Earl of Tankerville	c Small	1	b Lumpy	5
– Stone, Esq	c Small	0	b Brett	3
W. Bullen	b Lumpy	7	b Lumpy	1
J. Minshull	b Purchase	6	b Lumpy	8
J. Millar	b Nyren	16	c Sueter	12
– Colchin	not out	10	c Leer	19
T. White	b Brett	17	c Nyren	4
– Palmer	c Small	3	b Lumpy	5
J. Wood (of Seal)	b Nyren	27	c Brett	3
J. Frame	b Brett	1	b Purchase	3
T. Wood (of Surrey)	b Lumpy	0	not out	0
Total		88		64

*Captain.

winning 21 times and losing only 15, the remaining match being drawn. Their greatest year seems to have been 1779 when the Club beat England four times, including victory by an innings and 89 runs at Sevenoaks.

By 1779 however several of the players so graphically recorded by John Nyren had left the side: Thomas Brett 'beyond all comparison the fastest as well as straightest bowler that was ever known' came from the village of Catherington about five miles from Hambledon but seems to have finished playing in 1778 at the age of 31. Apparently he moved away to Portsmouth. William Barber, another of the principal bowlers, retired in 1777. He was a native of Sussex, but was persuaded to come to Hambledon by the patrons of the Club. William Hogsflesh was coupled with Barber by John Nyren as a bowler, but like Brett left off playing when young – in 1775, aged 32.

Of the 1779 players, pride of place goes to Richard Nyren, described by his son as: 'the chosen General of all matches, ordering and directing the whole.' The best batsman was John Small, sen. He is said to have begun playing in major matches in 1755 and his last match for Hampshire was in 1798 when he was aged 61. His innings of 136 against Surrey on Broadhalfpenny Down in 1775 was, it is believed, the highest ever made in a major contest up to that date. He was born in Empshott in Hampshire, but lived most of his life in Petersfield. He kept a shop where he sold cricket bats and balls which he made – originally he was a shoemaker. The following verse was written to his memory:

Here lies bowled out by Death's unerring ball,
A Cricketer renowned, by name John Small.
But though his name was Small, yet great his fame,
For nobly did he play the noble game;
His life was like his innings, long and good,
Full ninety summers he had death withstood,
At length the ninetieth winter came, when (fate
Not leaving him one solitary mate)
This last of Hambledonians, old John Small,
Gave up his bat and ball, his leather, wax and all.

George Leer acted as long-stop for Hambledon. He retired at the age of 33 and lived most of his life in Petersfield. The wicket-keeper was Thomas Sueter. John Nyren notes that: 'I have numberless times seen him stump a man out with Brett's tremendous bowling.' He was born and died in

Hambledon, playing until 1791, but not one of the extant scores credit him with a 'stumping', which is a little disconcerting. Edward Aburrow, another of the 1779 side and also a native of Hambledon, retired in 1782 at the age of 35. He was a noted long-field as well as a good batsman. Peter Stewart, known as 'Buck' on account of his sartorial elegance, was a sound batsman, whose playing days ended in 1779, and who was at one time landlord of the Green Man in Hambledon. Tom Taylor lived at Alresford, 'a most brilliant hitter, but his great fault lay in not sufficiently guarding his wicket; he was too fond of cutting, at the point of the bat, balls that were delivered straight.' Taylor played from 1775 to 1791.

James Aylward was a native of Warnford in Hampshire and a free left-hand batsman. He took over Small's record of Hambledon's highest innings, making 167 against England at Sevenoaks in 1777, but two years later Sir Horace Mann gave him a job as bailiff and he left Hambledon for Kent. Noah Mann, from Northchapel in Sussex, began appearing for Hambledon in 1777, travelling 20 miles once a week from his home in order to play at Hambledon. He had the ability to put a deceptive curve on his deliveries. Tragically, he died at the early age of 33. Going to sleep in a chair by the fireside, his clothes caught alight and the resultant burns caused his death.

One of the best batsmen of 1779 was Richard Veck, but perhaps in error Nyren does not mention him; Veck came from Alresford and appeared in the Hambledon side from 1776 to 1784.

The Earl of Tankerville played for Hambledon in two of the 1779 games, but he was more usually associated with Surrey, and Chertsey in particular, and employed two most famous cricketers, 'Lumpy' Stevens and William Bedster. Another Surrey man to play for Hambledon was Richard Francis, who came to live in the village, but later appeared for Kent.

David Harris lived at Crookham in Hampshire and began playing for Hambledon in 1782. He is credited with inventing, or perfecting, 'length' bowling and was for a time the premier bowler in England. Latterly he suffered from gout and used to arrive for matches on crutches!

Two sets of brothers who were notable players in the late 1780s and onwards came from Wrecclesham in Surrey, George and William Beldham and James and John Wells. William Beldham was the best known and as already noted he lived to a ripe old age; 'a most venomous hitter' Nyren calls him, and he certainly was one of England's best batsmen, his career continuing until 1821. Two other sets of brothers complete the catalogue of Hambledon's most celebrated men, Tom and Harry Walker from Churt, the former being recalled as 'Old Everlasting' on account of his steady batting, and Andrew and John Freemantle from Bishop's Sutton. Andrew's career spanned more than 20 years, but he only appeared for Hambledon from 1791.

The decline of the Hambledon Club began in the late 1780s and accelerated through the 1790s. The war with France depleted Hambledon's membership and the fact that two prominent members of the 1780–90s, Col Lennox and the Earl of Winchelsea, set up Thomas Lord on his new London Ground and helped to found MCC did nothing to encourage growth at Hambledon. Richard Nyren, who had looked after the Hambledon ground, first at Broadhalfpenny and then Windmill Down and whose inns, again first the Bat and Ball and then the George, had been the Club's headquarters, left the village, as did his son. His son noted: 'When Richard Nyren left Hambledon, the club broke up and never resumed from that day. The head and right arm were gone.'

The Hampshire team with the remnants of the Hambledon Club played MCC home and away in both 1797 and

The monument erected to mark the important place in cricket of the Bat and Ball Ground at Hambledon, frequently called the 'cradle of cricket'.
(Courtesy of Patrick Eagar)

1798. The county had one noteworthy recruit in John Bennett, a fine left-handed batsman from Kingsley in Hampshire. He played in important matches fairly regularly until 1818. The MCC in these four games were led by the Earl of Winchelsea and they won three out of four.

According to the Hampshire history published in 1957 (see bibliography), a Hampshire County Cricket Club was formed at Winchester in 1795; this detail originated in Waghorn's 'The Dawn of Cricket'. The actual reference reads:

> Aug 17 1795. The members of the Hampshire county club will please to take notice that the anniversary meeting will be held at the White Hart Inn, Winchester on Wednesday the 26th. Dinner at 3 o'clock.

This is the same county club noted by Ashley-Cooper in 'The Hambledon Cricket Chronicle' under his entry for Richard Brickenden, where it is specifically noted that it is not a cricket organisation.

There is a five-year gap, following 1798, in county cricket in Hampshire, but then, annually from 1803 to 1807 some games are played. It would seem probable that the Hampshire side of these years was raised by the Assheton Smiths – father and son. They were both christened Thomas and the father was elected a member of the Hambledon Club in 1786 and was President in 1794. He died in 1828. The son, who played in the majority of these 1803–07 Hampshire matches, played for Eton and then the Bullingdon Club (the premier side in Oxford in the 1790s). His country seat was not far over the Hampshire border in Wiltshire.

The outstanding figure to appear in the Hampshire ranks in this period was not however Assheton Smith, but Lord Frederick Beauclerk. Against England at Lord's in 1805 on his first outing with the county he hit 68 out of 140 and 129 not out out of 199 for 9; then in the return match he made 37 not out from 63 and 32 from 89. In his other two appearances he was not quite so successful but still made most useful contributions with the bat. At this time Lord Beauclerk was rated as the best batsman in England. He is said to have hung his gold watch on his wicket when practising, as a bait to the bowlers. He admitted that he made some 600 guineas a year out of cricket, through betting, and this brought much criticism since he was a cleric and for many years the vicar of St Albans! Essentially a selfish individual he, being more often than not captain, chose with care when to bowl in order to obtain most wickets and when to bat to make most runs. He was also not above bending the Laws to avoid defeat. His career lasted about 35 years and he was regarded as the authority on the game, possibly because no one dared contradict him, since his temper and language were not those one associates with men of the cloth.

When appearing for Hampshire most reports show him as a 'given man', but he certainly had connections with the County and is buried at Winchfield. There was a break of nearly ten years before Hampshire was again represented on the cricket field – two matches were played against MCC in 1816 and one against Epsom, a side which included the best Surrey players of the day.

Like Beauclerk, the man most prominent in the 1816 County side had only passing connections with Hampshire. William Ward, who owned some land on the Isle of Wight, was educated at Winchester, but his cricketing record at the school has long since been lost and it was not until he was all but 23 that he played his first game at Lord's. His name is forever linked to the record score of 278 which he made in 1820: he succeeded Lord Beauclerk as the best batsman in England. His best innings for the County was played on Sir John Cope's ground at Bramshill Park in 1823, when he hit 120 off the England bowlers and Hampshire won by five wickets. Two years later it was Ward who saved Lord's Cricket Ground from the builders by paying £5,000 for the lease from Thomas Lord – a price which was much higher than Lord had a right to expect. Ward immediately set about renovating and enlarging the pavilion, but within months of the alterations being made the building was burnt to the ground.

Although Hampshire were unable to replace the professional talent of the Hambledonians, two notable paid players did emerge during the early years of the 19th century.

Worthy Beagley, who is quite at the top –
With the bat he's first rate, a brick-wall at long-stop.

Thomas Beagley was born at Farringdon near Alton and first appeared for Hampshire in 1816 at the age of 26 – his career extended until 1844. For some years he was one of the outstanding professional batsmen and did particularly well in the Gentlemen v Players series of matches. Latterly he fell on hard times and came to live in London in the hope of finding work. In 1853 two benefit matches were played for him at The Oval in order to assist his financial problems.

T. C. Howard was an accomplished all-rounder from Elvetham, whose career spanned over 25 years. He was both a successful under-arm bowler, and a good wicket-keeper.

Two matches were arranged for 1826 when Sussex met the combined strength of Hampshire and Surrey at Petworth and Bramshill, but none of the teams was fully representative. Then in 1828 Hampshire opposed England at Lord's – William Ward and Howard were responsible for the County's eight-wicket win. It was just as well they proved to be in good form since Hampshire included three or four unlikely amateurs to fill up the team.

A long gap then occurs in the list of Hampshire county matches. *Bell's Life* in 1838 mentions the creation of a County Club: 'a great many gentlemen have enrolled their names'. This Club was organised by Thomas Chamberlayne of Cranbury Park near Winchester and is normally styled 'Gentlemen of Hampshire'. Another club based at Southampton and usually titled 'South Hants', but sometimes 'Hampshire', existed in the 1840s.

Thomas Chamberlayne was born in 1805 and succeeded to the Cranbury estate in 1834. He quickly laid out a cricket ground and began reviving the game in Hampshire, but much of his energy was also devoted to yachting and his boat, *Arrow*, won the major racing trophies of the day.

Following a series of lesser matches in the seasons 1838 to 1841, Thomas Chamberlayne's Hampshire side played MCC at Lord's in 1842 and beat the premier club by 235 runs; Chamberlayne himself opened the batting but scored only one run in two innings, the victory being mainly due to two professionals. Daniel Day and Richard Bodle. Day took ten wickets and hit 70, a score also achieved by Bodle.

At the behest of Chamberlayne, Day moved to Southampton from his native Surrey in 1842 and became landlord of the Antelope Inn and superintendent of its adjoining cricket ground, which then became the headquarters of Hampshire cricket. The problem of the titles of teams at this time is almost as complex as the earlier Hambledon/Hampshire confusion. Sometimes the sides are Gentlemen of Hampshire with one or more professionals as given men, at others plain Hampshire and just as often South Hants. According to Bodle's biography he was the professional with the South Hants Club from 1839 to 1858.

HAMPSHIRE *v* NOTTINGHAMSHIRE

Played at the Antelope Ground, Southampton, 20 and 21 July 1843

NOTTINGHAMSHIRE WON 39 RUNS

NOTTINGHAMSHIRE	FIRST INNINGS		SECOND INNINGS	
Rev H. Maltby	c Dorrington b Bathurst	2	b Bathurst	0
S. Redgate	c Martin b Bathurst	41	b Bathurst	0
F. Noyes, Esq	c Bodle b Day	31	c Weir b Day	5
J. Guy	c and b Day	46	c Dorrington b Day	14
*W. Clarke	c Martin b Day	12	c Day b Bathurst	30
A. Bass, Esq	run out	0	b Day	8
C. Creswell, Esq	c and b Day	43	c Barfoot b Bathurst	2
F. Noyes, Esq	c Barfoot b Bathurst	8	b Bathurst	9
H. Porter	not out	6	b Bathurst	1
J. Chapman	run out	8	c Weir b Bathurst	0
E. Patchitt, Esq	b Bathurst	0	not out	0
Extras	b 8, w 4	12	b 8, w 1	9
Total		209		78

HAMPSHIRE	FIRST INNINGS		SECOND INNINGS	
*T. Chamberlayne, Esq	c Patchitt b Clarke	2	b Clarke	0
Capt Weir	b Redgate	23	st Guy b Redgate	44
W. Brown, Esq.	b Clarke	22	c Noyes b Redgate	5
W. Dorrinton	c Noyes b Creswell	12	b Clarke	5
E. Martin	b Redgate	27	c Creswell b Clarke	4
G. Barfoot	c Noyes b Redgate	16	b Redgate	3
D. Day	b Redgate	3	b Redgate	1
R. Bodle	not out	3	b Redgate	49
Sir F. H. Hervey-Bathurst	c Noyes b Redgate	1	b Redgate	2
Hon. G. F. Hastings	b Clarke	5	b Clarke	0
A. M. Campbell, Esq	c Guy b Clarke	0	not out	0
Extras	b 11, w 6	17	byes	4
Total		131		117

The Hampshire team revived by Thomas Chamberlayne in the 1840s. W. Dorrinton of Kent played as a given man for Hampshire. A curiosity of this game was that Hampshire allowed Noyes to bat twice in each innings, because owing to an accident on the journey from Nottingham, the visitors had only ten men.

*Captain.

The first major match on Day's Antelope Ground was Hampshire with five given men *v* England on 5 and 6 September 1842. Despite the reinforcements, the County lost by an innings.

Season 1843 was Chamberlayne's most ambitious, when Hampshire played home and away games with both Notts and MCC. Hampshire lost all four matches and thereafter Chamberlayne lowered his sights. Chamberlayne's aspirations were not helped by the fact that the side arrived at Trent Bridge three men short and co-opted two locals and Chamberlayne's footman – they lost by an innings and 19 runs. The return game at Southampton is an historical curiosity. Barker, the Notts bowler, leapt out of a runaway cab crossing London and broke his leg. Hampshire in the circumstances allowed one Notts player to bat twice in each innings!

Of the variety of amateurs who assisted Mr Chamberlayne the most noted was Sir Frederick Bathurst. A fast round-arm bowler, Sir Frederick was educated at Winchester and began playing for MCC in 1831. He was a mainstay of the Gentlemen's side opposed to the Players. Ashley-Cooper noted:

> Bathurst was a member of the Club (MCC) from 1830 to 1881 and after his cricketing days was often seen at Lord's with the seals on his watch-chain plumbing a line clear of his toes.

After 1846 Hampshire matches were scarcely worthy of note outside the County itself – in 1847 Hampshire (so-called) were beaten by Portsmouth with an innings to spare. 'Strictly speaking Hampshire had no Eleven at this time', noted Haygarth. In 1848 the leading matches were played either at Bramshill Park, the team being basically the Gentlemen of Hampshire, or at Southsea on the ground of the East Hants Club. Brooke had taken over the Antelope Ground but the only match of interest played there in 1848 was Gentlemen of Hampshire against Players. Daniel Day had taken a ground at Itchen and William Clarke's All England Eleven opposed Fourteen of Hampshire on Day's new ground in September.

This fragmentation of Hampshire's cricketing talents continued right through the 1850s, just when the other leading cricketing counties were beginning to build their county clubs – Surrey and Sussex, Hampshire's eastern neighbours were well established by 1850, Kent could field a strong side and Notts were the all-powerful midland county. Rowland Bowen claimed that there was a 'lack of natural cricket interest in Hampshire' and this meant that there was little enthusiasm for a County Club. Surely the Hambledon Club, which relied largely on Hampshire-born players, disproves this remark. On the other hand, there has been a remarkable absence of Hampshire-born players in English Test cricket.

In 1861 the Hampshire side returned to Lord's, only to be beaten by MCC by an innings and 202 runs, but not long after the Gentlemen of Hampshire beat a similar side from Sussex on the Antelope Ground, and then playing at Cranbury beat I Zingari. Mr Chamberlayne, Sir Frederick Bathurst and friends were encouraged enough to think of laying the foundations of a new Hampshire County Cricket Club.

MORE DOWNS THAN UPS

ON 12 AUGUST 1863 'an influential meeting of the gentry of Hampshire' was held and a new County Cricket Club was formed. The President of the new body was the man who had spent many years trying to resuscitate Hampshire, Thomas Chamberlayne, and the Secretary was George Matthew Ede, the well-known gentleman jockey. Ede perished in tragic circumstances aged 36, when a horse he was riding at Aintree fell and rolled on top of him, Ede dying three days later of his injuries. A useful club cricketer, he made many runs in minor matches in and around his native Southampton. His twin brother, Edward Lee Ede, was also a founding member of the County Club and after playing for Hampshire, he acted as honorary scorer for 25 years, as well as being editor of the annual 'Hampshire Cricket Guide'. E. L. Ede was largely responsible for the first notable success of the new County. In 1864 Fourteen of Hampshire opposed Surrey at The Oval, and won a notable victory for the new County Club, E. L. Ede taking eight wickets. True, Hampshire had three more players than Surrey, but the latter were the Champion County of 1864 and in Jupp, Griffith, Caesar and Lockyer possessed four of the best professionals of the day, whilst Hampshire's four paid players were not of great value, the most famous, James Southerton, being at that time played as a batsman and not having yet acquired a name as a bowler.

The two years which followed saw Hampshire play Surrey on even terms and beat them twice. At Southampton in 1865, 'Our Sam' (S. Tubb) was brought into the Hampshire side at the last minute when one of the amateurs failed to appear and took seven wickets in the first innings to dismiss Surrey for 87. Hampshire went on to win by eight wickets, having lost the game at The Oval two weeks earlier by an innings and 221 runs! It was unfortunate for Hampshire that Tubb played so rarely – he was a well-known bookmaker and preferred racing circles to the cricket ground, despite his excellent fast left-arm bowling.

In 1866 Hampshire won at Southampton by a margin of ten wickets, with James Southerton being the most effective bowler. A native of Petworth, Southerton had been engaged by Hampshire due to his residence in Southampton. He had earlier played for Surrey and Sussex and he left Hampshire in 1867 to appear almost exclusively in the ranks of Surrey, being landlord of the Cricketers' Inn at Mitcham. So in Tubb and Southerton Hampshire lost their two best bowlers.

Apart from Surrey, Hampshire played Middlesex in 1864 twice and in 1865 once, the second game that season being cancelled by Middlesex at the last moment because most of the Middlesex players wished to watch Eton play Harrow. The Hampshire Secretary was not amused by this excuse and did not bother to try and arrange matches against Middlesex the following year.

The Hampshire newspapers in the late 1860s, no doubt to encourage their cricketers, proclaimed Hampshire victories when in fact the victories were obtained by the Gentlemen of Hampshire against similar opponents from another county. There was a world of difference between the full strength of most of the major counties of the 1860s and merely a team composed of amateurs of the county. For example the Gentlemen of Hampshire in 1864 played the Gentlemen of Sussex at Southampton and won, then on the following three

SOUTHAMPTON

The County Ground at Northlands Road, Southampton has been the home of Hampshire since 1885 and one record it holds is that of F. E. Lacey's 323 not out for Hampshire *v* Norfolk in 1887, a record in a minor county match which seems unlikely to be beaten.

No individual first-class triple hundred has been scored on the ground, the highest innings being 292 by L. C. H. Palairet for Somerset in 1896. C. P. Mead's 280 not out against Notts in 1921 remains the highest innings by a Hampshire batsman on the ground.

Curiously no Hampshire bowler has taken nine or ten wickets in an innings on the ground, but W. Mead for Essex performed the feat twice, having nine for 52 in 1895 and then nine for 40 in 1900. In the former match Mead ended with a total of 17 wickets, another record for the ground.

It was at Southampton in 1952 that Shackleton and Cannings bowled unchanged through both innings of Kent, dismissing that county for 32 in one innings.

days several Gentlemen on each side were dropped and replaced by professionals. The result was an easy win for Sussex – this happened again when the sides met at Hove.

HAMPSHIRE *v* SUSSEX

Played on the Antelope Ground, Southampton, 7 and 8 July 1864

SUSSEX WON BY 10 WICKETS

HAMPSHIRE	FIRST INNINGS		SECOND INNINGS	
Mr C. F. Lucas	c Ellis b Lillywhite	1	(2) c Horwood b Lillywhite	16
Mr J. C. Lord	c Wells b Lillywhite	11	(10) not out	4
H. Holmes	c Payne b Lillywhite	0	run out	7
Mr G. M. Ede	b Ellis	9	c Payne b Lillywhite	0
†Mr H. T. Frere	st Wells b Ellis	12	(8) c Fillery b Lillywhite	7
Rev C. H. Ridding	b Lillywhite	13	(9) c FitzGerald b Lillywhite	3
*Mr E. L. Ede	b Ellis	4	b Ellis	17
W. Humphrey	c Payne b Lillywhite	7	b Fillery	1
G. Ubsdell	not out	3	c and b Ellis	10
S. Tubb	c and b Ellis	2	(11) c Smith b Lillywhite	0
Mr G. H. Case	absent	–	(1) b Ellis	48
Extras	leg bye	1	b 1, lb 8	9
Total		63		122

1st inns: 1-5, 2-8, 3-13, 4-29, 5-34, 6-48, 7-58, 8-58, 9-63
2nd inns: 1-43, 2-57, 3-60, 4-67, 5-88, 6-91, 7-106, 8-117, 9-121

BOWLING	O	M	R	W	O	M	R	W
Lillywhite	21	9	22	5	35.2	11	58	5
Ellis	20.2	3	40	4	18	5	31	3
Fillery					17	11	24	1

SUSSEX	FIRST INNINGS		SECOND INNINGS	
Mr C. H. Smith	c Holmes b E. L. Ede	47	not out	0
Jas Lillywhite jun	c Lucas b Tubb	13		
Mr H. M. Hyndman	run out	11		
C. H. Ellis	b Holmes	17		
†G. Wells	b Frere	17	not out	1
J. Southerton	b Frere	1		
C. Payne	b Holmes	3		
R. Fillery	b Humphrey	35		
Mr C. Horwood	st Frere b E. L. Ede	11		
Mr M. P. FitzGerald	run out	8		
Mr Wyatt Gibbs	not out	6		
Extras	b 8, lb 8	16		
Total		185	(0 wkt)	1

1st inns: 1-35, 2-55, 3-72, 4-93, 5-99, 6-102, 7-132, 8-150, 9-166

BOWLING	O	M	R	W		O	M	R	W
Tubb	9	3	29	1					
Holmes	44	17	64	2					
E. L. Ede	15	2	56	2					
Frere	20	12	20	2					
Humphrey	1.3	1	0	1		0.3	0	1	0

Umpires: D. Day and J. Dean.
Hampshire won the toss.
Close of play: Hampshire 63; Sussex 185.
*Captain; †Wicket-keeper.

Hampshire tried to make the transition from a purely Gentlemen's side to a full-blown County side, but failed to do so despite repeated attempts. They thus remained for over 20 years in a kind of no-man's-land between the pukka 'first-class' counties – Notts, Surrey, Yorkshire, Lancashire, Kent, Sussex, etc. – and the less competitive world of Devonshire, Warwickshire, Berkshire and Buckinghamshire.

The cricket journalists, brought up on Nyren's tales and Pycroft, were always anxious to promote the cause of Hampshire and fan the embers of any club which tried to raise the Hampshire County flag.

Having beaten Hampshire twice in bona fide county matches in 1864, Sussex did not renew the fixture in 1865, but Hampshire found fresh opponents in Buckinghamshire, a county also trying to make a bid for 'first-class' status – Bucks won both matches, but retained the fixture for 1866, when each county had one success. Unfortunately Buckinghamshire then subsided back to obscurity and in 1867 only Kent played Hampshire. This fixture was abandoned for 1868, when a plaintive note appears: 'no matches this season for want of funds'.

In 1870, Captain H. M. Eccles, who had taken over as the Hampshire Honorary Secretary when Ede left, resigned and the Hon Charles North became the new Secretary. He arranged home and away fixtures with Lancashire. The Red Rose county, even with a weak team, won the Old Trafford fixture by ten wickets and the even weaker side which travelled to Southampton still won by 40 runs.

Depression set in and the only game of 1871 was a match against Gentlemen of Devon at the Torquay Cricket Festival. The following season the County sent an amateur side to Winchester College to play Gentlemen of Sussex – the

Hants v Sussex:
Southampton July 7, 8 1864
This was the first important inter-county match played by the newly formed Hampshire County Cricket Club. James Lillywhite, who was later to captain England in the First Test Match, bowled in fine form, taking ten wickets and bowling throughout both innings unchanged. The only home batsman to make any impression was George Case, a surgeon living in Fareham, who arrived too late to bat in the first innings, but opened the second. The scores were level when Hampshire had been dismissed a second time and thus the Sussex second innings was a formality.

college had recently laid out a new ground – but an announcement at the 1872 AGM of the South Hampshire Club stated that though the present officers of the Club would remain in their posts, no matches, no liabilities and no subscriptions were to be undertaken or demanded in the immediate future.

The Gentlemen of Hampshire played home (at Winchester) and away games with Sussex in 1873, actually beating Sussex at Hove, but only because they arrived a man short and were allowed to co-opt O. E. Winslow, who proceeded to hit the only fifty of the match.

At the end of September 1873 a match between the Players and Gentlemen of the County was organised on the Antelope Ground as a trial in the hope of finding players for a County side for 1874.

The most important match of 1874 however was promoted by Lord Londesborough, when Sixteen of Hampshire met Yorkshire United at Lyndhurst. Londesborough was a leading figure in the setting up of Yorkshire

WINCHESTER

The cricket ground at St Cross, Winchester, also known as the Garrison Ground, was the scene of only one first-class inter-county match, Hampshire opposing Sussex on the grounds on 1 and 2 July 1875. The Rev J. G. Crowdy, who was Precentor of Winchester Cathedral, was at the time captain of the Winchester City Club and was instrumental in not only resuscitating cricket in Winchester, but arranging for this county match to be played there. He appeared for Hampshire in the match and was joint-highest scorer in Hampshire's first innings, making 21.

Hampshire were easily beaten, Sussex winning by an innings and 27 runs. James Lillywhite jun, who was to captain England in the First Test in Melbourne two years later, took six for 42 and Richard Fillery nine for 98, as Hampshire were dismissed for 60 and 119.

At the turn of the century the ground was the headquarters of the 'Greenjackets' and a cricketer who made frequent appearances in regimental matches there was Prince Christian Victor, the only member of the Royal family to take part in first-class cricket. He was killed in the Boer War.

United in opposition to the official Yorkshire side run from Bramall Lane. The United survived only a few seasons.

Clement Booth assumed the combined offices of captain and Honorary Secretary for 1875 and home and away games were played against both Kent and Sussex. The former won both matches by an innings, but Hampshire beat Sussex at Hove, which provided the following comment: 'An unexpected victory for Hants, now low in the cricketing world'. The win was due entirely to A. W. Ridley who not only hit the highest score for his side, but also took 12 wickets. Ridley was in the Oxford side of 1875, having originally been awarded his blue in 1872. *Lillywhite's Companion* for 1876 describes him thus:

> Decidedly one of the best cricketers of the day. A great batsman against first-class bowling, his reach serving him in good stead; is probably the best slow under-hand bowler since the time of Clarke and surpassed by few as a fieldsman at point.

It was a blow to Hampshire cricket when the demands of business took Ridley to London. He was a Director of a large firm of brewers, and he transferred his cricketing allegiance to Middlesex. Clement Booth, the other major figure in the Hampshire Club of the 1870s, was a native of Lincolnshire. He had gained a blue at Cambridge in the 1860s, playing against Oxford for four years and had then attempted the daunting task of running a County Cricket Club in Lincolnshire. In the early 1870s he moved to Kilmeston, near Alresford and left the onerous burden of the Lincs Honorary Secretaryship for the even greater one of Hampshire. In 1875 he arranged four matches to be played at Winchester rather than the now neglected Antelope Ground (the name was changed in the same year to the 'Southampton Cricket Ground'), but the following year Hampshire returned to Southampton and replaced their Sussex fixture with two matches against Derbyshire, still retaining the Kent fixture. The outlook brightened considerably in 1876 and *Lillywhite's Companion* was delighted:

> Administrative energy, which we urged upon the Hants Executive in last year's Companion has had its effect, and the County Committee can look back upon the past season and the triumphs on the old Antelope Ground at Southampton, with feelings of satisfaction.

Three of the four matches were won, but it should be remembered that Kent and Derbyshire were the weakest of the major counties and that too much rested on one or two amateurs; since the emigration of Southerton, the ranks of professionalism in the County had been very thin indeed.

The same four home and away matches – *v* Kent and Derbyshire – were repeated in 1877, but this time all four were lost. Ridley and Booth were the leading batsmen, but Ridley's lobs were more expensive and though the professional, H. W. Tate, a fast round-arm bowler from Lyndhurst, did fairly well, the rest of the bowling was non-existent. Season 1878 almost repeated 1877, save for the fact that one match was drawn instead of lost. 'Hampshire appears to be going back to second childhood, and – so far as its sleepy condition is concerned – would seem again entitled to be called "the cradle of cricket",' was the opinion of *Lillywhite's Companion* in its review of the summer.

Ridley had left and there were no suitable replacements. In July 1879 Clement Booth resigned as Honorary Secretary and was replaced by Russell Bencraft of St Mary's, Southampton. Only one match was played and that was the Gentlemen of Hampshire *v* MCC. The new Secretary set about attempting yet another revival. The *Cricketer's Annual* sounded a trifle dubious when it came to review the results for 1880:

> The re-appearance of Hampshire in first-class cricket cannot fail to be satisfactory to those who remember the important part it played in the early history of the game. Whether the time chosen for its revival was opportune or not is best known to the authorities, but it certainly does not possess at present material stout enough to enable it to render a good account of itself with the more important shires.

In 1880 Hampshire did in fact beat MCC twice, but they lost twice to Sussex and indeed to Devonshire and Somerset. The results in 1881 proved even more discouraging to young Russell Bencraft (he was only 21 years old when he volunteered to take on the problems of the County Club): all five matches were lost. F. E. Lacey, the Cambridge University cricketer, topped the batting table. He was to represent the County until 1897 after which he became the Secretary to MCC and stayed in that important post for nearly 30 years,

SIR FRANCIS EDEN LACEY

A barrister by profession – he entered the Inner Temple in 1889 – Francis Lacey was eminently suited to the job which he took in 1898 and retained for the next 28 years, that of Secretary of the MCC. When he was appointed the Club was run in rather a haphazard manner, but he soon set matters to right and was a major force in the administration of cricket both at Lord's and through the ICC for more than quarter of a century.

As a cricketer he had an outstanding career at Sherborne, scoring no less than six centuries in his final year (1878) in the school eleven. He captained the school at both cricket and rugby. His first taste of county cricket was for his native Dorset, but in 1880 he began to play for Hampshire and continued with that county on and off until 1897. He will be remembered as the scorer of 323 not out for Hampshire against Norfolk in 1887 – a record score in a minor county match. A sound batsman, he could hit the ball hard especially in front of the wicket. He also bowled slow round-arm with some success and was a good fieldsman in any position.

In 1926 he was knighted for his services to cricket and was made a Trustee of the MCC. He died on 25 May 1946, aged 86.

being in 1926 knighted for his services to cricket. Captain F. W. Lipscomb played one or two good innings, but at 47 was hardly a batsman with a future.

In 1882 A. H. Wood of Froyle Park, Alton was appointed as joint secretary with Bencroft, but lasted only one year, being replaced by Captain James Fellowes. Fellowes it was who was mainly responsible in 1883 for obtaining the lease of eight acres of land off Bannister Road in Southampton for the use of the County Club as their headquarters.

In 1883 and 1884 the County continued to use the old Antelope Ground. In the former year their only victory worth much was at the expense of Sussex, though they beat Hertfordshire, Somerset and Uppingham Rovers as well. In 1884 Kent and Somerset were beaten, but all the remaining six matches ended in defeat. Lacey scored 211 out of 414 in the first innings of the game with Kent and 92 not out of 148 for 7 in the second, as Hampshire won the high-scoring game by three wickets. Kent had followed on nearly 200 in arrears and then made 344 in their second attempt.

Lacey also demonstrated his batting skill in May 1885 when the new County Ground at Bannister Road was first used. Lacey hit 181 not out for the South of the County against the North. The ground was officially opened by the Countess of Northesk, wife of the County Club's President.

THE HAMPSHIRE CRICKETER'S GUIDE

This first Hampshire annual appeared for six years from 1885 to 1890. The retail price of each issue was 6d ($2\frac{1}{2}$p) and the venture does not seem to have met with much success, there being four different publishers involved over the six issues. The cover goes through three colour changes and the sizes also are not uniform, though all are roughly five inches by three inches. The Honorary Secretary of the County Club acted as Editor and provided a short Preface to each edition: 1885–87 by Lieutenant-Colonel J. Fellowes and 1888–90 by Russell Bencraft. The general editorial content is however not distinguished, though apart from the first issue, the scores of county matches are given.

Copies of this Guide are exceedingly rare and this will be reflected in the price listed in dealers' catalogues.

James Fellowes, now a Lieutenant Colonel, took over as sole Honorary Secretary in 1885, but he watched over a sad decline, even by the modest standards set in the last few years, of the County's fortunes. Eight matches were lost, five by an innings margin, and included in those was the first major county match on the new ground – against Derbyshire on 25 and 26 June. The cause of Hampshire's troubles was easily seen in the season's averages: no less than 39 players were called upon for the ten matches. The two professionals of the team were W. C. Dible of Lyndhurst and F. G. Willoughby, who the following year became coach at Winchester, but neither was good enough to worry the best batsmen of the day. A. H. Evans, the Oxford blue and useful Somerset all-rounder, appeared in three games for Hampshire in 1885 and took ten wickets. Two other useful all-rounders of the early 1880s were C. E. Currie and H. H. Armstrong. The former was at Marlborough and Cambridge without obtaining a place in the eleven at either!

The pavilion, which had been erected in 1884–85, was extended for the 1886 season and the ground further improved by the addition of a concrete practice wicket, but on the field Hampshire showed no improvement. Of the six matches against first-class counties all were lost, four by an innings. Victories were achieved only against Norfolk and Hertfordshire. After the 1885 season, the Cricket Reporting Agency had acted to define which counties should be regarded as first-class and had confined Hampshire to the status of 'second-class'. The results obtained in 1886 confirmed the opinion of the Agency.

Lieutenant-Colonel Fellowes gave way to Russell Bencraft and H. K. Grierson as Honorary Secretary in 1887 but this in no way helped Hampshire's immediate problems. The only victory of the summer remains high in the record books due to the batting of F. E. Lacey. He hit 323 not out against Norfolk at Southampton and Hampshire won by an innings and 342 runs, Norfolk making 77 and 139 in response to 558. Lacey's innings is the largest ever in a match between two Minor Counties.

The new Second Class Counties Competition was inaugurated by *Wisden Cricketers' Almanack* in 1888, with ten counties competing. Hampshire were placed sixth, having just one success to their name, the victims again being Norfolk at Southampton. In 1889 they did no better. Lacey, who had taken on the captaincy a year or two back, could

PORTSMOUTH

Hampshire played their first inter-county game on the United Services Ground at Portsmouth in 1888, but the first first-class match on the ground took place on 17, 18 and 19 August 1882 when Cambridge University Past and Present opposed the Australians and beat them by 20 runs. 'The scene at the end was one of wild excitement', noted the report. The remarkable feature of the cricket was the hitting of the giant Australian, Bonnor, who made 66 out of 79 in 30 minutes. A. G. Steel took five for 24 to cause the tourists to collapse in their second innings.

In a similar type of match in 1893, the Australians scored 843, which created a new record for first-class cricket in England. The innings lasted ten hours and the two largest stands were 232 for the seventh wicket by Bruce and Trumble and 136 for the fifth, while the ninth pair added 121. The University side employed ten bowlers, four of whom conceded over 100 runs. According to the reports the Australians did not declare because they wished to beat the highest score ever made up to that time in any match, namely 920, but this they failed to do and in the process ruined the game, since the home side did not start batting until the middle of the third morning.

Hampshire use Portsmouth regularly, as they have done since the County was re-admitted to first-class status in 1895. The highest individual innings on the ground was 302 not out by P. Holmes for Yorkshire in 1920.

only play once or twice. The bowling was in the hands of W. C. Roberts, a medium-pace left-arm bowler who came from Farley near Winchester. The best innings of the year was Russell Bencraft's 195 against Warwickshire.

Season 1890 at last saw an upturn in the county's record. Six out of twelve matches were victories. Captain E. G. Wynyard, who had played on and off since 1878, was able to play regularly and improved the batting strength of the side. A regular army officer, he had spent much of the 1880s in India, but in 1890 was at home. He was a stylish batsman who hit the ball hard and scored very heavily in military cricket. He was also a skilled footballer and appeared in the FA Cup Final of 1881. The Hampshire bowling table of 1890 was also topped by a military man, Captain C. G. Barton, who like Wynyard played much of his cricket in India. Barton was a native of Hampshire, being born at Romsey, and bowled slow left-arm.

Captain Barton had a wonderful season for Hampshire in 1891, his 42 wickets being captured at a cost of nine runs each. He was ably assisted by four other bowlers. The 20-year-old A. J. L. Hill had gained his blue at Cambridge in 1890 and was a fast bowler who could make the ball come very quickly off the wicket. His career with Hampshire was to span more than 30 years and he was the second native of the County to appear in Test cricket. An all-round sportsman, he captained Hampshire at rugby football and hockey. Third in the bowling table was H. W. Studd, later Brigadier-General Studd, another fast bowler from Cambridge, who had been in the Eton XI of 1888 and 1889 and in 1890 had been tried in one game for Middlesex. He was a member of the well-known cricketing brotherhood.

The other two bowlers were professionals whose names were to be linked with Hampshire for many summers to come. Henry Baldwin came from Wokingham, but lived at Winchfield and in 1891 was a coach at Eton. A slow right-arm bowler he appeared in the ranks of his adopted county until 1905. The other professional was Tom Soar, who was engaged by the Hampshire County Club as the groundsman at Southampton. He was a most useful fast bowler and occasionally made runs.

Hampshire's weakness was the batting. Only one player achieved an average above 20 and not a single hundred was scored in any of the eleven matches. In the two Surrey matches the side were dismissed for 86 and 66 then 109 and 85; against the much weaker Sussex attack a similar story, 99 and 60, 108 and 57. As a result the County could only obtain three wins and in the table of Second Class Counties came 5th out of 7.

A new face joined the County ranks in 1892 and ended the summer at the head of both the batting and bowling tables. 'Bombardier' Victor Barton, a regular soldier stationed in Kent, had played for that county with some success in 1889 and 1890, having first made a name for himself with the Royal Artillery cricket team. In 1891 he bought himself out of the army in order to go on tour to South Africa with the team captained by W. W. Read. Described in 1892 as 'a magnificent all-round cricketer', Barton was a very attractive batsman and a medium-pace bowler. Born in Netley, he was for some years the proprietor of the Alexandra Hotel in Southampton and would have achieved even greater fame if his career had not been cut short by ill-health. He died at the early age of 38.

Soar and Baldwin both did well with the ball in 1892, the former taking 62 wickets at 14 runs each. Bombardier Barton hit 161 *v* MCC and another hundred against Oxfordshire. Lacey re-appeared and had one outstanding innings, but otherwise the batting still left much to be desired and Hampshire won one solitary match in the Second Class Counties Competition.

The highlight of 1893 was the victory over Sussex when Soar took 12 for 84 and Sussex were dismissed for 160 and 88, but Hampshire still fared badly in the Second Class Competition. Wynyard managed to play in a few games and hit the highest innings of the season for Hampshire, 154. The only other hundred came from the bat of Bombardier Barton and once more the batting let the side down.

There seems to be more than a little confusion over who was officially the captain of Hampshire during the early 1890s. In 1892, for example, *Wisden Cricketers' Almanack* gives F. E. Lacey, *Lillywhite's Annual* gives H. W. Forster and H. S. Altham, in his 1957 history, gives Russell Bencraft. Most probably all three led the side in some matches. Forster, who appeared for Hampshire from 1885 to 1895 and represented Oxford in the University matches of 1887, 1888 and 1889 was a stylish right-hand batsman. Though born in Kent, he lived at Exbury near Southampton and later became a noted politician, being Conservative MP for Sevenoaks for over 25 years and later Governor-General of Australia.

On 30 April 1894, the captains of the nine first-class counties resolved unanimously to place before the MCC at the Club's Annual General Meeting the following proposals:

> That the matches played by the following four counties: : Derbyshire, Warwickshire, Essex and Leicestershire against the nine counties at present styled first-class, and also against one another and against the MCC should be regarded as first-class matches . . .

The Committee of the MCC duly accepted this proposal, but the admirers of Hampshire cricket were not happy:

> Rightly or wrongly the selection of the four counties

seems to have produced something of a grievance. The bitter cry of outcast Hampshire has, indeed, found expression in the columns of the press.

The supporters of Hampshire reminded the public of the county's historic past, but in truth their record in 1892 and 1893 was not as good as Cheshire, who were placed fifth in the Second Class Competition in both years, one position above Hampshire.

Hampshire, however, did improve their lot in another direction. H. K. Grierson proposed that the County Club should buy the freehold of the County Ground at Southampton from the owner, Sir Edward Hulse. The agreed price was £5,400 plus £600 for the buildings. The Hampshire County Ground Company was formed and shares were issued and it was not long before the necessary sum had been raised to complete the purchase, thus securing the future of the County Club in Southampton. It was now up to the cricketers to prove that a mistake had been made when Hampshire were not included among the counties raised to first-class status.

The first half of the County's 1894 programme – the six matches played up to the end of July – produced a grim record. Only one match was brought to a successful conclusion and that against a nondescript MCC side. On the other hand, Warwickshire, Leicestershire and Sussex all beat the County and Derbyshire had the better of a drawn game.

August however saw a welcome transformation, beginning at Leyton on the fourth, when despite a deficit on first innings Hampshire ended by beating Essex – one of the new first-class counties – by nine runs. A. J. L. Hill scored 114 in Hampshire's second innings and once the stand between McGahey and Rowe was broken, the home county's batting collapsed. Soar was the most successful Hampshire bowler. The Hampshire team then went to Derby, where Wynyard hit 90 of the side's 204, then Derbyshire were dismissed cheaply by Baldwin and the follow-on enforced. Baldwin again proved the most difficult bowler, returning match figures of 12 for 112 and after that only several breaks for rain threatened to prevent Hampshire's victory, which came by a margin of five wickets. Directly after their win Hampshire returned to Southampton to meet Warwickshire. A stand of 172 for the third wicket by Bombardier Barton and H. F. Ward gave Hampshire a 60-run lead on first innings.

Ward was a 21-year-old amateur from Northwood near
Winchester. A most promising stylish batsman, he contracted typhoid in 1897 and died still in his mid-twenties, a
great loss to the County. Soar dismissed Warwickshire in
their second innings, leaving Hampshire needing 180 to win.
Barton and Ward again batted well, but the rest struggled
and the match was won amid great excitement by just two
wickets.

The next visitors to Southampton were Sussex. Ward and
A. J. L. Hill batted well to bring Hampshire a first-innings
lead of 109, but the old Australian captain, Murdoch, batted
some six hours, making an undefeated 172, and then
declared, setting Hampshire the difficult proposition of 241 in
180 minutes. Hill and Wynyard came together when the first
wicket fell at 17 and added 173 in two hours, of which
Captain Wynyard made 117, 'a most brilliant display of
hitting'. Hampshire won by six wickets with three minutes
to spare.

Rain ruined Hampshire's next game, but not before
Wynyard had notched another hundred, Barton 81 not out
and Ward 68, giving Hampshire a commanding first innings
lead with only four wickets gone. The County's final match
simply confirmed Hampshire's form. Wynyard hit yet
another hundred, this time off the Essex attack at Southampton. He batted 150 minutes for 108, twice hitting the ball out
of the ground. Essex could only make 146 in their first
innings and made an even worse mess of their second, being
dismissed by Baldwin and Steele for 75. A local amateur,
D. A. Steele was a useful all-rounder, whose career in county
cricket continued until 1906. Hampshire therefore brought
their programme to a close with an innings victory, and even
before this win a petition was being circulated round the
first-class counties asking for their support in the promotion
of Hampshire to first-class status.

In October 1894 the Committee of MCC issued a circular
which if passed would regulate the County Championship
Competition, including the status of the counties. Hampshire
were listed among the 14 to take part in the 1895
Championship. This scheme was subsequently agreed and
thus Hampshire regained first-class status.

A moment's glance at the Hampshire averages for 1894
shows how the County improved its standing compared
with any of the last three seasons. Wynyard of course topped
the batting table with an average over 66, but Ward, Hill and

Barton all exceeded an average of 40 – in previous years if two players exceeded 25 it was regarded as an improvement. Baldwin and Soar came first and second in the bowling. Two questions which must have been uppermost in the mind of Russell Bencraft, the captain and secretary, during the winter of 1894–95 were: how would the bowling fare against the major first-class counties, and how many of the talented amateur batsmen would be available on a regular basis, in view of the increased number of matches involved in Championship cricket?

THE FIRST YEARS IN THE CHAMPIONSHIP

Hampshire's first County Championship side, 1895. Back row, left to right: H. Baldwin, Captain Barton, G. W. Lewis, C. Heseltine, T. Soar. Front row: C. I. Robson, E. G. Wynyard, Dr R. Bencraft, A. J. L. Hill, H. F. Ward. On ground: F. H. Bacon, V. Barton.

THE SIDE WHICH REPRESENTED HAMPSHIRE in its first Championship match of 1895 was: C. Robson, A. J. L. Hill, E. G. Wynyard, V. A. Barton, H. F. Ward, F. H. Bacon, C. Heseltine, H. W. R. Bencraft, T. Soar, H. Baldwin and C. G. Barton. The game took place on Somerset's County Ground at Taunton and at the half-way stage appeared to be an easy win for the home side, who had dismissed Hampshire for 94 and thus gained a lead of 127. Following on, Ward and Bacon added 131 and with other useful contributions made sure that Somerset needed 188 in their final innings. F. H. Bacon was one of the few pre-First World War cricketers to appear as a professional and then change to amateur status. A useful batsman, he never really sustained his early promise. On the last morning Somerset needed only 44 with five wickets in hand; Soar then bowled with such success that he took three wickets for 13 and Hampshire won by 11 runs.

Their margin of victory was much more pronounced for the second game, which was the first at home, Derbyshire going down by an innings and 79 runs. Soar and Baldwin bowled unchanged through both innings, the former taking 11 for 113 and the latter eight for 93. The large crowd which attended on both days (the game being completed without the use of the third day) was fully satisfied with the result, especially as military duties prevented Wynyard from playing and an injured finger deprived the side of the regular wicket-keeper, Robson. As substitute wicket-keeper the County brought in Dean, who had last appeared in first-class cricket 15 years before in the ranks of Surrey.

Hampshire made a special effort to entertain the next county to visit Southampton and on the first evening of the match a banquet was laid on for the Yorkshire team, since Lord Hawke and the Yorkshire executive had more than anyone else pressed for Hampshire to be raised to first-class status. Rain ruined most of the first day, but Yorkshire made up for lost time and won with comparative ease. Essex also beat Hampshire and the County brought James Wootton, the old Kent bowler, who was now coach at Winchester, into

BASINGSTOKE

May's Bounty at Basingstoke has been the scene of Hampshire first-class matches since 1906. Basingstoke were most fortunate to have a generous cricket patron in Lt-Col John May. He stepped in when the local cricket ground, known as the Folly, was being sold for building land, bought the ground and later gave the field to the trustees of Basingstoke and North Hants Cricket Club.

He also enlarged the ground and in 1901 erected a new pavilion on it. The first County match was against Warwickshire and the Hampshire captain, E. M. Sprot, most sportingly continued batting in Hampshire's second innings despite the fact that he could easily have brought the match to a premature conclusion since rain was falling heavily. However, Hampshire batted out their innings in the wet and lost the match. Lilley, the Warwickshire wicket-keeper, noted: 'There is yet, I am glad to perceive, at least one County that plays the grand old game without too particular attention to phraseology of rules'.

SOMERSET *v* HAMPSHIRE

Played on the County Ground, Taunton, 30, 31 May and 1 June 1895

HAMPSHIRE WON BY 11 RUNS

SOMERSET	FIRST INNINGS		SECOND INNINGS	
Mr. L. C. H. Palairet	c Bacon b Baldwin	96	(2) c and b Soar	33
*Mr S. M. J. Woods	c Robson b Soar	7	(6) c and b Soar	16
Mr R. C. N. Palairet	c Robson b Soar	26	b Soar	13
Mr G. Fowler	b Soar	2	c Wynyard b C. G. Barton	52
A. E. Clapp	not out	60	c Hill b Soar	1
Mr V. T. Hill	b Baldwin	0	(1) c Bencraft b Baldwin	4
Mr E. W. Bartlett	run out	6	c Wynyard b Soar	40
Mr C. E. Winter	c Bacon b Baldwin	9	c sub b Baldwin	5
E. J. Tyler	c Hill b Baldwin	8	c Ward b Soar	3
G. B. Nichols	c Robson b Soar	0	c Hill b Soar	0
†Rev A. P. Wickham	c Soar b Baldwin	7	not out	1
Extras		0	Byes	8
Total		221		176

1st inns: 1-49, 2-102, 3-104, 4-166, 5-166, 6-177, 7-186, 8-200, 9-202
2nd inns: 1-35, 2-49, 3-62, 4-66, 5-84, 6-166, 7-166, 8-171, 9-175

BOWLING	O	M	R	W	O	M	R	W
Soar	25	2	89	4	30.2	8	71	7
Baldwin	19.2	5	62	5	27	7	72	2
Capt C. G. Barton	12	2	45	0	7	2	16	1
Hill	6	0	25	0	3	0	9	0
Heseltine					1	1	0	0

HAMPSHIRE	FIRST INNINGS		SECOND INNINGS	
†Mr C. Robson	b Tyler	9	b Tyler	41
Mr A. J. L. Hill	run out	24	run out	14
Capt E. G. Wynyard	c L. C. H. Palairet b Woods	1	c Wickham b Tyler	11
V. A. Barton	b Woods	1	c Hill b Nichols	11
Mr H. F. Ward	c Wickham b Tyler	8	c Bartlett b Hill	71
F. H. Bacon	c Fowler b Woods	15	c Tyler b Hill	92
Mr C. Heseltine	b Woods	6	b Tyler	10
*Mr H. W. R. Bencraft	b Woods	16	lbw b Tyler	10
T. Soar	b Tyler	9	not out	38
H. Baldwin	c and b Woods	4	b Tyler	0
Capt C. G. Barton	not out	1	c and b Tyler	1
Extras		0	b 11, w 4	15
Total		94		314

1st inns: 1-10, 2-14, 3-26, 4-43, 5-52, 6-64, 7-71, 8-88, 9-90
2nd inns: 1-43, 2-67, 3-84, 4-84, 5-215, 6-230, 7-243, 8-287, 9-300

BOWLING	O	M	R	W		O	M	R	W
Tyler	18	3	46	3		44	9	117	6
Woods	17.4	6	48	6		30	9	68	0
Fowler						9	1	30	0
Nichols						23	6	51	1
Hill						7	0	33	2

Umpires: H. Draper and A. Millward.
Somerset won the toss. Close of play: 1st day: Hants 61-1 (Robson and Wynyard not out); 2nd day: Somerset 143-5 (Woods and Bartlett not out).
*Captain; †Wicket-keeper.

the side against Somerset, but Hampshire's batting failed and a further loss was recorded. Another Winchester man who was co-opted into the side and brought a surprise victory over Yorkshire at Bramall Lane was E. H. Buckland, an assistant master at the college. He had obtained his blue at Oxford in the 1880s and as a slow bowler had played a few matches for Middlesex. On his Hampshire debut he returned figures of 16.1-4-30-5, dismissing Yorkshire for 110 – Soar took five for 21 in the second innings and Hampshire won by two wickets.

Hampshire finished 1895 with six wins and nine losses, a record which put them tenth out of the 14 counties. It had been expected that Hampshire's strength would be in its batting, while the bowling would not be up to first-class standard. The reverse was the case. The slows of Baldwin picked up 102 Championship wickets at 16 runs each, whilst at the other end Soar had 89 victims at 18 runs each. Wootton, who had been absent from Championship cricket for four years, also returned good figures. The great trio of batsmen, Wynyard, Barton and Ward, had a poor season and A. J. L. Hill did little better; the batting table was headed by Captain F. W. D. Quinton of the Royal Artillery, due to his one great innings of 178 against Leicestershire. His brother also played for the County, but with no success.

Russell Bencraft retired from the captaincy at the end of 1895 and was succeeded by Captain Wynyard. Unfortunately neither he or Captain Quinton could play as often as in the previous year and the batting was further depleted by the decision of A. J. L. Hill to spend the summer in South Africa (he had toured that country in the previous winter). By way of compensation Victor Barton and H. F. Ward enjoyed

COLONEL CHRISTOPHER HESELTINE

Christopher Heseltine represents a good example of the relative strengths of cricket at Eton and Cambridge in the 1880s and 1890s. He was unable to gain a place in the eleven at either establishment, but was considered good enough to play for Hampshire at the age of 20 – in 1890 – and at the end of an intermittent first-class career had taken 170 wickets at an average of 24.53, as well as having played for England in the two Tests of 1895–96 in South Africa. He was a deadly fast bowler when used in short spells.

Against Worcestershire in 1899 he achieved the unusual feat of taking a wicket with the opening ball in each innings, the unfortunate batsman being Bromley-Martin. Playing for Hampshire against Surrey, he also managed to dismiss the much more formidable Robert Abel twice without scoring.

Apart from South Africa he toured both India and West Indies, and was frequently seen in good-class club cricket for MCC, I. Zingari, Free Foresters, Eton Ramblers and Quidnuncs. Although born in London, he resided at Brambridge Park, Eastleigh. He was appointed President of the Hampshire County Cricket Club in 1925 and was still in that office when he died in 1944 aged 74.

better seasons. E. I. M. Barrett, the Cheltenham College boy, played in three games in the holidays and looked a most promising batsman. Like so many Hampshire amateurs of his generation he joined the armed services and his appearances in Championship cricket were restricted, though his last appearance for the County was not until 1925.

The attack was handicapped by an injury to Soar and a distinct falling-off in the effectiveness of Baldwin, whose 70 Championship wickets cost 25 runs each. Kitchener, a fast bowler from Hartley Row, took five for 21 against Sussex in the second match of the summer, giving Hampshire a win by 76 runs, but did little subsequently. Captain E. R. Bradford, whose father was Chief Commissioner of Police, made many runs for the Aldershot Division as an opening bat and was brought in to the County side for this reason, but being put on to bowl after Soar, Baldwin and Wootton failed, took six for 28 against Essex in the first innings and a further five for 40 in the second, bringing Hampshire an innings victory. A fast bowler, Bradford's action was not all it might have been and he was one of the bowlers no-balled for throwing during Lord Harris's purge.

Despite their difficulties Hampshire won five matches and moved up from tenth to eighth in the Championship. The season of 1897 saw the County continue to occupy a place in the middle of the Championship table. Military duties prevented Captain Wynyard from leading the side until July, but for the second half of the summer his batting was so consistent that he was invited to tour Australia with the England side of 1897–98 – again military matters forced him to decline. H. F. Ward scored 40 and 39 in the opening match, but suffered sunstroke during the game and died 14 days later. The re-appearance of A. J. L. Hill went some way to filling the gap left by Ward's tragic death. Hill, of course, was in addition to his batting a useful bowler and since Soar was not at all himself, the bowling needed all the support Hampshire could muster. Another amateur bowler who proved more than useful – indeed his record of 38 Championship wickets at 15 runs each placed him at the head of the Hampshire averages – was Christopher Heseltine. It is curious to note that he failed to get into the eleven either at Eton or Cambridge, but played for England in the 1895–96 Tests against South Africa. He continued to appear on and off for Hampshire until 1904.

The professional A. S. Webb had a regular place in the side as a middle-order batsman and hit a splendid hundred off the Sussex attack at Portsmouth, being in about 180 minutes and not giving a chance. E. C. Lee, the old Winchester boy, played in 11 Championship games and looked promising without making any large scores. Captain Luard, the former Gloucestershire batsmen, appeared in five games, but did nothing and H. F. Ward's brother was also tried but with no concrete results. F. E. Lacey was available for seven matches and hit a delightful hundred in the drawn game with Derbyshire – Hampshire gained a large first innings lead, but rain prevented any play on the final day. Rain and high scoring increased the number of Championship matches which were drawn, so though Hampshire only won four games out of 18 they still managed to come ninth.

In 1898, the captain, Wynyard, played in only three Championship matches, pleading that military duties prevented his appearance, but on at least two occasions, when he ought to have been supporting the County, his name was found in other cricket teams. This did not go unnoticed. Lacey was appointed MCC Secretary and thus even his

BRIGADIER-GENERAL ROBERT MONTAGU POORE

Regarded as the finest swordsman in the British Army, a brilliant polo player, a noted tennis player and a champion shot, R. M. Poore took to cricket whilst serving in Bombay under Lord Harris in the early 1890s. His first-class cricket began with the European Team in the Bombay Tournament, and then on his transfer to South Africa, he appeared for Natal, hitting a brilliant undefeated hundred for that side against the 1895–96 English touring team. It was an innings which gained him a place in the South Africa Test side of that summer.

He came to England in March 1898 and was given a place in the Hampshire team. His debut was quite remarkable, for he carried his bat through the County innings for 49 not out in a Hampshire total of 97. He played one or two equally fine innings, but the transition from matting to grass and the variety of bowling in English cricket soon uncovered his weaknesses – Poore maintained that he learnt his batting from the 'Badminton Book of Cricket', which he studied as he would a textbook for an exam. Some critics wrote him off after his moderate 1898 performance, but in 1899 he created all sorts of records with first-class figures of 21 innings, four not outs, 1,551 runs, 304 highest score, average 91.23. He hit two separate hundreds in a match for Hampshire and a third in his next innings, as well as his famous 304 against Somerset, which involved the 411 partnership with Captain Wynyard.

Military duties made it impossible for him to play regular county cricket – in the period 1898 to 1906, he appeared in only 36 first-class Hampshire matches. After 1906 his cricket was very limited, though in 1923 he toured the West Country with MCC, and at the age of 57 hit three consecutive hundreds off good-standard club bowling.

The feature of his batting ws the power of his off-drives. He made the full use of his height (6ft 4in) and build both to attack the bowling and, by playing well forward, to get to the pitch of the ball.

fleeting appearances with the County Club ceased. A. J. L. Hill was the outstanding all-rounder, but the County found a really notable recruit – as so many others from military circles – in Major R. M. Poore. Poore had been for some years a prolific batsman in Indian cricket and when posted to South Africa had been chosen to represent that country in the Tests against England in 1895–96. Poore developed into one of the outstanding batsmen of his generation and in his first summer of Championship cricket he hit 659 runs at an average of 34.68. His largest innings of the season came in a run glut at Derby, when the home side tore the Hampshire attack to ribbons making 645, with four individual hundreds. Hampshire made only 240 in reply of which Poore hit an undefeated 121. Captain Quinton hit a hundred in the follow-on and saved the game.

With Soar injured for most of the year the bowling was in the hands of Baldwin, Hill and Heseltine, plus an odd asortment of amateurs and professionals of whom Ted Tate from Lyndhurst, a slow bowler, seemed the only one likely to bother the batsmen. Only two matches were won. Tate took eight for 51 against Somerset at Bournemouth which gave Hampshire one of their two victories. Bournemouth was added to Southampton and Portsmouth as one of Hampshire's home venues and proved financially successful.

Hampshire in 1898 fell to 12th place in the Championship. Next season saw a slight improvment, with four victories out of 20 matches, Worcestershire being met for the first time and therefore the Hampshire fixture list being increased by two matches. Major Poore appeared in nine matches and took the cricket world by storm, hitting 1,399 runs at an average of 116.58. He topped the first-class averages for the season and *Wisden* understated the situation when it announced that it would be difficult to find a parallel to the sudden fame experienced by Poore's batting feats. Wynyard had an excellent summer including 225 against Somerset at Taunton, but no one challenged Poore's 304 in the same match. The pair added a record 411 for the sixth wicket in 260 minutes and for once Hampshire's bowlers did not let them down, so the County won by an innings and 151 runs.

It was the attack which failed more often than not – 17 bowlers were tried during the year. Baldwin took easily the most wickets, but they cost 27 runs each and those of Heseltine, who was the second most successful, cost 32. Soar was unable to bowl in August due to rheumatics and A. J. L. Hill, who owing to business could only play in eight matches, scored plenty of runs, but failed as a bowler. Tate, after his good showing in 1898, fell away. T. Sutherland, a fast bowler and useful bat, was tried in seven Championship games but his four wickets cost 300 runs.

The overall results in 1899 produced four Championship wins, which meant that Hampshire ended the season in tenth place, equal with Notts.

SOMERSET *v* HAMPSHIRE

Played on the County Ground, Taunton, 20, 21 and 22 July 1899

HAMPSHIRE WON BY AN INNINGS AND 151 RUNS

SOMERSET	FIRST INNINGS		SECOND INNINGS	
Mr H. T. Stanley	b Soar	28	c Steele b Heseltine	9
Mr C. A. Bernard	c Robson b Heseltine	42	c Steele b Baldwin	7
E. Robson	b Soar	74	run out	19
Mr R. C. N. Palairet	c Robson b Soar	29	run out	27
Mr J. Daniell	c Robson b Baldwin	0	c Lee b Baldwin	57
G. B. Nichols	b Baldwin	64	c Lee b Wynyard	13
G. C. Gill	c Steele b Heseltine	8	c Webb b Wynyard	6
*Mr A. E. Newton	c Robson b Wynyard	46	c Steele b Baldwin	33
E. J. Tyler	not out	15	c English b Baldwin	10
†Rev A. P. Wickham	b Wynyard	1	not out	0
B. Cranfield	absent	–	b Wynyard	3
Extras	lb 7, nb 1	8	b 19, lb 1, w 2	22
Total		315		206

1st inns: 1-63, 2-81, 3-159, 4-164, 5-194, 6-204, 7-290, 8-309, 9-315
2nd inns: 1-16, 2-26, 3-63, 4-78, 5-98, 6-114, 7-189, 8-199, 9-206

BOWLING	O	M	R	W	O	M	R	W
Heseltine	26	4	80	2	19	2	58	1
Baldwin	39	13	84	2	25.4	13	53	4
Lee	6	1	15	0	3	1	10	0
Steele	7	1	34	0	4	0	14	0
Soar	19	4	74	3	15	5	31	0
Wynyard	11.3	3	20	2	10	3	18	3

HAMPSHIRE	FIRST INNINGS	
†Mr C. Robson	c and b Tyler	15
V. A. Barton	lbw b Tyler	12
Major R. M. Poore	st Wickham b Tyler	304
Mr E. A. English	b Gill	0
Mr E. C. Lee	c Nichols b Cranfield	11
T. Soar	c Cranfield b Gill	95
*Capt E. G. Wynyard	c Bernard b Tyler	225
H. Baldwin	not out	1
A. S. Webb	not out	2
Mr C. Heseltine		
Mr D. A. Steele		
Extras	lb 3, w 4	7
Total	(for 7 wkts dec)	672

1st inns: 1-26, 2-31, 3-38, 4-62, 5-258, 6-669, 7-670

BOWLING	O	M	R	W
Gill	44	8	127	2
Tyler	63	6	201	4
Cranfield	22	3	113	1
Robson	22	4	75	0
Nichols	21	2	104	0
Stanley	3	0	26	0
Daniell	4	0	19	0

Umpires: G. Burton and H. Pickett.
Somerset won the toss. Close of play: 1st day: Hants 65-4 (Poore 24, Soar 2); 2nd day: Hants 672-7.
*Captain; †Wicket-keeper.

The Boer War affected Hampshire more than any other county in 1900. Captain Wynyard's military duties meant that he resigned as captain and handed the reins over to Charles Robson, the wicket-keeper. Robson's career in county cricket had begun with his native Middlesex in the early 1880s, when he was an attacking opening batsman and fair change bowler. On moving to Hampshire in the 1890s, he was drafted in as wicket-keeper and his work behind the stumps had an adverse effect on his batting – he later regretted that he had been persuaded to become the County wicket-keeper.

Besides Wynyard, Hampshire lost Poore, Heseltine and, for most matches, Quinton, as well as two or three more who had been occasionally in the side, to the military authorities. As they failed to recruit any worthwhile replacements, the Hampshire season was a total disaster. Not a single game was won and 16 of the 22 Championship matches ended in defeat.

No less than 40 players were called upon. Barton and Webb, the two professional batsmen, appeared in every match. Baldwin missed one game and took the most wickets, 84 at 28 runs each. For some unknown reason, the most economical bowler, Soar, appeared in only eight games. E. M. Sprot, the old Harrovian, was available on a regular basis and hit a maiden hundred off the Warwickshire attack – Sprot was to be seen in the Hampshire side for many years to come, but Newton, who like Sprot, appeared in 17 games with fair results, made this his only summer in county cricket.

Two men changed the face of Hampshire cricket in 1901. The South African, C. B. Llewellyn, had played for the County in 1899 against the Australians and in 1900 against

Hants v Somerset: Taunton July 20, 21, 22 1899
At the close on the first day Somerset appeared to have a firm grip on the match, Hampshire having lost four wickets for 63 in response to Somerset's 315. A partnership of 411 between Poore and Wynyard on the second day completely changed the situation. Poore batted six hours 50 minutes and was lucky to be missed three times, as was Wynyard. Hampshire declared on Saturday morning and Somerset made a poor attempt to force a draw, Baldwin and Wynyard being the most successful bowlers.

MAJOR EDWARD GEORGE WYNYARD, DSO

Over six feet in height and a fine figure of a man, Wynyard excelled at many sports, but notably cricket and soccer. Educated at Charterhouse, though born in Bengal, he made his first-class debut for Hampshire in 1878 at the age of 17 and played his last match for the county 31 seasons later, but his appearances were very intermittent, due to his military career. He was a distinctive figure of the cricket field, for he normally wore an I Zingari cap of polo shape complete with strap under chin, even in county matches. His batting mainly consisted of attacking strokes in front of the wicket, but he liked to drop down on one knee and drive the ball over mid on! Twice he was invited to go to Australia with the MCC side but had to decline; he did, however, tour New Zealand in the autumn of 1906 only to snap a tendon in his knee during the third match and return home. The following year he led the MCC team to America. In 1905 and 1909 he toured South Africa.

The only time in England that he appeared in Test cricket was in 1896 against Australia, but he also appeared in the 1905–06 series against South Africa. In the 1880s he played in many matches in India, whilst stationed out there. A prominent member of MCC, his final first-class game was for the Club v Oxford University in 1912. He made regular visits to Lord's in later life and assisted in the management of the Ground.

As a soccer player his most outstanding match ws the Cup Final of 1881, when he represented Old Carthusians, who beat Old Etonians at The Oval. He was also a noted figure skater. He died at his residence, The Red House, Knotty Green, Beaconsfield on 30 October 1936 aged 75. His cousin, F. W. Wright, represented Lancashire from 1869 to 1875.

THE HAMPSHIRE COUNTY CRICKET CLUB GUIDE

Compiled under the supervision of the County Cricket Club Committee, this Guide was bound in blue cloth with gold lettering. The price was 6d (2½p). The publication, which was issued by G. Buxey, lasted only four years and the Guides are actually numbered one to four. The contents had not materially altered from its predecessor, the *Hampshire Cricketer's Guide*, though the editorial content had expanded – it included racing, lawn tennis, the Boat Race and athletics, as well as cricket. In 1893 a full list of Hampshire members is printed for the first time, and the list of County Club officials seems rather large, with eight Trustees, 18 Vice-Presidents and a Committee of 20.

The 1895 issue tells of Hampshire's re-admission to the first-class county list.

the West Indians, whilst waiting to qualify by residence. He had performed well in these matches, but it was still a most pleasant surprise when he took 115 Championship wickets in 1901 at a reasonable cost, as well as scoring two centuries. Captain J. G. Greig, the second debutant, had made a name for himself in Indian cricket as a brilliant batsman and he now brought his expertise on to English grounds. He hit five scores over 100, including 249 not out off the Lancashire bowlers at Liverpool, when he was at the wicket 320 minutes.

Six matches were won and Hampshire climbed to seventh place. In addition Llewellyn put his former colleagues to the sword when the South African tourists came to Southampton, hitting 216 in 180 minutes and finishing off the match with a second innings analysis of 6-3-6-4, as the visitors lost by an innings and 51 runs. The most satisfying of the County victories was against Kent at Bournemouth, again largely due to the all-round cricket of Llewellyn, who made 121 runs and took six wickets.

E. I. M. Barrett and Wynyard both played occasionally and their form showed what the County was missing when they were absent. The professionals Webb and Victor Barton had good seasons, the latter taking wickets as well as making runs. In contrast Baldwin and A. J. L Hill showed a marked decline. Soar was the most economical bowler, but again was played in only eight games.

Captain Greig was back with his regiment in India when the 1902 season came round. Barrett was fighting in South Africa and Wynyard's duties meant that even his fleeting appearances disappeared. The famous Lancashire batsman, A. C. MacLaren, was qualified by residence for the County and had announced he would play, but then decided to remain with the Red Rose contingent. In addition Victor Barton was suffering from opthalmic trouble and missed several matches. His one day of success was with the ball when he took five for 33 and enabled victory to be achieved against the strong Surrey eleven. In fact this was one of only two victories Hampshire claimed in 1902, the other being at the expense of Somerset at Portsmouth.

Llewellyn topped both batting and bowling tables by a fair margin and was the scorer of the County's only hundred, a point which indicates clearly how badly Greig, Wynyard, Barrett and Poore (he played twice) were missed. Second in the bowling table was H. V. Hesketh-Prichard, whose attributes are neatly summed up in 'The Cricket Blue Book': 'Takes up the summer game as a recreation, and generally does an amount of execution with his fast bowling.' He was soon to become a popular novelist and well-known traveller. A. C. Johnston, who had topped the Winchester batting during the summer was drafted into the side at the end of July, but his day was still to come and like so many others he chose an army career. W. H. B. Evans, who had made a name for himself in Public Schools cricket, being the oustanding all-rounder for Malvern in 1901 and as a result playing in the holidays for Worcestershire, switched his loyalties to Hampshire but played in only four matches. He joined the Egyptian Civil Service, which restricted his County appearances, and then in 1913 was tragically killed in a flying accident at Farnborough.

Hampshire were at the foot of the Championship table for 1902 and 1903 saw no upward movement at all – the number of wins even dropped from two to one. This victory came in the first home game – against Derbyshire at Southampton – due to the bowling of Hesketh-Prichard who took ten wickets in the match. At the close of the year he had more wickets than any other Hampshire bowler, though it should be added that this was a modest 45.

CHARLES BENNETT LLEWELLYN

Discovered by Colonel Poore, whilst he was serving in South Africa, C. B. Llewellyn was persuaded to come to England and qualify by residence for Hampshire. What struck Poore was Llewellyn's orthodox slow left-arm bowling, but the South African not only learnt the art of the 'chinaman', but developed into the best run-getter Hampshire possessed.

At the age of 24, in his first summer in English cricket, Llewellyn became the first Hampshire cricketer to achieve the 'double' – and to the embarrassment of his former South African colleagues hit a double-century off their attack in the first first-class match that country ever played in England. He repeated the feat of the 'double' in 1908 and 1910, but at the close of the latter season left Hampshire over a disagreement on terms and spent the winter of 1910–11 with the first South African team in Australia.

Returning to England he became a League professional, but was co-opted into the South African side for the 1912 Test, hitting a brilliant 75 against England at Lord's. After that season he was not seen again in first-class cricket. Llewellyn lived to see Hampshire win the Championship in 1961. He died in 1963, aged 87.

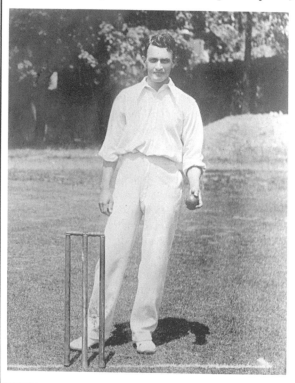

E. M. Sprot took over the leadership from Robson. Sprot was one of the few amateurs who had played regularly for Hampshire in the Boer War period and in 1903 was easily the best of the regular batsmen, averaging 36.30, with Llewellyn, immediate below him, achieving only 20.07. Barrett, Wynyard and A. J. L. Hill came above both, but had three, six and nine innings respectively. Nothing was seen of Poore and Greig. Victor Barton was forced by ill-health to retire and died, aged 38, in 1906.

Of the young hopefuls, W. H. B. Evans couldn't play, but A. C. Johnston turned out in eight matches and continued to improve. A local fast bowler, who had made one appearance in 1902, came into the side in mid-season and ended at the top of the averages with 42 wickets, at 13.95 each. W. T. Langford almost won the Warwickshire match at Southampton. He took 11 for 71 and the Warwickshire tail-end just managed to hang on for a draw. With Hesketh-Prichard also bowling well during the year, it was a terrible pity that Llewellyn seemed to lose his skill with the ball completely. His 39 wickets cost 39 runs each, so the County were forced to fall back on the veteran Soar, who when required bowled as well as ever.

Apart from Robson, another familiar face had retired after the 1902 season, that of Russell Bencraft, who handed over the secretarial duties to F. H. Bacon. Bacon became the first paid Secretary, but Bencraft remained nominally in charge as Honorary Secretary until the following year.

For the third successive year, 1904 found Hampshire with the wooden spoon. Llewellyn's decline was even more pronounced. Evans and Wynyard put in two appearances each, the former hitting a hundred against Worcestershire. Major Poore did manage nine matches, but failed to show his best form, though both A. J. L. Hill and A. C. Johnston, also playing in about half the games, batted well and with the captain, E. M. Sprot, very reliable, the batting got by. The bowling however was feeble. Only the ageing Baldwin supported Hesketh-Prichard. Langford was mastered, Soar's days were finally done. The professional, James Stone, had taken over as wicket-keeper and he now began to make some runs. Webb, now in his final year, was given a benefit, but support for the County was at such a low ebb that he received only about £150.

Season 1905 was yet another at the bottom. The bowling, with Hesketh-Prichard coming only for five matches, was in

ALTON

Hampshire have played just one first-class match at Alton – on the Recreation Ground *v* South Africans, 7 and 8 July 1904. The tourists completely overwhelmed the County, winning by an innings and 19 runs. Kotze virtually dictated the result of the game on the first evening. The County went in after the South Africans had made 380 and then Kotze's fast bowling took five wickets as Hampshire collapsed to 87 for seven. On the second day Llewellyn, playing against his compatriots, hit a brilliant 60, but the home side's position was hopeless and the game ended inside two days.

The ground used for this match was laid out only in the last years of the 19th century, the old town ground being The Butts, and on this ground, Alton played cricket against many of the neighbouring towns and villages back into the 18th century. Thomas Scott, who was born at Alton in 1766, played for Hambledon in the 1790s, but more famous are the three brothers Beagley, Thomas, Henry and John. Thomas was the first player to hit a century in the well-known Gentlemen *v* Players series of matches – at Lord's in 1821. The family was involved with the Alton side for many years.

even worse shape. Only Baldwin took more than 50 wickets and his cost 30 runs each. E. M. C. Ede, son of the old amateur, E. L. Ede, sent down some useful slow left-arm stuff and had 26 wickets in his seven matches. H. W. Persse, the Southampton amateur, aged 19, looked a good fast bowling prospect, but he joined the ever-growing band of Hampshire players who could not find time for regular county cricket.

Captain Greig (nine matches) and A. J. L. Hill (eight matches) both batted well – they both managed the feat of hundreds in each innings of a match, Greig *v* Worcester and Hill *v* Somerset. It was a statistical oddity that Llewellyn also performed the same feat in the course of the summer. Although of the amateur batsmen, only the captain played in more than half the matches, there were enough of the irregulars to make the opposition work hard, but however many runs were piled on the board, there were too few for the Hampshire bowlers, except in the Derbyshire game at

ARTHUR JAMES LEDGER HILL

Hill's career with Hampshire spanned the seasons 1890 to 1921, but unfortunately for the County he could not play regularly. Recognised as one of the finest amateur batsmen in England, Hill combined a sound defence with an array of attacking strokes dominated by the drive, both on the leg and off sides.

He went on three overseas tours under Lord Hawke, including the 1895–96 visit to South Africa, when he took part in all three Tests, and in the game at Newlands saved England by scoring 124 out of an all-out total of 265.

Hill's most memorable game for Hampshire was in 1905 against Somerset. He scored hundreds in both innings and in the second innings formed a curious first-wicket partnership with Major Wynyard. Hill reached 50, when Wynyard had made only two, and 80 when Wynyard had reached seven. In this innings, Hill was lame, but his partner, owing to a bad thumb, could bat with only one hand.

Playing for the Hampshire Hogs in 1901, Hill hit 50 off two consecutive overs from E. R. Kinnersley – 28 and 22. Towards the close of his county career, he actually appeared in the same Hampshire side as his son, A. E. L. Hill.

In his younger days at Marlborough, where he was in the eleven for three years, and at Oxford, playing four times against Cambridge, he was a more than useful fast bowler, but later he took to bowling lobs with occasional success.

Southampton, when Hampshire's novelist took eight for 32 and dismissed the Peak team for 58 – it was Hampshire's solitary win of 1905.

On the face of it, the only major innovation for 1906 was the newly qualified batsman, Philip Mead, who had won fulsome praise whilst on the staff at The Oval. A left-hand batsman aged 19, he scored 60 and 109 off the Yorkshire attack in the season's first home game. His 109 was a most mature innings and the critics were looking forward to some fine batting from him. He did not live up to their expectations – at least for the rest of 1906 – and the man who in effect dragged Hampshire out of the depths was John Badcock, a native of Christchurch, who had had the odd game with Kent Second Eleven. A fast bowler, he brought Hampshire their first win of the year – after four successive defeats – when he captured nine Derbyshire wickets. Badcock also bowled well in the return with Derbyshire which brought another win and also the two victories over Northants and Leicestershire. His season's record of 92 wickets at 24.71 runs each was an outstanding performance from an unknown. Both Llewellyn and Langford benefited from Badcock's success and had better bowling records. F. J. C. Wyatt, a medium-pace bowler, was selected for four games and took 22 wickets but he could not find the time to play and joined the irregular brigade.

With the batting still strong – Greig appeared in many matches, Barrett, Hill and Poore in some – the County enjoyed its best season for a long time. Seven wins placed them eighth in the Championship.

Although much of the military element was absent in 1907, Hampshire fielded a more settled eleven – four players appeared in all 24 Championship games and three more in at least 20. Badcock did not do as well as in his first year, but H. W. Persse, totally absent in 1906, played all summer and obtained 60 wickets at 23.20 each. In addition Llewellyn bowled better than for some time. The result was that six wins were obtained, the best of which was against Kent, though the side gained almost as much credit for forcing Yorkshire on to the defence in the final game at Bournemouth.

Jack Newman, who had played once or twice in 1906, gained a fairly regular place by virtue of his medium pace bowling. A local man from Southsea he was to become an essential member of the side, as was Alec Kennedy, whose seven wickets for 83 runs put him theoretically on top of the bowling table. R. W. F. Jesson, the Sherborne schoolboy, who was at Oxford, though not in the eleven, took some wickets with his leg breaks, but scored few runs.

Of the batsmen, Mead reached a thousand runs as did E. M. Sprot and Alec Bowell. The last named had his most successful season so far and had developed into a most attractive batsman – his County debut had been made in 1902 and he was now aged 27.

Sprot created a sensation in the 1908 Northants match at Southampton, when, with more than a day lost through rain, he declared the Hampshire innings closed although still 24 runs behind on first innings. This action, which later became a commonplace, was most successful, since Philip Mead with seven for 18 bowled out Northants for 60 in their second innings and then Hampshire went on to win by nine wickets, Sprot himself making 62 of the 85 required. That was one of seven Championship wins for Hampshire and maintained the County's position in mid-table.

A. J. L. Hill headed the batting table, appearing in nine matches. Sprot and Mead came second and third, both averaging 33, followed by Bowell and Llewellyn. Captain W. N. White made 12 Championship appearances and confirmed that he was yet one more army man who might have made a name in county cricket if he had been able to afford the time, a remark which also applied to the Haileybury boy, G. N. Bignell.

The bowling was mainly in the hands of the three professionals, Newman, Llewellyn and Badcock. Wyatt bowled well in the four games for which he was available and H. C. McDonell, the old Cambridge and Surrey slow bowler, appeared under residential qualification and did well against Warwickshire.

In 1909 a much greater personality took advantage of a residential qualification to switch his counties. C. B. Fry, the eminent England all-rounder, left Sussex for Hampshire. He hit a hundred against Warwickshire at Bournemouth which, together with the bowling of Newman and McDonell, brought victory by an innings. Fry made 132 – the next highest score in the whole match was 46.

Seven wins placed Hampshire in eighth place, which was most satisfactory, especially when considered in relation to the first game of the season, in which Surrey won by the overwhelming margin of an innings and 468 runs – Hobbs and Hayes both made double hundreds for the victors.

CHARLES PHILIP MEAD

Having a trial with his native county of Surrey as a slow left-arm bowler, Philip Mead failed to impress, and in search of another opportunity he moved to Hampshire in order to qualify by residence. Gaining a regular place in the County side in 1906, Mead reached 1,000 runs in every season from then until his retirement 30 years later. Tall and angular, he had the odd mannerism of walking around in a little circle before addressing the ball and then fiddling with his cap, as if saluting the bowler. Despite his consistency, he failed to obtain a regular place in England's Test side and had the curious experience of going to Australia with the 1911–12 MCC side and then not again until 1928–29.

The basis of his success was his sound defence, but although he did not appear to score quickly, he kept the scoreboard ticking over with carefully judged singles, as well as being severe on any loose deliveries on the leg side. He was the first left-handed batsman to compile 100 centuries and at the time of his retirement, only Hobbs and Hendren had scored more.

Twice Mead reached 3,000 runs in a season; on seven other occasions he topped 2,000. His greatest year was 1921 when he not only headed the first-class averages but also hit 182 not out against Australia at The Oval, his highest Test score.

The County suffered its usual problem of having talented amateurs who could not play in many matches. Fry easily topped the batting table but appeared only nine times. First and second in the bowling were W. H. B. Evans and McDonell, who played in seven and nine matches. The professional strength was at last growing, and this went some way to producing a more balanced team. Newman, Kennedy, Bowell, Llewellyn and wicket-keeper Stone were joined by George Brown. Brown, at this stage described as a fast bowler, became a cricketer of many parts, who on his day was an outstanding all-rounder, a term which included being a wicket-keeper. His career lasted to 1933.

So Hampshire appeared to have a bright future, with a collection of very talented young players on their staff. It was also pleasant to note from the Statement of Accounts that, following years of financial embarrassment, 1909 saw a profit of £200 on the year's workings, disregarding the additional sum given to the Club as part of the Test Match profits.

W. H. B. Evans and C. B. Fry could only come for two matches each in 1910. A few years back to lose their two most talented amateurs meant disaster – no more, however, for the professionals, notably Mead and Newman and a rejuvenated Llewellyn, were almost a side on their own. Newman created a new Hampshire record when he took 156 Championship wickets, and with Llewellyn taking 133, the pair completely dominated the bowling – McDonell took the third most wickets, his total being 33. Mead was fast developing into the most difficult batsman to dismiss in Hampshire and England. He scored most runs, followed by Llewellyn and A. C. Johnston. Captain Greig was available for 12 matches and did well considering the wickets hardly suited his style.

No less than ten matches were won, which put Hampshire sixth. The record would have been even more outstanding had it not been for an unfortunate period in August. Hampshire set Lancashire 404 to win with five hours' playing time left. Sharp and Makepeace added 242 in 160 minutes and Lancashire won with half an hour in hand. Just as exciting was the Yorkshire game ten days later. Hampshire needed 240 and on a drying wicket lost four for 26, but Captain White batted so well, that the game was lost by only six runs. The proudest moment of the season was the victory over Surrey, the first time since 1902 that Hampshire had been successful against that county.

CHARLES BURGESS FRY

The outstanding sports personality of the Edwardian era, Fry's cricket was mainly with Sussex, and it was not until he was 37 that he joined Hampshire under residential qualification in 1909. The highest score of his first-class career was 258 not out for Hampshire *v* Gloucester at Southampton in 1911 and in the following season he led England in the six Tests of the Triangular Tournament.

His final year with Hampshire was 1921. According to his autobiography, Fry was invited to captain England when Douglas failed in the First Test of that summer, but Fry recommended to the selectors that they should pick Tennyson for the job. As Fry forecast, Tennyson was relatively successful with the bat.

In 1920, Fry was the assistant to Ranjitsinhji with the Indian delegation to the United Nations and then Fry went to India and was there in 1922 when the Prince of Wales made his famous tour of the country. It was at this time that Fry made his final appearance in first-class cricket, playing for the Europeans in the Bombay Tournament.

Fry's son, Stephen, played occasionally for Hampshire from 1922 to 1931 and his grandson, Charles Anthony, played in five Hampshire matches in 1960.

Llewellyn would not accept the contract offered to him by Hampshire for the 1911 season, preferring to play for South Africa and in the League. This decision immediately removed half the 1911 county attack and as is so often the case, Llewellyn's bowling partner, Newman, found life very much more difficult. His decline was quite startling – 67 wickets at 33 runs each compared to 156 at 18. Brown and Kennedy improved on their 1911 totals and D. M. Evans, the brother of W.H.B., played in nearly half the fixtures, picking up 45 wickets at a reasonable cost, but these three could in no way make up for the missing Llewellyn and the out-of-form Newman.

Mead continued his methodical advance, his Championship run total being 1,706 at an average of 58.82. Fry, batting in 10 matches, was in great form. He hit 258 not out off the Gloucestershire attack and two hundreds in an innings off Kent at Canterbury. Fry ended the summer at the head of the national first-class averages, with Mead in second place, the latter finishing his season with two brilliant innings, 223 for Players against Gentlemen at Scarborough and then 101 in the Rest of England *v* Champion County at The Oval.

Seven matches were won, but ten lost and the County dropped five places. The financial position of the County was now much stronger and the membership continued to grow. A new scoreboard, at a cost of £105, was erected on the Southampton Ground.

Only seven matches were brought to a successful conclusion in 1912, but the reason was mainly because rain forced a draw in many matches, a state of affairs which affected all the counties, and therefore Hampshire rose up the Championship table again. Fry, though missing many matches due to Test calls, scored 612 Championship runs at an average 102.00. At the end of the year, Hampshire batsmen had improved even on their 1911 showing in the first-class averages, for they occupied not only the first two places, but also the third – Fry came first, A. C. Johnston second and Mead third, and the fact that E. I. M. Barrett was in tenth place made the County the strongest batting combination in the country. If the bowling had matched up Hampshire might well have claimed the title. As it was the attack consisted of Kennedy and Newman, and then Newman and Kennedy. Making the ball swing, Kennedy had his best season to date, and in Championship games took

112 wickets at 17 runs each; Newman's figures were 86 at 22. The only other bowlers of any consequence were H. C. McDonell and Hesketh-Prichard, but they were available very infrequently.

The best win of the season was against Middlesex at Portsmouth, when victory was achieved by nine wickets, due to some good all-round cricket rather than exceptional play by one or two – Fry was absent for this game. The County also beat the Australians for the first time ever, Mead making an undefeated 160 and Kennedy taking 11 wickets – Hampshire supporters were baffled by the non-selection of Mead for any of the six Test Matches.

With their three brilliant amateurs more or less absent all year, Hampshire's position in the Championship fell in 1913. Fry and Barrett were not seen at all and Johnson only appeared six times. Mead, however, had a tremendous summer and came top of the first-class averages, as well as scoring most runs: 2,627, average 50.51. Two young batsmen came to the fore and it was unfortunate that neither was available for the full season. The Hon Lionel Tennyson and Lieutenant C. H. Abercrombie created something of a sensation in the match at Leyton. Essex made 507 and Hampshire were then dismissed for 190 and the follow-on enforced. Tennyson then hit a century in 80 minutes without giving a chance and Abercrombie made 165, and with G. Brown added 325 in 210 minutes. Tennyson had been in the Eton Elevens of 1907 and 1908, without doing anything exceptional. At Cambridge he had failed to obtain a blue and had then entered the Army. It was in military cricket, therefore, that he made his name and came to the attention of Hampshire. After his 100 against Essex he then hit a second in the following match at Trent Bridge and ended the year second to Mead in the Hampshire averages, though playing in only nine games. He was to dominate Hampshire cricket for much of the period between the wars. Abercrombie's reputation was made when he hit a century for the Royal Navy against the Army at Lord's in 1912. He was given a trial for Hampshire in the match against Oxford University on 30 June and signalled his debut with a century, made without a blemish. With Bowell he added 100 in 55 minutes. Three matches later he hit a second hundred, off the Worcestershire attack at Dudley, and in the game which followed made his hundred against Essex. Abercrombie's cricket was sadly

The side which beat the Australians in 1912. Back row, left to right: E. R. Remnant, J. Stone, J. Newman, G. Brown, C. P. Mead, A. Bowell, A. S. Kennedy. Front row: G. N. Bignell, C. B. Fry. E. M. Sprot, E. I. M. Barrett, Rev W. V. Jephson.

confined to 1913 – in 1914 his naval commitments prevented any County appearances and in 1916 he was killed at the Battle of Jutland, whilst serving aboard HMS *Defence*.

Whilst these two exhilarating young batsmen hit the headlines, the two mainstays of Hampshire cricket were Kennedy and Newman, who came first and second in the Hampshire bowling table. Both had productive years, as did Brown, whose 83 Championship wickets cost 26 runs each. One new bowler was Arthur Jaques. He had failed to get into the Cambridge Eleven, but had played much club cricket, especially with the Trojans, and had toured West Indies with the 1912–13 side. A fastish in-swing bowler, he played in Hampshire's second match of the season and then remained in the team more or less for the rest of the campaign. He was to die on the Western Front in 1915.

Hampshire's results in 1913 were remarkable for the number of close finishes. Surrey won at Southampton by five

HAMPSHIRE COUNTY CRICKET GUIDE

After the 1895 edition of *The Hampshire County Cricket Club Guide*, published by G. Buxey, the County Club decided that due to the continued financial loss incurred by the annual they could not afford to subsidise it any longer. The local newspaper, the *Hampshire Advertiser*, took over the responsibility for 1896, and published by H. King and edited by E. L. Ede, this third Hampshire annual, the *Hampshire County Cricket Guide*, continued until 1910. As with the second annual it was bound in blue, and the general production was excellent.

In 1899 an illustration appeared for the first time – being a portrait of the County Club President, L. G. Bonham-Carter. Illustrations however did not appear in every edition. A list of Births and Deaths of Hampshire players first appeared in 1900 and included details of the famous Hambledon cricketers.

The retail price remained 6d (2$\frac{1}{2}$p) and as late as 1964 the Hampshire County Cricket Club still held some issues in stock!

runs and in the next game on the same ground, Notts wanted eight to win with two wickets to fall when time was called. More successful for Hampshire was the game against Worcestershire, which they won by two wickets.

Although the club's finances were much better than in the past, a loss of £200 was made on the year's workings and it was pointed out at the County's Annual General Meeting that an annual income of £2,000 from subscriptions was desirable to ensure the future.

Jaques perfected his leg theory bowling for 1914, Pitching the ball on or about the leg stump and using a ring of fieldsmen close in on the leg side, he took 112 Championship wickets and, apart from the occasional McDonell, topped the Hampshire bowling averages. Kennedy, with 148 wickets came close behind him, with Newman and Brown giving good support as change bowlers and Hampshire achieved a record 13 Championship wins which gave them fifth place – the highest in their history so far.

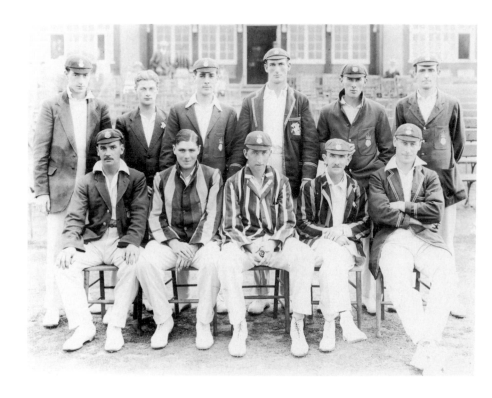

Hampshire in 1914. Back row, left to right: H. H. Livsey, J. H. Down, A. S. Kennedy, G. Brown, A. Bowell, J. Newman. Front row: J. Stone, H. A. Haig-Smith, A. Jaques, J. G. Greig, C. P. Mead.

The batting aspect was not so happy, but that was not important so long as Mead ground out his runs, which he did with remarkable consistency, coming third in the first-class averages behind Hobbs and Hearne. The amateurs were not freely available. Fry appeared four times, Tennyson three, Johnston three and Greig nine. Apart from Mead only Newman and Bowell completed 1,000 Championship runs. The Cambridge blue, A. C. P. Arnold, another who was shortly to die in action, played in 11 matches, and the Felsted schoolboy Alastair MacLeod batted most promisingly in five, as did Lieutenant-Commander G. C. Harrison, who had come into the side following success in the Royal Navy side. In the professional ranks the main change was the inclusion of Walter Livsey as wicket-keeper, replacing Stone. Livsey, a Yorkshireman, was to remain the County's wicket-keeper through the 1920s.

It was a pity that the success Hampshire attained on the field of play was not reflected in the Treasurer's department,

but the outbreak of war made a very large difference to the
accounts and a deficit of over £700 was recorded. The most
satisfactory feature of the match results was the double
victory over Kent, but they also beat Leicestershire,
Derbyshire and Somerset home and away.

Hampshire were thus at their strongest when the First
World War ended first-class cricket. It was to be five years
before the team reassembled.

PROLIFIC MEAD AND DASHING TENNYSON

IN THE ABSENCE OF ANY INTER-COUNTY MATCHES during the First World War, the County Ground at Southampton was used for Charity games and numerous military matches. The County Club held its Annual General Meeting each year despite the absence of cricket and enough members renewed their subscriptions to pay for the various overheads which still occurred. At the 1916 AGM the subject of winter pay for professionals was discussed. Russell Bencraft spoke strongly against such payments, saying that professionals earned a good deal of money during the season and that he did not think it right that strong, healthy young men should be idle for seven months of the year.

During 1918, E. M. Sprot indicated that he did not wish to continue as captain when cricket resumed and the Committee elected the Hon Lionel Tennyson for the post. The death of Jaques and the absence of Newman left the attack relying on Kennedy and Brown for the first matches of 1919, but the latter proved useless, his five wickets costing 59 runs each. Tennyson was forced to open the bowling and his seven wickets cost 58 runs each. Commander A. E. Evans – another brother of W.H.B. – helped Kennedy beat Surrey at The Oval in the second match of the summer. Kennedy took 12 wickets and Evans, bowling medium pace and making his Hampshire debut, took seven. There followed three drawn matches and a defeat at the hands of Yorkshire. The Hampshire Committee in their search for bowlers engaged Frank Ryan, an American-born slow left-armer. He had served in the Royal Flying Corps and was qualified by residence. His bowling enabled the County to beat Sussex at Hove, when he took five for 57 and Sussex collapsed for 119 all out in their second innings, having been left two hours to make 184.

H. C. McDonell returned to the eleven in the second half of the year and further bolstered the attack. Three matches were won in August and Hampshire were happy to end the season in seventh place. Five wins in 16 matches might appear modest, but 1919 was the year of the great experimental two-day county match programme and the very dry summer made the task of obtaining definite results very difficult.

THE THIRD BARON TENNYSON
(HON LIONEL HALLAM TENNYSON)

Receiving a telegram, Tennyson read it, rolled it into a ball, tossed it in the air and caught it, remarking: 'Good gracious, they've asked me to captain England.'

He took up his appointment for the Third Test against the Australians in 1921, injured his hand whilst fielding, but insisted on batting against the ferocity of Gregory and McDonald and, going in last but one, hit 63 one-handed.

It cannot be said that Tennyson, a grandson of the Poet Laureate, was ever a reliable batsman, but the more desperate the situation, the more likely he was to succeed. Indeed he twice confused all the pundits – at school he was an excellent fast bowler, but as soon as he arrived in first-class cricket he more or less abandoned bowling for batting; then he hit 110 on his first-class debut for MCC and within a month or so had made two hundreds for Hampshire and ended his first season fifth in the first-class averages, with an invitation to tour South Africa as part of the England side of 1913–14. He hit fifty on his Test debut at Durban, having been in first-class cricket only six months. Tennyson played for Hampshire from 1913 to 1935, and captained the County from 1919 to 1933.

Leveson-Gower said that Tennyson ought to go down in history as the laughing cricketer, and the more outgoing crowds in the West Indies – where he toured five times – and in India relished his personality and his style of cricket.

MAJOR THE Hon.
L.H.TENNYSON
.2.

Turning to the batting, Mead was now firmly established as the best left-hander in England and his figures proved it. In Championship games he hit 1,332 runs at an average of 60.54. His limitless patience and impregnable defence wore down even the best bowlers. Brown, having lost his bowling, showed very good form with the bat and came second to Mead, whilst in third place was the South African Oxford blue, Dr B. G. von B. Melle, who opened the innings for nearly all the fixtures. Before the war he had been a better bowler than batsman. Commander G. C. Harrison scored runs at a tremendous rate when set – his 111 *v* Gloucestershire at Southampton came in 90 minutes – and a newcomer, T. O. Jameson, another noted military batsman, also hit some useful runs. The captain, Tennyson, however, could not find his form at all.

THE RED GUIDE

Although officially known as *Hampshire County Cricket Guide,* the title of its predecessor, the fourth series of guides, which commenced in 1911 is better known as *The Red Guide.* Bound in red paper covers, the page size was $6\frac{1}{2}$ by $3\frac{1}{2}$ inches generally, though some issues varied slightly. The number of pages varied but was normally about 250, with the 1929 edition running to 270 pages and being the largest. Whilst the County scores and list of County Members continued to be published, the Guides also contained 'Notable Performances in Club Cricket' and 'Facts in Hampshire Cricket History' as well as photographs and biographies of many of Hampshire's famous players and administrators.

The Guide was published by the *Hampshire Advertiser* until 1923, then the *Hampshire Advertiser and Echo* until 1927 and from 1928 until the last issue in 1939 by Southern Newspapers Ltd. From 1911 to 1914 the price actually halved to 3d (approx 1p), but after thge First World War it was normally 6d ($2\frac{1}{2}$p), except in 1922 when 9d (approx 4p) was charged.

As 1919 was something of a curiosity, a couple of Hampshire oddities for the year would not come amiss. In the Gloucester game, Pothecary, the Hampshire No 11 played the ball into the top of his pad and then shook the ball out into the hands of the wicket-keeper. He was pronounced out 'caught'. This decision however was contrary to the Laws. In the Hampshire averages, Mr G. Newcombe is featured playing 18 innings and scoring 358 runs. Mr Newcombe was in fact G. N. Bignell, the pre-war Hampshire amateur, using an alias, a fashion which had generally died in the 19th century.

The following season, 1920, started full of hope. Newman returned to strengthen the bowling and Captain E. I. M. Barrett was to be available for most matches, but the team was taken apart by Leicestershire, one of the weakest of the counties, in the first match and then narrowly lost at The Oval. Though the third match – against Worcester – brought victory, the next three games were all defeats by substantial margins and from this poor beginning the County never recovered. The reason for the defeats was inexplicable batting collapses. Mead was as good as ever and Brown also was in good form. Both hit six Championship hundreds, two of Brown's being over 200, including one off the Yorkshire bowling at Headingley. This match illustrated how brilliant Hampshire could be when everything came together. Hampshire scored 456 for two declared, with Brown 232 not out and Mead 122 not out. Kennedy and Newman then took full advantage of a drying wicket to dismiss Yorkshire twice and produce an innings victory.

Of the regular players, the batsmen with the best record, after the two left-handers, were Captain Barrett, Tennyson and Bowell, but all three were inconsistent. Colonel Greig batted well when able to come and C. B. Fry, only appearing twice, hit 137 off the Notts bowlers at Southampton. It was a superb display and more especially so for a 48-year-old veteran not in practice. Another ancient of the same age, A. J. L. Hill, hit 74 in 90 minutes off the Middlesex attack – Middlesex were the County Champions of 1920 – but Hill also only played twice.

Kennedy was easily the County's best bowler with 164 wickets at 17 runs each. Newman also took over a hundred but was more expensive. Ryan, the find of 1919, fell away and dropped out of the side. McDonell likewise was not so effective. Support for Kennedy and Newman came in some matches from the left-arm slows of E. R. Remnant, who had played for the County since 1908 with variable success as an all-rounder.

On paper the opening of the 1921 season was even more miserable for Hampshire supporters than that of 1920, but the fixtures fell in such a way that the County met the strongest opposition, Yorkshire, Middlesex, Kent and Lancashire, first. Once the programme moved on and the weaker Counties arrived, Hampshire rose quickly up the table. Ten of their last 13 matches were successes and sixth place in the table was attained. The total number of Championship victories was 14, a record for the County.

Too much depended on the bowling of Kennedy and Newman. Each put in a tremendous amount of work sending down more than 1,000 overs each. Newman also scored a thousand runs and with the aid of not outs managed a batting average above 30.

Tennyson was chosen to captain England in three Tests against Australia and he had a reasonable batting average, but remained very inconsistent. Brown had the rather odd experience of being chosen to keep wicket for England in three Tests, though he was not Hampshire's regular wicket-keeper, that post still being occupied by Livsey. Even more odd was Brown's 1921 batting record. He averaged 24 in Hampshire Championship games and 50 in Test cricket, scoring 250 runs in his five innings.

Season 1922 also contained an oddity, but of a different sort. In the game at Trent Bridge, Newman was barracked by the crowd for the amount of time he spent adjusting the field to suit his bowling. Tennyson ordered Newman to stop wasting time, whereupon Newman replied to his captain in no uncertain manner. Tennyson then told him to leave the field, and in doing so Newman kicked down the wicket. Subsequently there were apologies all round and Newman was reinstated in the side the next day. Notts won the game by nine wickets, this being one of six Championship defeats suffered by Hampshire. On the other hand they claimed 13 victories and retained their position of sixth in the table.

Even though the Championship table had been expanded as long ago as 1895, the counties then promoted still, in 1922, failed to make much impact on the race for the title. The very occasional success of these 'new' counties was even now greeted as a nine-day wonder. In 1922, for example, Hampshire beat Lancashire for the first time since their 1895

promotion and this was treated in the press as quite extraordinary. Hampshire also beat Yorkshire at Bradford. The report on this game commences: 'In this match Yorkshire met with their second defeat and very sensational it was.' Both these historic wins occurred in August and were due to the bowling combination of Kennedy and Boyes, Yorkshire being dismissed for 56 and 116, Lancashire for 139 and 77.

Kennedy had his best season to date and achieved the feat of taking 200 wickets (190 for Hampshire) and scoring 1,000 runs. Boyes had turned out as an amateur for Hampshire in a few games in 1921, but had since become a professional, and as a slow left-arm bowler he exploited the wet wickets of 1922, ending with 94 Championship wickets at 18 runs each. With Newman also in form the County now had three regular bowlers instead of the usual two plus occasional amateurs.

As well as a bowling discovery, Hampshire found a new run-getter of note. H. L. V. Day, the international Rugby footballer, who had saved England at Twickenham in February, was chosen for the Hampshire side against Kent at

The Hampshire side which won the famous victory over Warwickshire in 1922, after being all out for 15 and following on. Back row, left to right: G. Brown, umpire, W. H. Livsey, G. S. Boyes, W. R. Shirley, A. S. Kennedy, umpire, J. Newman. Front row: A. Bowell, A. S. McIntyre, Hon L. H. Tennyson, H. L. V. Day, C. P. Mead.

WARWICKSHIRE *v* HAMPSHIRE

Played at Edgbaston, 14, 15 and 16 June 1922

HAMPSHIRE WON BY 155 RUNS

WARWICKSHIRE	FIRST INNINGS		SECOND INNINGS	
L. T. A. Bates	c Shirley b Newman	3	c Mead b Kennedy	1
†E. J. Smith	c Mead b Newman	24	c Shirley b Kennedy	41
Mr F. R. Santall	c McIntyre b Boyes	84	b Newman	0
William Quaife	b Newman	1	not out	40
*Hon F. S. G. Calthorpe	c Boyes b Kennedy	70	b Newman	30
Rev E. F. Waddy	c Mead b Boyes	0	b Newman	0
Mr B. W. Quaife	b Boyes	0	c and b Kennedy	7
J. Fox	b Kennedy	4	b Kennedy	0
J. A. Smart	b Newman	20	b Newman	3
C. C. Smart	c Mead b Boyes	14	c and b Boyes	15
H. Howell	not out	1	c Kennedy b Newman	11
Extras	leg byes	2	b 6, lb 4	10
Total		223		158

1st inns: 1-3, 2-36, 3-44, 4-166, 5-177, 6-184, 8-200, 9-219
2nd inns: 1-2, 2-77, 3-85, 4-85, 5-85, 6-89, 7-113, 8-143, 9-147

BOWLING	O	M	R	W	O	M	R	W
Kennedy	24	7	74	2	26	12	47	4
Newman	12.3	0	70	4	26.3	12	53	5
Boyes	16	5	56	4	11	4	34	1
Shirley	3	0	21	0				
Brown					5	0	14	0

HAMPSHIRE	FIRST INNINGS		SECOND INNINGS	
H. A. W. Bowell	b Howell	0	c Howell b W. Quaife	45
A. S. Kennedy	c Smith b Calthorpe	0	b Calthorpe	7
Mr H. L. V. Day	b Calthorpe	0	c Bates b W. Quaife	15
C. P. Mead	not out	6	b Howell	24
*Hon L. H. Tennyson	c Calthorpe b Howell	4	c C. C. Smart b Calthorpe	45
G. Brown	b Howell	0	b C. C. Smart	172
J. Newman	c C. C. Smart b Howell	0	c and b W. Quaife	12
Mr W. R. de la C. Shirley	c J. A. Smart b Calthorpe	1	lbw b Fox	30
Mr A. S. McIntyre	lbw b Calthorpe	0	lbw b Howell	5
†W. H. Livsey	b Howell	0	not out	110
G. S. Boyes	lbw b Howell	0	b Howell	29
Extras	byes	4	b 14, lb 11, w 1, nb 1	27
Total		15		521

1st inns: 1-0, 2-0, 3-0, 4-5, 5-5, 6-9, 7-10, 8-10, 9-15
2nd inns: 1-15, 2-63, 3-81, 4-127, 5-152, 6-177, 7-262, 8-274, 9-451

BOWLING	O	M	R	W	O	M	R	W
Howell	4.5	2	7	6	63	10	156	3
Calthorpe	4	3	4	4	33	7	97	2
William Quaife					49	8	154	3
Fox					7	0	30	1
J. A. Smart					13	2	37	0
Santall					5	0	15	0
C. C. Smart					1	0	5	1

Umpires: A. J. Atfield and B. Brown.
Warwickshire won the toss. Close of play: Warwickshire 223, Hampshire 15 and 95 for 3; 2nd day: Warwickshire 223, Hampshire 15 and 435 for 8.
*Captain; †Wicket-keeper.

Southampton at the beginning of June and on this, his first-class debut, made 91 and 56, coming in at No 7 against the bowling, among others, of Woolley and Freeman. Like so many of his Hampshire predecessors, Day was a military man, being a Lieutenant in the Royal Artillery, and though he hit 1,000 runs in 1922, his appearances in future seasons were to be very restricted.

Hampshire's batting in 1922 relied much too much on the efforts of Mead, who had yet another prolific summer – 2,270 Championship runs at 63.05. Day came second with 1,042 at 40.07. No one else averaged as much as 25.

Two amateurs playing fairly often about this time, who made names for themselves in cricket administration later in life were Ronald Aird and H. S. Altham. Twenty-year-old Aird, a stylish right-hand bat, gained his blue at Cambridge in 1923 and is now best remembered as Secretary of MCC in the 1950s. H. S. Altham, on the staff at Winchester College, had obtained a blue at Oxford before the war and had played a few times for Surrey. He appeared in 24 matches for Hampshire between 1919 and 1923 as a middle-order batsman, but with little success. He was a member of the MCC Committee for 25 years and wrote a history of the game.

Results in 1923 were not quite as good as in 1922, but with ten championship wins, the County were in seventh place. The season began well and a brilliant win was obtained over Middlesex at Lord's in late July by means of good cricket by

Hants v Warwickshire: Birmingham June 14, 15, 16 1922

Quite one of the most remarkable matches ever played. The dramatic collapse of Hampshire in their first innings was simply a freak performance, since the wicket did nothing out of the ordinary. Following on Hampshire lost six wickets for 186 and an innings defeat appeared certain. Shirley then helped Brown to put on 85 runs and, after McIntyre failed, Livsey hit a century without giving a chance. Kennedy and Newman went on to dismiss Warwickshire cheaply and Hampshire won the most incredible victory.

GEORGE BROWN

'He is a daring field at silly-point, but so far has escaped decapitation', noted the 1934 *News Chronicle Annual*. Brown was indeed a remarkable fielder, not only at silly-point, but also deeper, where he obtained numerous 'run out' by deceiving the batsmen into a sense of false security. In emergency he was called upon to keep wicket, not only for Hampshire, but also for England, and he performed that duty in a most efficient manner.

As batsman he could improvise, using strokes not seen in any textbook, but he was strongest on the leg side, either hooking or driving. His Test career was confined to matches against Australia in 1921 and in South Africa in 1922–23. His best run-getting season was in 1926 when he exceeded 2,000 runs for the only time in his career, which spanned 26 years.

A new-ball bowler of something above medium pace, he might well have been employed more often by the County in that capacity.

For all his obvious talent, Brown was at times a volatile character and this was reflected in his cricket – his form varied from season to season and match to match and, rather like his captain, Tennyson, he tended to do better in adversity.

It was Brown who changed the course of that extraordinary match against Warwickshire in 1922, when Hampshire were dismissed for 15 in their first innings. Brown scored 172 in the second.

After retiring from county cricket he stood as a first-class umpire for several seasons. He died, after being in ill health for some years, at Winchester in 1964 aged 77.

the whole team rather than one or two individuals. A week prior to this Hampshire had beaten Notts for the first time ever. They needed 323 to win in the fourth innings and again it was a team effort with Bowell, Brown, Mead and Tennyson all making fifties.

By the end of July Hampshire, though still well behind Yorkshire and Notts, were fourth in the table. Everything went wrong in August, and of the ten games played that month, only one – against Somerset – was a win.

The batting had been to some extent a two-man band in 1922. In 1923 it was Mead alone. The left-hander hit 2,265 runs, average 64.71. The next best average was Kennedy's 26.04. Day could not get time to play more than three games. Two amateurs, P. E. Lawrie and C. P. Brutton, both hit individual hundreds but otherwise did little. Lawrie was a 20-year-old Old Etonian in his second year at Oxford, who appeared very infrequently for the County up to 1928. C. P. Brutton, whose father had made a solitary appearance for Hampshire in 1904, had learnt his cricket at Winchester and played for the County until 1930, but never again made a first-class hundred and later appeared for Denbighshire, Dorset and Cheshire.

The bowling was weakened by the mysterious decline in Boyes and this threw a great strain on Kennedy and Newman, both of whom proved more expensive than in the previous year. The Eton fast bowler, W. R. de la C. Shirley, who was up at Cambridge, though he failed to be selected for a single first-class game for the University in 1923, came into the Hampshire side in the vacation and took some useful wickets – he gained his blue in 1924, but did not appear in county matches after 1925.

Quite a number of amateurs popped in and out of the eleven but without making a name for themselves. A. E. L. Hill, the son of A. J. L., had six innings in 1923, but his highest score was 24 and despite further odd appearances up to 1930, he never improved on that. F. G. B. Arkwright hit the headlines when he took 175 runs off the Winchester attack in 1923 whilst playing for Eton. Having a birth qualification for Hampshire he was immediately given a trial, but in five innings his highest was 14. He joined the regular army and played with success in military matches. The Cambridge undergraduate, H. D. Hake, hit an undefeated 81 off Lancashire at Southampton, but could only manage 48 in his other nine innings for the County.

WALTER HERBERT LIVSEY

A native of Todmorden, Livsey was given a trial with Surrey Colts in 1912, but since the experts at The Oval were not favourably impressed and anyway Herbert Strudwick was firmly in residence behind the wicket, he moved on to Hampshire. Whilst waiting to qualify for a Championship match, Livsey appeared for the County in a mammoth scoring game against Oxford, and did well to concede only three byes in a total of 554. In 1914 he took over as the County wicket-keeper, only to find his career interrupted by the First World War.

He resumed his place in the team in 1920 and, making a good impression on the county circuit, was selected to go to South Africa with the 1922–23 MCC side. He had the misfortune to break a finger whilst playing in the sixth match and thus missed the major portion of the tour. Apart from his wicket-keeping, Livsey could score runs on occasion, being a very hard-hitting batsman. He hit a famous 110 in the great match against Warwickshire in 1922 and in 1928 hit 109 not out in 85 minutes against Kent at Dover, whilst against Worcester in 1921 he helped Bowell to add 192 in 110 minutes for the 10th wicket.

Ill-health brought his career to an abrupt halt at the end of the 1929 season. Livsey died in London in 1978, aged 84.

Realising that the success of the County in the years 1921 to 1923 was based too often on the efforts of a few and that young amateurs were not as prolific or talented as they had been in years past, the Hampshire Committee decided to set up a Nursery to groom young hopefuls at the County Ground. This scheme could hardly be expected to provide new players instantly and in 1924 the County found itself slipping down the table. The summer, which was generally wet, began badly. Only one of the first 11 engagements ended in success and although matters improved in mid-season, there was a further tailing away in August. A total of five Championship wins placed Hampshire 12th.

The batting averages told a now-familiar story. Mead hit 1,543 runs, average 44.08. No one else averaged 30. Bowell, now in his forties, was left out of the side for the first half of the summer, but was brought back and came second to Mead. Aird played in most matches and reached 1,000 runs. The professional all-rounders, Brown, Kennedy and Newman all failed miserably with the bat. It was a pity that Captain Fowler – the famous all-rounder of the Eton *v* Harrow match of 1910 – who was outstanding in Army cricket, could appear in only three Hampshire matches. Tragically he was to die in June 1925. The 21-year-old amateur leg-break bowler, F. A. Cross, looked the most promising of the younger brigade.

The number of wins was increased by one in 1925 and by dint of picking up points for first-innings lead, Hampshire rose to ninth place, but on the whole the season was little more successful than its predecessor. The batting was again in the hands of Mead, but Tennyson played much better than for some time and slaughtered the Middlesex attack at Southampton with an innings of 184 made at more than one a minute. Captain Jameson, the amateur squash champion, hit his maiden hundred for Hampshire against Warwickshire in under two hours. He was a noted exponent of the square cut. In the same innings A. L. Hosie, on leave from India, made 53 and played one or two other fine knocks. Aird however was not so successful as in the previous year. Kennedy picked up 132 Championship wickets, but his partner Newman had a difficult year and it was as well for the County that Boyes found his form once more.

In 1926 it was Kennedy's turn to have an off-season, but Newman more than filled the gap and Boyes took over 100 Championship wickets. The County made a marvellous start to the season and in late May and June picked up six wins in seven matches, putting them third in the Championship. July produced three more wins, but August was one long nightmare – not a single victory in eight contests and Hampshire watched as Kent, Notts, Surrey and Middlesex overtook them, whilst at the top Yorkshire and Lancashire moved on and out of sight. Thus Hampshire remained the best of the 'new' counties, but unable to break the grip which the ancient ones still held.

Mead hewed out his 2,000 runs, and the occasional amateurs, Aird, Jameson and Day were useful when in the mood. A. K. Judd, an interesting batsman, played in his vacation from Cambridge, but was later to disappear to Nigeria. J. P. Parker, a local amateur from Portsmouth, came in down the order in the Canterbury game and then helped Mead add 270 in 170 minutes – Parker hit 156. McBride, who was shortly to become a double blue at Oxford (he was a good goalkeeper), came to strengthen the bowling, but his medium-pace deliveries were not designed to annoy professionals.

Financially the club had a happy year with a record profit of £1,700 and to help encourage the youngsters they engaged the old Sussex pro, Robert Relf, on a five year contract.

The nine-wicket win over Surrey at Bournemouth, a very creditable win against the odds over Kent and the fact that Notts had to fight desperately hard to save the game at Portsmouth were all bright spots of 1927. Around these, however, hung a very gloomy picture. Only Newman and Kennedy had bowling averages under 30 and both these stalwarts had too often to trundle on knowing the change bowling to be of doubtful content. Newman completed the 'double' and thus was also to help Mead and Brown in the batting department. Mead had the incredible Championship average of 75.19, scoring 2,331 runs. He also had the satisfaction of completing his 100th first-class hundred, being only the fourth batsman ever to accomplish that feat.

The serious aspect of 1927 was the apparent absence of any worthwhile young players, amateur or professional. Utley, the RAF cricketer, was a useful fast bowler and took 20 Championship wickets, but his County cricket was very limited. W. E. N. Scott, a spinner from the Isle of Wight, played in five matches, but was never seen again.

Mead ploughed his lone furrow in 1928. He hit no fewer

JOHN ALFRED NEWMAN

Achieving the 'double' five times, Jack Newman's best all-round feat in a match occurred against Gloucestershire in 1926, when he scored 66 and 42 not out and took 14 for 148. He and Kennedy were the mainstays of the Hampshire attack for some years and twice they bowled unchanged through both innings, the first time against Sussex in 1921 and the second v Somerset in 1923.

Newman began his county career as a bowler of a little more than medium pace, but later added the variety of off breaks. He achieved a hat-trick against the 1909 Australians at Southampton and at Hove in 1923 took three wickets in four balls against Sussex. In 1927, when approaching the veteran stage, he hit two hundreds in the same match – v Surrey at The Oval – and by coincidence Jack Hobbs managed the same feat in the same match.

The incident at Trent Bridge in 1922 when he kicked down the stumps in anger was entirely out of character, and after being ordered of the field by Lionel Tennyson, Newman apologised profusely to all involved. In his early days he acted as coach to the boys of the training ship *Mercury*, and late in life, after nine years as a first-class umpire, he emigrated to South Africa where he resumed coaching. He died in Cape Town on 21 December 1973, aged 89.

NEWMAN. HANTS CC

than 12 hundreds and in all first-class matches topped 3,000 runs. His average in Championship games was 81.22 – of the regular players, Hosie came second with 31.23. To cap it all, Mead actually headed the bowling table, his 14 wickets costing 17 runs each. Yet, once again, he failed to appear in a Test match that year; he was, in fact, to play for England only once more, against Australia in A. P. F. Chapman's 1928–29 tour.

Three wins in August, out of a total of five, saved Hampshire from being classed with Glamorgan and Worcestershire, and they ended in 12th place. Fleet of foot and keen to punish anything loose, Hosie, home on leave, hit three hundreds and completed 1,000 runs. Aird played twice, hitting a hundred off the Leicester bowlers, saving the side from defeat. Harfield, a local professional, who batted in the middle of the order, was given an extensive run in the first eleven without doing much. Sprinks, an amateur fast bowler, played in 13 games, but could claim only 18 wickets at 51 runs each. With Boyes, Kennedy and Newman all rather expensive, the best bowling return came from Utley. The remarkable schoolboy bowler, Ward, was given a few matches but with no positive result. Some people were beginning to label the cricket nursery an expensive white elephant.

Catastrophe hit Hampshire in the fourth match of 1929 when Mead had his thumb broken. He had to stand down from nine matches. Tennyson had broken a finger in an earlier season preliminary match and then Boyes strained his bowling arm and Brown was the victim of a motor-cycle accident. Kennedy and Newman, however, soldiered on. Kennedy, who had cut down his run, grew more subtle with age and his season's Championship figures of 140 wickets at 17 runs each were well deserved. Boyes also had a good year, and third in the averages came Herman, the Oxfordshire professional, who qualified by residence in May and, bowling right-arm fast-medium, took 53 Championship wickets.

Several other young players were tried: Harfield, who played in nearly every game, reached 1,000 runs without scoring a hundred; W. L. C. Creese, son of the old Transvaal cricketer, looked a promising all rounder, being left-handed both as a batsman and bowler; Bailey, another left-hander, was a local product from Winchester; and Arnold, a second cricketer from Oxfordshire, and a useful soccer player,

ALEXANDER STUART KENNEDY

There was never a greater hearted trier than Kennedy, nor was there a fairer bowler – that opinion was expressed by H. L. V. Day, on learning of Kennedy's death in 1959.

Although born in Scotland, he moved with his parents to Southampton whilst a child and would spend hours at the County Ground willing to bowl to anyone and everyone. On leaving school at 14, he joined the Hampshire staff and at 16 made his first-class debut for the County. His enthusiasm for bowling continued for a span of 30 years and when, at 65, he was invited to bowl a ceremonial over to launch a benefit game, he insisted on sending down eight accurate overs and picking up several wickets into the bargain.

Of strong physique and stamina he combined with Newman to form Hampshire's attack for most of the inter-war period, but at the same time he built up a reputation as a batsman. He had begun his career at No 11, working his way slowly up the order until on several occasions he was involved in an opening partnership of a hundred and more. His batting, like his bowling, was tempered to suit the situation and he was as effective as a hitter as he was carefully defending.

In all he performed the 'double' five times and his best season with the ball was 1922, when he took 205 wickets at an average of 16.80. He went to South Africa with the 1922–23 team and it was on this tour that he made his only Test appearances, opening the England bowling in all five matches and being England's outstanding bowler with 31 wickets, average 19.32.

After the Second World War Kennedy spent five years coaching in South Africa, but then returned to England and died at Hythe, Southampton in 1959 aged 68.

seemed a useful acquisition. So Relf's nursery was now having its effect on the County. Most interesting of the young amateurs were Stephen Fry, son of C.B., who was mistakenly invited to open the innings, when he would have flourished better in the middle of the order, and G. C. A. Adams, who had gone up to Cambridge and gained a rugby blue. His fielding let him down.

To some extent all this new blood covered for the various injuries previously noted, but with eight championship wins the County had to be content with 11th place. Their only success over one of the 'Big Six' came on 1 July at Southampton, when Surrey were beaten in two days, Boyes dismissing the visitors in their second innings for 95 – he took five for 20 on a wicket which was ideal for him. Wicket-keeper Livsey was not too happy about the brevity of the match, for he had chosen it as his benefit game.

The big talking point of 1930 was the decline of Mead. By normal standards his record of 1,305 runs at an average of 31.07 in the Championship was quite respectable, but put in the context of his performances over the previous 20 years it was decidedly modest. With Mead not flourishing, it was a tragedy that young Harfield was taken ill and unable to play

ALDERSHOT

Hampshire staged their first first-class match on the 'Officers' Ground' at Aldershot on 25, 26 and 27 May 1905, when Surrey were the visitors. Walter Lees, the Surrey fast bowler, came in at No 9 and celebrated the christening of the new County ground by hitting a century in an hour, Surrey reaching 482 all out. Hampshire made 227 and were obliged to follow on. A. J. L. Hill hit a hundred in the second innings, but he could not save the game and Surrey won by seven wickets.

The ground has been used only for the occasional Championship game since then. The first pavilion was built on it in 1887. This was replaced in 1936.

The Army side have used the ground regularly, possibly the best attended game being the one between the Army and the Australians in 1938. Bill O'Reilly took seven for 33 as the Army collapsed in their second innings and lost the match by an innings and 67 runs.

all summer; but Arnold, now qualified, came to the rescue and in his first Championship season headed the batting table. Brown, who took up the wicket-keeping duties on a full-time basis because Livsey could not play, was the only other batsman to appear regularly and be consistent. Hosie appeared in some matches in order to captain the team in Tennyson's absence, and scored useful runs. Apart from Arnold, Mead, Hosie and Brown no one attained a batting average of 22. Creese and Bailey did not advance on their promise of 1929. Boyes, Newman and Kennedy had the lion's share of the bowling. Herman's average was much enhanced by nine wickets against Northants – in his other 13 appearances he took 28 wickets at considerable cost.

Pothecary, the Southampton professional, was given an extended trial and as a middle order left-hand batsman scored some runs, as well as picking up wickets with left-arm slows. Baring, a tearaway bowler in his second year at Cambridge, took 32 wickets at 40 runs each, but bowled much better than his figures suggest.

Although Hampshire managed only five wins all summer and dropped to 13th place, they still had an influence on the destiny of the title, for they were the only side to beat Notts. This proved Hampshire's best match. Newman dismissed Notts for 69 in their first innings, taking five for 18. Some good hitting by Brown gave Hampshire a lead and though Notts batted better in their second innings, Hampshire needed only 171 to win. The extra half hour was employed on the second evening, but when seven o'clock arrived Hampshire needed one run to win. Stumps were pulled up and on the third morning Notts fielded in ordinary clothes. Kennedy hit four off the second ball and brought victory by five wickets.

Mead recovered his form in 1931, Arnold made further progress and Brown just managed 1,000 Championship runs. Aside from the occasional bright innings, those three constituted the entire batting strength. Harfield returned, but in 20 matches could only muster 620 Championship runs. Bailey's best innings was 104 on a plumb wicket at Bournemouth in late August. Kennedy hit a hundred off Northants, but his seasonal average was only 13.77.

The bowling was in similar straits since Newman was unable to play in any matches. Kennedy bowled as well as ever and Baring gave excellent support, but of the rest only Boyes and Herman achieved anything of note. The absence

JOHN ARNOLD

Son of an Oxfordshire wicket-keeper, Johnnie Arnold helped his native county win the Minor Counties Championship in 1929, before moving on to Hampshire in 1930 and a year later opening the batting for England against New Zealand at Lord's. At that time he was a painstaking defensive batsman, but he later developed some very powerful attacking strokes, and by the time illness ended his career in 1950, he had reached 1,000 runs 14 times.

A talented outside-left at soccer, he played for Southampton and Fulham, gaining an England international cap against Scotland at Hampden Park in 1932–33. His speed on the wing was put to good use in the outfield and he was noted for his powerful and accurate throws from the boundary edge, or in the covers.

Soon after leaving the Hampshire playing staff, he joined the Minor Counties umpires' list and later graduated to the first-class grade. He died in 1984 in Southampton aged 76.

of Tennyson for many matches did not help to bring the best out of the eleven. Aird, Baring, young Fry and Mead all acted as captain. Neither was the wicket-keeping situation very satisfactory. Brown had taken over from Livsey, but the side really required a specialist keeper. Lieutenant-Commander E. L. D. Bartley, who kept for the Royal Navy, stood in in two games, as did Stephen Fry – Fry was captain and wicket-keeper during some odd happenings at The Oval. Today such 'arrangements' are commonplace, but Fry caused a great outcry when he declared Hampshire's first innings closed at lunchtime on the third day with the score 127 for no wicket and Hampshire 118 in arrears. The Surrey captain responded by batting for 75 minutes in his second innings and then declaring to set Hampshire 222 in 165 minutes. Hampshire were 125 for five at the close. The authorities argued that the spread of 'freak' declarations would reduce the Championship to an absurdity.

Of the young players, Arnold, as noted, had a good year and was selected for one Test against New Zealand (destined to be his only England appearance), but the two left-handers, Creese and Pothecary, though brilliant in the field, were still below County standard as batsmen.

Hampshire's overall record for the season showed very little change from the results of the previous year, but they managed some improvement in 1932. The younger players, though not producing any outstanding feats, made substantial contributions. Arnold developed into a very sound batsman and he and Brown formed a good opening pair. Bailey dropped down the order and had some good days with both bat and ball, but for several weeks in mid-summer could do little right. Pothecary and Creese both improved. McCorkell was the discovery of the year. He was given a place in the second match as wicket-keeper and appeared in every match afterwards. He also batted well on occasion, being particularly strong in defence.

Eight Championship matches were won and the County came eighth. The best win occurred at Headingley, when Kennedy took ten wickets and Tennyson batted well. By coincidence these two cricketers were prominent when Hampshire had last beaten Yorkshire ten years before.

Batsmen dominated the dry summer of 1933 and it was Hampshire's great disadvantage that they possessed no fast bowler to exploit the hard wickets to the full. The result was that whilst Hampshire's batsmen churned out big scores (16

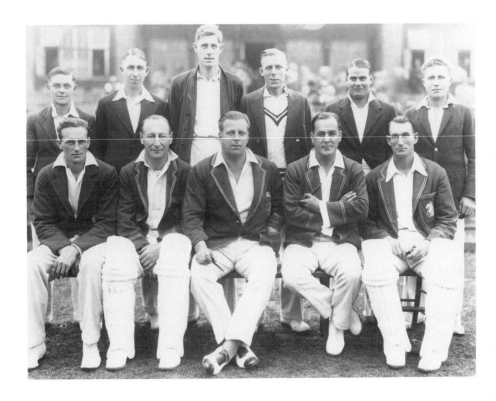

Hampshire in 1932. Back row, left to right: N. McCorkell, W. L. Creese, O. W. Herman, A. E. Pothecary, J. Bailey, J. Arnold. Front row: G. S. Boyes, C. P. Mead, Lord Tennyson, A. S. Kennedy, G. Brown.

times the County topped the 300 mark and on six of these occasions the total went above 400), Hampshire's opponents also enjoyed a feast of runs. It was therefore hardly surprising that 17 of the 28 Championship games were drawn and only two ended in victory to give the County one of its worst years in modern times.

Mead, now aged 46, managed ten hundreds and with 2,478 runs at 68.83 was in full spate. Creese and Pothecary each had two hundreds and 1,000 runs to his name, while Brown and Arnold also reached a four-figure aggregate. With Kennedy, Bailey, Boyes and McCorkell all capable of good scores the tail was reduced to just Herman.

The bowling told a very different story and too often only Boyes and Kennedy looked likely to take wickets. Herman's 76 wickets cost 36 runs each, but he held his place in the side because none of his possible rivals made much progress. Baring had dislocated both knees in a motor accident and this had prevented him playing in 1932. He reappeared in 1933 but was not the same man. Cadogan, a fast bowler from

Winchester who was stationed in India, looked useful but was not available very often.

Illness overtook Lord Tennyson and with no amateur willing to take over the leadership, six players captained the team at various times, including the Rev. Gilbert Jessop, son of the legendary hitter. The 19-year-old amateur, R. H. Moore, hit 159 in the final home game of the season at Bournemouth and he seemed to have a bright future. It was in this game that Essex declared at lunch on the last day in the hope of bowling out Hampshire and obtaining a win by an innings. The umpires, due to a misreading of the Laws, added an extra 15 minutes on to the lunch interval for rolling the wicket. Happily this did not affect the outcome, since Creese and Pothecary batted well enough to save the match with ease.

Tennyson handed over the captaincy to W. G. L. F. Lowndes in 1934. An Oxford blue of 1921, Lowndes had made a few appearances for Hampshire commencing in 1924, but had never played regularly in first-class county matches. He proved a useful all-round man, but his presence did little to solve the weakness in the bowling. Creese improved as a bowler, but Boyes found the wickets against him. Kennedy, at the age of 43, was the leading wicket-taker, but at the season's end he decided the time had come to retire; he had first played for the County in 1907.

With Moore appearing in every match and hitting over 1,500 runs and both Mead and Arnold in good form, the batting remained as formidable as in 1933 and thus drawn games were a major feature of Hampshire's results. Three matches were won and Hampshire remained in 14th place.

Two notable absentees were Brown, who joined the first-class umpires' list and Bailey, who in December 1933 announced that he was moving to Middlesex in order to qualify for that county. Gerry Hill, a 21-year-old all-rounder, and C. G. A. Paris of King's School, Canterbury, a very defensive batsman, both had long runs in the first eleven and seemed to be prospects worth further encouragement.

The problem of the captaincy recurred in 1935. Lowndes could only play in about half the games and an assortment of amateurs led the County in the rest of the matches. Another disadvantage which handicapped the side early in the season was that Moore caught scarlet fever and thus missed all but five matches. McCorkell was promoted to open the innings with Arnold and the pair provided a sound start to many

HAMPSHIRE *v* WARWICKSHIRE

Played at Dean Park, Bournemouth, 28 and 29 July 1937

HAMPSHIRE WON BY AN INNINGS AND 143 RUNS

HAMPSHIRE	FIRST INNINGS	
*Mr R. H. Moore	lbw b Hollies	316
†N. T. McCorkell	lbw b Mayer	33
W. L. C. Creese	b Paine	45
J. Arnold	lbw b Paine	13
Mr C. G. A. Paris	b Hollies	75
A. E. Pothecary	c Wyatt b Santall	2
O. W. Herman	c Croom b Hollies	3
D. F. Walker	c Kilner b Hollies	2
G. Hill	st Buckingham b Paine	0
G. S. Boyes	retired hurt	8
G. E. M. Heath	not out	2
Extras	b 8, lb 2	10
Total		509

1st inns: 1-108, 2-188, 3-220, 4-427, 5-444, 6-457, 7-474, 8-475, 9-509

BOWLING	O	M	R	W
Mayer	23	4	90	1
Wyatt	11	2	51	0
Hollies	49.5	9	205	4
Santall	11	0	56	1
Paine	32	7	97	3

WARWICKSHIRE	FIRST INNINGS		SECOND INNINGS	
N. Kilner	c sub b Creese	64	c Paris b Moore	7
A. J. W. Croom	b Herman	15	c Paris b Creese	22
W. A. Hill	run out	7	lbw b Creese	22
*Mr R. E. S. Wyatt	run out	13	c McCorkell b Creese	0
H. E. Dollery	b Creese	0	c McCorkell b Creese	0
F. R. Santall	c McCorkell b Herman	32	c and b Heath	69
J. S. Ord	c Moore b Creese	8	c McCorkell b Heath	36
†J. Buckingham	b Herman	12	c Walker b Creese	0
G. A. E. Paine	b Herman	2	c McCorkell b Creese	4
J. H. Mayer	c Paris b Herman	16	not out	6
W. E. Hollies	not out	1	b Creese	2
Extras	b 10, lb 5	15	b 9, lb 4	13
Total		185		181

1st inns: 1-40, 2-69, 3-111, 4-111, 5-111, 6-127, 7-150, 8-150, 9-174
2nd inns: 1-27, 2-45, 3-45, 4-45, 5-68, 6-151, 7-168, 7-170, 9-175

BOWLING	O	M	R	W	O	M	R	W
Herman	17.4	5	42	5	8	2	12	0
Heath	10	4	19	0	15	0	40	2
Creese	23	4	74	3	22.3	3	85	7
Hill	16	4	35	0	5	0	22	0
Moore					7	5	9	1

Umpires: W. Bestwick and A. Skelding.
Hampshire won the toss. Close of play: 1st day: Hampshire innings completed.
*Captain; †Wicket-keeper.

innings, but this weakened the middle order. It was bowling, however, which was the weak link. Hill, who appeared to bowl his off-breaks off the wrong foot, improved his action and with it his results. At the end of the year he had taken 93 Championship wickets at 24 runs each. Kennedy, now coach at Cheltenham, helped the County in August and topped the bowling table. Boyes and Creese had reasonable seasons with the ball, but Herman was expensive.

The County ended 1935 second from the bottom. A considerable number of players were tried in a vain attempt to improve the overall results. Fenley, the old Surrey leg spinner, appeared in three matches; Collins, who had played for Notts in 1921, had two games. Lloyd Budd, later to become a Test umpire, played in 22 Championship matches, but his 17 wickets cost 54 runs each. W. Lancashire, the Southampton schoolmaster, and H. M. Lawson, whose father played in seven matches before the war, were tried, as were several others. Various injuries to Creese and Pothecary made team selection even more difficult.

Two changes at the top brought a breath of fresh air to Southampton. Alastair MacLeod, who had appeared on the odd occasion for Hampshire since 1914, was appointed Secretary and Moore was given the captaincy. MacLeod virtually assumed the role of manager as well, and having lead the staff in pre-season training began a process of rebuilding a team-spirit. The number of players used in Championship games dropped from 27 in 1935 to 18 in 1936; the batting, so long dependent on a good innings by Mead, became the collective responsibility of seven players, all regulars – Creese, Mead, Arnold, Pothecary, McCorkell, Paris and Moore, and six of those seven completed 1,000 Championship runs. The bowling was not particularly strong, but at least, in Boyes, Creese, Herman, Hill and Lawson there were five regulars to share the burden.

Hants v Warwicks: Bournemouth, July 28, 29 1937
The match in which Moore broke the record, held by Poore, of the highest individual innings for the county, proved to be Hampshire's best win of the season as well. Moore, last man out, batted six hours and 20 minutes, hitting 43 fours and three sixes. Boyes twisted his knee and could not bowl, but in Warwickshire's first innings Herman made the ball lift uncomfortably and in the second Creese bowled his left arm slows accurately, so that the home county won inside two days.

The determination of the side was plain to see and it was reflected in the results. Seven Championship matches were won and the team rose six places in the table. The fielding which had not been of a high standard for some time was excellent – Arnold in the deep, Pothecary in the covers and Boyes and Creese close to the wicket were outstanding. Behind the stumps, McCorkell was challenging Ames for a place in the England side.

1936 marked the end of an era. At the close of the season it was announced that Mead had been released by the County. He had appeared in exactly 700 matches for Hampshire, his astonishingly prolific career stretching back 32 years. A public subscription was opened for him during 1937.

Moore continued as captain in 1937, providing the public with the most enterprising cricket in the Championship. He accepted each and every challenge and on several occasions this led to the defeat of the County; the number of losses rose from five to 16, though the wins remained the same at seven. Moore led by example and opening the batting he attacked the bowling to the point where, on occasion, he could be accused of being reckless. His great innings came at Bournemouth in July when he made 316 in 380 minutes – it was the highest score made for Hampshire, overtaking Poore's 304 in 1899. Herman and Creese then dismissed the opposition – Warwickshire – twice and Hampshire won by an innings.

Herman, with his high, easy action, made the ball rise sharply off the wicket and had a very successful summer with 133 Championship wickets at 21 runs each. He found an excellent new ball partner in Heath, a professional from Bournemouth. Heath, who had appeared in Club and Ground games in 1935 and 1936, was drafted into the side and his ability to make the ball dip in confused the best batsmen. His 67 Championship wickets at 23 runs each was a very good return for a man new to County cricket.

Hampshire also undercovered a worthwhile new batsman in D. F. Walker, who had previously appeared for Surrey Seconds. In contrast to the carefree batting of Moore, he had unlimited patience and late in the season he was moved up to No 3 in the order, which added some stability to the batting.

Owing to pressure of work Moore was compelled to give up the captaincy in 1938. Paris replaced him, though Moore appeared in a few matches and with the aid of two hundreds topped the batting table by a large margin – McCorkell,

NEIL THOMAS McCORKELL

A talented wicket-keeper-batsman, McCorkell was considered unlucky not to be selected for England, but he was in competition with Ames and then Gibb. He represented the Players *v* Gentlemen at Lord's in 1936, then just missed out on the MCC team to Australia in the winter which followed.

Short, and of compact build, he carried out his duties behind the stumps with the minimum of fuss. He was a product of the Hampshire cricket nursery and having become the County wicket-keeper in 1932 he gradually developed his batting, which initially was dominated by defensive strokes. In 1935 he was asked to open the Hampshire innings due to R. H. Moore's absence through illness. His most effective stroke was the square cut, but he also made many runs through drives on both sides of the wicket. Not the most elegant of batsmen, he was at his finest in a crisis and could thwart the best of bowlers.

He twice dismissed seven batsmen in a match: 4 ct 3 st *v* Glamorgan at Bournemouth in 1932 and 5 ct 2 st *v* Lancashire on the same ground in 1947. In the innings when Leicester hit 535 for eight in 1938, he did not concede a single bye.

After retiring in 1951, McCorkell went to Johannesburg as coach at Parktown Boys High School.

now the most consistent batsman in the side, scored most runs. In contrast Arnold abandoned his free-flowing style in favour of nudges and deflections which proved a poor substitute and he failed to reach 1,000 runs or score a hundred. Bailey, having changed his mind regarding a qualification for Middlesex, became Accrington's professional and played in a few Hampshire mid-week matches. The chief supporters of McCorkell were Pothecary and Creese, though the Rev. J. W. J. Steele, an Army Chaplain from Winchester, was a most useful newcomer.

Boyes had the satisfaction of hitting the highest score of his career when Hampshire broke new ground by playing at Newport on the Isle of Wight and in the same match – v Northants – he took his 100th wicket of the season and came out at the head of the bowling averages, though closely followed by Heath. Herman also reached a hundred wickets, but was overbowled and lost form as the season drew to a close.

Although Moore was no longer captain the club policy of striving for a definite finish and avoiding draws was continued and this meant that though Hampshire won nine matches, they finished below four teams who claimed fewer wins, having suffered more losses than any side bar Northants. The team's form was unpredictable and the end result, considering the paper strength of the side, was disappointing.

Another change of leadership for 1939 did nothing to build up morale. Paris resigned and a local solicitor, G. R. Taylor, who had been in the Lancing eleven in the 1920s, but had virtually no experience of county cricket – he had played once for Hampshire in 1935 – was made the new captain. It was still a case of an amateur leader at all costs.

The batting was fairly sound – Arnold, who was nearly sacked after his 1938 efforts, recovered his form, Bailey left the Leagues and played regularly and D. F. Walker batted well. But the bowling became progressively weaker – Heath was asked to do too much and broke down, Hill was disappointing and Boyes seemed to lose interest. Baring was useful when he played and the young Southampton amateur, C. J. Knott, was promising. Right at the end of the season, an 18-year-old leg-break bowler, Dean, was brought in. In his second game he took four Worcester wickets in five balls and in his only other appearance returned figures of five for 58 against Yorkshire.

The final season before the outbreak of the Second World War found Hampshire down in 15th place, claiming just three victories as against 17 losses. The cricketers could hardly realize that they would have to miss six summers before having a chance to rebuild their reputations.

NEWPORT, ISLE OF WIGHT

In August 1938, Hampshire played their first County Championship match on the Isle of Wight, when they opposed Northants on the Newport Ground. The match belonged to Boyes, who not only hit 104, the highest score of his career, but provided Hampshire with an unexpected victory by taking six for 40 in Northants second innings. Rain had more or less washed out the second day's play and the game seemed certain to peter out as a draw. In the event Hampshire required 69 to win in the final innings in quick time and McCorkell hit a six with just five minutes playing time remaining to produce a seven-wicket win.

When Hampshire returned to Newport in June of the following year, rain allowed only an hour's play on the first day, but produced a spinner's wicket on the second, with quite remarkable results. Middlesex were the visitors and Robertson and Edrich hit 215 between them, the former making 97 and the latter 118, but the side were dismissed for 261, with Boyes again the leading wicket taker with five for 45.

Hampshire however, had an even more miserable time. The home county were dismissed for 93, forced to follow on and lost the match by an innings.

BUILDING TOWARDS A TITLE

THE COUNTY LOST ONLY ONE LEADING PROFESSIONAL during the Second World War – Pilot-Officer D. F. Walker was killed whilst flying over Holland. Two of the other regulars, Creese and Boyes, retired, whilst Pothecary was appointed grounds-man at Southampton and Sam Staples, the old Notts and England spinner, was coach.

The County Ground had been used throughout the war, though only once before 1945 did a Hampshire team take the field. The ground had been kept in good condition, but the pavilion had suffered from enemy action and the Club launched an appeal for £20,000 to make repairs due to bomb damage and general dilapidation. Unfortunately the appeal failed and various other ways of persuading the public to support the County Club had to be tried.

In October 1945, the Committee appointed Desmond Eagar as captain and Secretary for 1946. Eagar had played occasionally for Gloucestershire before the war and had gained a blue at Oxford in 1939. He was destined to remain the guiding light of Hampshire until his death in September 1977.

Six years may have come and gone, but Hampshire in 1946 remained as unpredictable as ever. They were the only county to beat the Champions – Yorkshire. This was no freak declaration game, but a straight win by ten wickets, with Yorkshire dismissed for 135 and 130. Lancashire, who came third in the table, were overcome at Old Trafford, being dismissed for 151 and 182. On the other hand Hampshire lost 15 matches and could command only tenth position in the Championship.

For most of their successes they owed a great debt to the cleverly flighted off-breaks of C. J. Knott, who took more wickets in the season than any amateur had ever done before, 121 in all first-class matches. Hill's off-breaks put him second to Knott in terms of average, but Herman, who bowled a variety of deliveries ranging from fast in-swingers to off-breaks was the more effective, and like Knott completed a hundred wickets. Dean, the youthful prospect of 1939, was erratic and Heath rather expensive.

The batting let the side down too often. McCorkell could

Charlie Knott played for Hampshire for 16 years, spanning the Second World War, and was later chairman of the cricket committee.

not find his form and had to be relieved of his opening position. Arthur Holt, who had played with occasional success before the war, but was better known on the soccer field, as a forward for Southampton, was promoted to partner Arnold. The England double international was at his most dependable – he hit over 1,500 runs, but scored only one hundred – and his chief help came from Bailey. Hill and Eagar had modest returns. Much was expected of Neville Rogers, the professional from Oxford. He hit 90 on his debut, but could average only 17 in Championship matches. The Rev J. R. Bridger, a wartime Cambridge blue, played in two games at Bournemouth in July, opened the batting and scored 50, 39 and 142. The County desperately needed him on a full-time basis.

The glorious summer of 1947 gave the batsmen time to find their feet, but played havoc with the bowlers. Knott struggled to make his off-breaks turn and in despair tried medium-pace instead, but with equal lack of success. Hill and Herman fared little better. The most exciting game of the year was the fixture at Bournemouth against Lancashire. The result was a tie. Hampshire declared to set their opponents

221 in 135 minutes. Place and Washbrook knocked up 142 in 90 minutes, then Bailey took six wickets for 29 runs in six overs. Lancashire were unfortunate in having Roberts, their last man, in hospital with a broken finger.

The medium-pace of V. J. Ransom headed the bowling averages, but even his 54 Championship wickets cost 27 runs each. Ransom, a Surrey-born amateur, had made a name for himself in London Club cricket with Malden Wanderers. Strongly built and over six feet tall, he had a short run and created a great impression on his debut, taking eight Sussex wickets and providing Hampshire with one of only four of their 1947 victories. He had been specially registered. Of the other bowlers only Heath managed an average below 30. Dean proved completely ineffective and played in only six Championship games.

McCorkell, Arnold and Rogers all had good summers with the bat and Eagar hit his maiden hundred for his new county. Two professionals, both surnamed Dawson but unrelated, joined the staff as batsmen. Gilbert, from Bradford, hit a century in the final match of the year against his native county, when he was asked to open the Hampshire innings in place of the injured Arnold. Harold, from Todmorden, appeared in five Championship matches without scoring many runs.

Although the day of the occasional amateur was drawing to a close, the County still had two – the Rev J. R. Bridger and Lieutenant-Commander J. E. Manners, who, having last appeared in 1936, appeared only once in 1947, and hit 121 out of 192 in 160 minutes against Kent at Canterbury.

The County finished the season in 16th place, but despite this dismal record the membership figure for the Club climbed above 5,000 and a record 113,078 spectators paid through the turnstiles.

Supporters of the County were amazed by the apparent transformation of the side in the first half of the 1948 season, and by mid-July Hampshire were in fifth place in the table with an outside chance of taking the title – nine matches had been victories. The main reason for this about-turn was not a new recruit, or youngster coming good, but the Indian Summer enjoyed by the veteran Bailey. In both the batting and bowling tables of 1947 he had been in the also-rans, but in 1948 he headed both lists, 1,310 runs, average 32.75, and 109 wickets, average 17.97. G. Dawson and Eagar both completed 1,000 Championship runs for the first time. Dawson

had the satisfaction of making a hundred off the Derbyshire attack at Portsmouth, Derbyshire at that time being a very strong bowling side.

Having performed so well up to 27 July, Hampshire then began a period of almost total failure, achieving just one more win, and that by the narrow margin of two wickets. So the County had to settle for ninth place – an intense disappointment after such an auspicious beginning.

Hampshire in 1948. Back row, left to right: G. Hill, G. Heath, T. A. Dean, G. Dawson, N. H. Rogers, N. McCorkell, J. Arnold. Front row: V. J. Ransom, C. G. A. Paris, E. D. R. Eagar, J. Bailey, C. J. Knott.

One of the best pieces of cricket seen at Southampton during the year was the dismissal, by Knott and Bailey, of the all-conquering Australians for 117, which gave Hampshire a first-innings lead of 78. Miller and Johnston, however, struck back and in the end the tourists won by eight wickets.

The team was handicapped for several weeks when McCorkell broke a finger. C. J. Andrews, the brother of the Somerset professional, and an outstanding club wicket-keeper, was co-opted into the side for four matches, but as he could not afford the time for more frequent appearances, Leo Harrison, a promising young batsman, was given the job behind the stumps and acted very well in that capacity. It was unfortunate that he was the side's best outfielder, and as several of the team were not the fastest of movers in the field, this created problems.

In the spring of 1949, Hampshire signed a new coach, Arthur Holt, who replaced Sam Staples. Holt had played as a

The Rev. J. R. Bridger was one of Hampshire's clerics, appearing from 1946 to 1954.

batsman for Hampshire since 1935, but had never really made his mark. Now, however, he found his niche and was a vital member of the club over the next decades, responsible for the development of many county cricketers.

The County obtained special registrations for two new players for 1949, Cliff Walker, from Yorkshire, a stylish batsman, and A. W. H. Rayment from Middlesex, as a promising batsman. Both played in County matches during the year, the former with some success. Much more important, though, was the emergence of the fast-medium bowler Derek Shackleton from Todmorden, who had joined the staff the previous year. He took 92 wickets in the Championship at 26 runs each. It was as well that Shackleton was effective, for the team's attack lacked Ransom, Herman and Heath virtually all year – Ransom turned out in five games and Heath four. To support Shackleton, therefore, only Knott and Bailey remained and the latter was rather expensive. The wicket-keeping was another problem. McCorkell, although past his best as a keeper, remained a splendid batsman and topped the averages by a margin of six runs. Several younger players were tried behind the wicket before Harrison ended by taking over the post for the second time.

Although six matches were won, the team ended the season in 16th place. For the 1950 season, Vic Cannings the Warwickshire opening bowler, was engaged – Cannings had a birth qualification for the County. Herman, Heath, Bailey and Dean, as well as the batsman, G. Dawson, all left the County and it was agreed that the eleven would be very much an experimental one during the coming season, building for the future. It was something of a surprise to find Hampshire in third place in the Championship in mid-June – wins had been obtained against Middlesex, Leicester and Sussex and a tie against Kent. In this last low-scoring game, none of the four innings totals reached 200. Hampshire required 22 to win when the last man, Knott, joined Cannings. The pair added 21 before Knott was caught in the slips. Kent, however, had suffered misfortune earlier in the game when Ames strained his back and was forced to retire hurt with his score at 55.

Hampshire obtained two further wins in June, but their remaining 15 matches produced only two more victories and they had to settle for 12th place. This was much more satisfactory than in 1949, especially considering the makeshift nature of the eleven – Eagar for example fractured a finger and missed several games and Arnold was forced to drop out due to illness. The old international appeared in 15 out of 28 Championship matches and headed the batting table, in what proved to be his farewell summer. The now established and dependable Rogers, opening the innings with McCorkell and scored most runs. Cliff Walker, coming in usually at No 5, reached 1,000 runs for the first time.

The attack revolved round Shackleton and Knott, though Cannings gave good support. Eagar frequently gambled with the idea of putting his opponents in to bat, but his experiments failed – five times the match was lost and on the other occasion it resulted in the tie with Kent.

Considering that not a single Hampshire batsman figured in the top 20 in the 1951 averages, and only Shackleton appeared in the similar bowling table, the County were fairly content to find themselves in ninth place in the Championship. The season began in the same fashion as 1950, with the club doing very well in the first month, having three successive wins, against Kent, Notts and Middlesex in mid-May. Thereafter they could achieve just two more victories.

Neville Rogers was a reliable opening batsman for the ten years following the Second World War.

With Knott conceding many more runs per wicket, the bowling became very much a two-man attack – Shackleton and Cannings. The batting also relied far too much on the opening pair of Rogers and McCorkell. Gray, a Southampton-born professional, and Harrison both completed 1,000 runs for the first time, but their averages, both 30, owed much to the number of not-out innings involved.

McCorkell decided to retire at the close of 1951 to take a coaching post in South Africa. Gray was given the job of opening the innings with Rogers in 1952, and had a very good year, so one of the County's immediate problems was solved. But there remained the weaknesses of the support bowlers. Knott was available for only five matches, leaving the County's spin department exceedingly thin. So whilst Shackleton and Cannings provided a seam pair equal to that of any county, when they stopped bowling, the opposition started to enjoy themselves, although Gray managed one or two good days with his medium-pace stuff, notably seven for 56 against Notts at Bournemouth. Dare, from Blandford, an outstanding fielder, played in nearly every match as a left-arm spinner, but his 54 wickets cost 33 runs each. Usually batting at No 10 or 11, Dare caused something of a stir by coming in at No 9 against Worcester at Bournemouth and hitting an unbeaten 109.

Of the seven 1952 victories, the outstanding one was against Kent at Southampton, when Shackleton and Cannings bowled unchanged through both completed Kent innings, a feat which in post-war cricket is almost unknown. Shackleton took 12 for 67 and Cannings eight for 55; Kent were all out for 32 and 91.

Hampshire were 12th in the Championship and though this was a decline on the previous year, a number of the younger members of the side were developing into useful cricketers: Prouton from Southampton became the regular wicket-keeper and kept very efficiently to the fast bowling, but was not really tested standing up; Rayment just reached 1,000 runs in all matches and added to the number of brilliant fieldsmen in the side. Ingleby-Mackenzie, the left-hand batsman, who had an outstanding season at Eton in 1951, played in six matches and showed belligerent promise.

Knott appeared in seven Championship matches in 1953 and his 38 wickets cost only 13 runs each – it was a great loss to the County that he was not available more often, and his success when he did appear merely served to underline the paucity of the Hampshire spin attack. Shackleton and Cannings continued to fulfil their roles, but they could not make Hampshire an effective force on their own. Rogers, after a good beginning, injured his thumb, and when he returned to the side seemed to have lost his form: Cliff Walker and Gray came above him in the batting table, as did the Rev J. R. Bridger, who only appeared in three games, but hit an unbeaten hundred at Worcester. Henry Horton, the Southampton soccer player, qualified by residence and looked a useful batsman – he had previously appeared for Worcestershire – but by and large the batting line up was

VICTOR HENRY DOUGLAS CANNINGS

Few cricketers can have won two county caps within a few weeks of appearing for each county. Vic Cannings was awarded his Warwickshire cap after only nine weeks in first-class cricket and his Hampshire cap within a month of his first game for his native county. Owing to the Second World War – Cannings was in the Palestine Police Force for seven years – he did not make his Championship debut until he was 28. Three seasons were spent with Warwickshire, then in 1950 he transferred to his native Hampshire and immediately established himself as Shackleton's opening partner. His pace was scarcely above medium and his main asset the outswinger, though his accuracy was a byword in the 1950s.

A professional who took his cricket very seriously, he might have joked about his batting whilst in the dressing room, but not when at the crease and on several occasions he made useful runs at the end of a Hampshire innings, notably when he hit 43 off the Sussex attack, raising the Hampshire total from 147 for eight to 236 all out in a game Hampshire went on to win. He took 100 wickets in a season four times, his best year being 1952 with 112 wickets, average 21.56.

He travelled the world as a cricket coach, and was regarded as the best teacher of the bowling arts.

rather thin. Six matches were won and the County went a two further places down the table. It seemed that if the two or three main batsmen failed, the rest of the side panicked and the opposition soon disposed of them.

Qualifying for the County in 1953 and scoring runs in minor matches – he hit a hundred against The Army, for example – was the West Indian, Roy Marshall. Hampshire could not improve on the 14th place in 1954, whilst Marshall still kicked his heels. In a nutshell, the batting remained in the hands of Rogers and Gray and the bowling with Shackleton and Cannings. Ingleby-Mackenzie was given a permanent place in the eleven, but the soft pitches were all against his swashbuckling style. Prouton gave way to Harrison behind the wicket, but the latter, apart from a hundred at Burton on Trent, did little with the bat. Barnard, the Portsmouth footballer, reached a maiden hundred against the Pakistani tourists and played several useful knocks.

There was a trio of young bowlers who looked as if they might give valuable assistance to Shackleton and Cannings in the near future. Peter Sainsbury, a slow left-arm bowler from Chandlers Ford, appeared six times whilst on leave from the Army. Malcolm Heath, a 20-year-old from Bournemouth, was a fast bowler who picked up 17 wickets in the closing matches at a very reasonable cost. The third was also a local product, Mervyn Burden, an off-break bowler, who was introduced into the team at the beginning of July and played for the rest of the year, capturing 46 Championship wickets. If any two of these three could make the grade, then Hampshire would move out of the lower reaches of the Championship.

For Eagar, who had struggled to keep the team going for nine years, everything suddenly fell into place in 1955. The risk that had been taken by persuading Roy Marshall to spend two blank summers qualifying paid off with a dividend to the tune of 1,890 runs at an average of 36.34. All three young bowlers took wickets at a reasonable cost, as did Shackleton and Cannings. In fact if Marshall's bowling efforts are included, Hampshire had the enviable bowling statistics of every one of their six bowlers taking their wickets at less than 23 runs each.

The effect of this flowering of talent was a rapid climb up the Championship ladder. Whilst it would be idle to pretend that Hampshire challenged for the title – in 1955 this, in the end, was a battle between Surrey and Yorkshire – they

*Hampshire in 1955. Back row, left to right: P. J. Sainsbury,
J. R. Gray, A. W. H. Rayment, M. Heath, R. E. Marshall,*

*M. D. Burden, H. Horton. Front row: D. Shackleton, N. H. Rogers,
E. D. R. Eagar, L. Harrison, V. H. D. Cannings.*

finished 14 points above fourth-placed Sussex. It was the highest position the County had ever achieved.

Hampshire gained 16 Championship wins, the most satisfying being a comprehensive victory over Surrey at Bournemouth. Hampshire scored 368 for seven dec and 180 for seven dec, yet managed to bowl out the Champions twice for 245 and 174, Heath taking five wickets in the first innings and Sainsbury five in the second. The youngsters had come of age. Sainsbury also had a great match at Bradford, where Yorkshire found themselves dismissed for 62 and 119, Sainsbury nine for 62. The County won that game by an innings.

Although in 1956 Hampshire beat Surrey at Portsmouth on 12 June, Burden taking six wickets in the first innings and Marshall six in the second as the previously unbeaten Surrey were dismissed for 126 and 108, they then lost three games before the end of June, and this in effect removed any hopes

Malcolm Heath took over 500 wickets for Hampshire in the 1950s and 1960s.

HENRY HORTON

Horton's ungainly stance – bottom jutting, knees bent, bat at an angle of 45 degrees – caused amusement around the county circuit for more than 20 years, but after a hesitant start he became a very workmanlike cricketer.

In his youth he was overshadowed by his elder brother, Joe, who played for Worcestershire for several seasons prior to the Second World War, and when county cricket resumed in 1946, Henry was more interested in bowling left-arm spin than in batting. He had a trial as an amateur with Worcestershire in 1946 and the following year went on the staff at New Road, but had little opportunity to bowl and was unable to gain a regular place as a batsman.

Though his cricket career at this stage was unsuccessful, he began to become noted in the soccer field, as wing-half for Blackburn Rovers. In 1951–52 he was transferred to Southampton and in August 1952 he was persuaded to play for Hampshire Club and Ground – his last match for Worcester had been in 1949. He was invited to join the Hampshire staff in 1953 and by 1955 had gained a regular place in the County side. Twelve times he reached 1,000 runs in a season, and his best year was 1959 with 2,428 runs, average 47.60. His defensive batting saved many matches for Hampshire, but he could also attack the bowling, scoring most of his runs in front of the wicket by putting a great deal of power behind his 'pushes'.

they might have entertained of the title. Injuries to Cannings and Heath allied to Marshall's difficulties on the generally damp wickets accounted for Hampshire's slight decline. They won nine Championship games and were sixth at the close of the season.

Brought up on the hard pitches of the West Indies, Marshall found the ball coming through slower and this proved his downfall too many times, at least before August, when the weather improved. In contrast his opening partner, Gray, was just the batsman for such a summer. His careful approach paid dividends and both his aggregate and average increased. Horton also flourished, and though failing to hit a Championship hundred, he scored 1,249 runs at an average of 31. Outside these three, the batting remained a rather mixed bag. Rayment could play a delightful innings and then a few days later look like a novice. Some idea of the weakness in the middle order is clearly shown by the fact that Barnard usually came in at No 5 or No 6, yet his season's average was 16. Pitman, from Bartley, was also a middle-order batsman who was given 11 Championship matches in the course of the summer – he managed just 122 runs at an average of 8.71.

Shackleton had a splendid year – he played in every Championship game and captured well over a hundred wickets. Sainsbury, following his success in 1955, was rather disappointing, but to an extent the fielding was to blame, far too many catches being spilled. Burden was another whose wicket total suffered from missed chances.

The talent which Holt had uncovered ought to have developed further in 1957, but for some inexplicable reason Barnard, Sainsbury, Rayment, Pitman and Heath, all of whom were given ample opportunity – the County used only 14 players in the 28 Championship matches – progressed marginally or not at all. Since Cannings suffered injury and missed a third of the matches, the attack fell too heavily on the shoulders of Shackleton. The batting remained in the hands of Marshall, Gray and Horton – no one else averaged above 25.

Only one of the last eight matches – the final one of the season – provided a victory and a total of seven wins put Hampshire in 13th position. Again the critics put some of the blame on dropped catches and in August this fault became more serious, since Barnard, the best slip field, went off to play soccer for Portsmouth.

Marshall was now rated one of the most attractive batsmen

in England and justified this description against Kent at Southampton, when he hit 100 in 66 minutes, the fastest of the season and the fastest for Hampshire since 1927. At Portsmouth against Glamorgan he managed a hundred before lunch and showed his talents to the full in the disastrous match against Surrey, also at Portsmouth. Surrey scored 386 for six declared. Lock and Bedser then dismissed Hampshire for 120, of which Marshall made 56. The follow-on was enforced and this time Lock shared the wickets with Laker as Hampshire were again bowled out and lost in two days. Marshall made 111 out of 231 in that second innings and, the report noted: 'treated all four Surrey bowlers with scant respect'.

At Portsmouth in the return match, Marshall was unable to come to the rescue, much to the embarrassment of the local dignitaries. The Queen and the Duke of Edinburgh had been invited to the City to celebrate the 700th anniversary of the first charter and a visit to the cricket match was on the programme at tea on the second day: Hampshire were defeated before three o'clock on that day, being dismissed for 66 and 108. An exhibition game was hastily devised to amuse the royal party.

The year was a sad one for Desmond Eagar for it was his last as captain, and with all the potential available it was unfortunate that a man who had given so much to the County should bow out when the team was in the doldrums. His successor was to be Ingleby-Mackenzie, who had played in virtually every match and in all first-class cricket completed 1,000 runs in the season.

If things went badly for Eagar in his final year, the reverse was true of Ingleby-Mackenzie's first summer in charge. It was a year of high humidity – ideal for the swing which Shackleton imparted to the ball; only Lock took more wickets in 1958. Cannings, however, had come to the end of the road, but Shackleton found an effective partner in Heath, who far exceeded anything he had previously achieved and in Championship matches took 119 wickets at 16.32 each. The spin attack, though not as good as the seam bowling, improved and both Sainsbury and Burden had quite respectable figures. For some reason Marshall almost gave up bowling – in his first years in county cricket his off breaks had provided a most useful back up.

Although the West Indian remained the dominant batsman, Ingleby-Mackenzie outscored him on occasion,

EDWARD DESMOND RUSSELL EAGAR

On the field, Desmond Eagar's greatest asset was his close catching. He was a fearless short leg, easily distinguishable by his Harlequin cap in an era when such exotic headgear was going out of fashion. As a batsman he was elegant and attacking, and successful against all but the highest class of bowlers. A slow left-arm spin bowler, he put himself on when all else failed and sometimes surprised himself by taking a wicket.

Even as a schoolboy he was a notable captain. *Wisden* of 1937 comments: 'Eagar kept his side (Cheltenham) always on their toes, and their keenness in the field furnished a real tribute to his captaincy.' This quality he retained when he was appointed Hampshire's captain in 1946 and he gradually built up the County's self-respect and image on the Championship circuit, which had been none too distinguished in the years between the wars.

His work as Hampshire's Secretary meant a continual round of mundane tasks, which others might have regarded as chores, but Eagar attended dinners and other functions with a keen enthusiasm and he tried to persuade the other Hampshire players to sell themselves and county cricket to the public at large. In doing so he built up the membership of the County Club. Eagar was Chairman of the Hampshire Cricket Association and thus helped to encourage local cricket, as well as county cricket. He believed in the standards of the 'Golden Age' of cricket and in later life was concerned that cricket was becoming too much a part of show business. He died whilst on holiday in Kingsbridge, Devon, on 13 September 1977.

notably against Somerset at Bournemouth, when his hundred came in 61 minutes and only rain prevented Hampshire from an innings victory, and at Southampton against Kent. In this match Hampshire were set 305 in 270 minutes and won with half an hour to spare because the captain hit his hundred in 98 minutes. The other two players to make runs were Gray and Horton, though the former Worcester cricketer tried a little too hard to emulate the flashing blades of Marshall and Ingleby-Mackenzie and would have done better to play his more solid role, especially as the others – Pitman, Barnard, Harrison and Rayment – were still very unreliable.

After a moderate start to the year, being beaten by Notts and Lancashire, Hampshire began to win with some frequency and by the end of June were leading the Championship. They continued to be the front runners until the middle of August, when two very close contests went the wrong way. At Eastbourne, Hampshire needed 180 to win, but lost four wickets for 22. Then Pitman and Ingleby-Mackenzie added 70 in 50 minutes. The rain clouds were now gathering, and though Sainsbury and Harrison added a further 56 for the eighth wicket, the left-arm spinner, Bell, took three for six and extinguished Hampshire's hopes. The following match, with points now of vital importance, ended as a draw, Hampshire being just six runs short, having been set 170 in 120 minutes. Marshall hit 55 in 45 minutes, but with no other major innings materializing the chase could not be maintained. All hope of the title finally vanished at Bournemouth, the scene of the next game. Rain prevented any play on the last day with Hampshire requiring 270 in the fourth innings. Hampshire afterwards lost the last match of the season when they were dismissed for 61 by Derbyshire, but it was of purely statistical importance. So Hampshire were the runners-up, 26 points behind Surrey.

Beating Glamorgan and Gloucester in the first two matches of 1959, Hampshire began the summer at a gallop, but the pace soon slackened, when three successive defeats were incurred, all by fairly large margins. Although the County did not feature in the final exciting battle for the title, they finished· in eighth place only 18 points behind the runners-up and registered 11 victories. It was a summer of glorious weather, with counties needing accurate fast bowlers to dismiss the oposition. Hampshire had Shackleton, but all his partners had poor records. Cannings, in his final

LEO HARRISON

By the age of 12 Leo Harrison was already a member of his village team of Mudeford on the edge of the New Forest. In those days he was a left-handed batsman, but by the time he had joined the County staff in 1937 he had become right-handed. The following year, still only 16, he was opening the innings with Arthur Holt in Club and Ground matches and in 1939 his form for the second eleven was such that he made his County Championship debut. The war then intervened, and for six years Harrison served in the RAF, with few opportunities for cricket. However in 1946 he was given the job, almost by chance, of wicket-keeper in some Services matches and proved so successful that he kept for the Combined Services. When he rejoined Hampshire his appearances at first were restricted by the presence of McCorkell. Problems with his eyesight did not help his batting and it was not until 1954 that he really gained a secure place in the County side and showed such skill that in 1955 he was selected for the Players *v* Gentlemen at Lord's.

He continued to appear in the County side until 1966, having the previous year succeeded Arthur Holt as Hampshire's coach.

year, appeared in less than half the Championship matches, Heath had a dismal time and gave way eventually to young White, the Sutton Coldfield fast bowler, who sent down some very rapid deliveries indeed.

Of the spinners, Sainsbury was ill and missed some games, Burden's wickets cost 30 runs each and he lost his place in the eleven. Baldry had been signed from Middlesex, but was even more expensive – his main forte was batting and he scored 151 on his Hampshire debut. Wassell, a 19-year-old youth from Fareham, appeared in ten games and bowled his left-arm slows with some guile.

In all Hampshire first-class matches, Horton, Gray and Marshall each reached 2,000 runs, an event unique in the County's History. The initial batting was thus at its strongest, but after the first three the rest continued to be very inconsistent. Baldry went in at No 4, but the County failed to discover a good No 5, Pitman, Barnard and another youngster, Flood, all being given a chance, whilst the captain occupied the No 6 slot with his usual flair.

On 11 June 1960, the County stood third in the table. From that date on they gradually sank until they rested at 12th. The bright spot of the year was the rapid improvement in the fast bowling of White, who took over 100 wickets at 18 runs each. If he had not been no-balled for throwing, he would probably have been chosen for the MCC winter tour. Shackleton therefore had an excellent partner with whom to open the bowling. Heath had a better year and played in about two thirds of the matches, but the spin bowling consisted very much of one man, Sainsbury. Burden remained expensive, Baldry and Barnard scarcely bowled and accomplished little when they did. Piachaud, the Oxford blue, was brought in during his vacation and his brand of off-break was tried in a dozen matches in place of Burden; but there was little to choose between the two.

The batting was very much a repeat of 1959, except that Sainsbury improved and Baldry declined. Danny Livingstone from Antigua, who had averaged over 100 in Club and Ground matches in 1959, was qualified for Championship games in 1960, but could not command a regular place in the eleven, though he looked a promising batsman. Harrison, still the regular wicket-keeper, chipped a bone in his right hand in mid-season and his understudy, Timms from Ropley, gave a good account of himself, but did nothing to bolster the batting.

ROY EDWIN MARSHALL

Only 15 when he made his first-class debut for his native Barbados in 1946, Marshall was the youngest member of the famous 1950 West Indian team which took England by storm, and although he hit 1,117 runs at an average of 39.89 on that tour, he failed to obtain a place in any of the Tests. The following English season he returned as a pro for Lowerhouse in the Lancashire League and then gained selection for the 1951–52 West Indies team to Australia. On that tour Marshall appeared in two Tests against Australia and a further two when the side went on to New Zealand, but his best innings was a splendid century against New South Wales. Marshall spent a second year in the Lancashire League in 1952, but in September of that year he was offered a contract with Hampshire and decided to take a chance and stay in England to qualify by residence. In 1955 he began his County Championship career and completed 1,000 runs every season from then to his retirement in 1972.

His batting style emulated the great West Indians: fast scoring, unorthodox but very effective. His most productive scoring strokes were those square of the wicket, but his drive off the back foot could also be used with deadly certainty.

Marshall's best season was 1961, when he hit 2,607 runs at an average of 43.45. His three double-centuries were all for Hampshire, the highest being 228 not out against the Pakistan tourists in 1962. He could also bowl a deceptive off-break.

In 1960 the County had 5,382 members and receipts from membership created a new record of over £10,000. But against this the number of paying spectators was the lowest since the war, and the Club showed a loss of nearly £6,000 on the year's workings. Hampshire's fortunes, in fact, seemed at a distinctly low ebb.

THE HAMPSHIRE HANDBOOK

After the Second World War, the County did not have an annual until 1950, when the first *Handbook* appeared edited by K. Peskett for the County Club. In the years 1951 to 1953, Sports Publications issued the annual, but it was not a financial success and no issue appeared in 1954. M. L. Pepper (Publicity) Ltd issued a new *Handbook* in 1955 on the Club's behalf – this firm was responsible for the production of several other counties' annuals at this time. The 1955 *Handbook* retailed at one shilling (5p) and contained 120 pages, the page size being the same as at the present time. The annual of 1955 contained the full County Championship scores, the club's annual report and three or four articles. The price however soon doubled to two shillings (10p) and later to half-a-crown (12½p).

In 1968 the County Club resumed responsibility for the production. By 1974 the size had increased and the plain cover given way to a coloured photograph. The present production, in terms of the comprehensiveness of the statistics and match score details, is not matched by that of many other counties.

CHAMPIONS AT LAST

HAVING ENDED THE 1960 SEASON in 12th place the bookmakers did not rate Hampshire's chances of the title for 1961. The County had not imported any new players and no dramatic advance was expected from the youngsters on the staff, but at least the breaking of Surrey's stranglehold on the Championship in 1959 had left the competition much more open. Yorkshire had claimed the honours in 1959 and 1960, but as *Wisden* pointed out, they took the title in 1960 without showing really outstanding form and went through some shaky periods when they looked quite moderate. Lancashire, who had come second in 1960, were not a very happy crew, and at the end of 1960 Wharton went off to Leicestershire, Dyson disappeared and Barber's captaincy was on occasion somewhat controversial and not to the liking of members of the County Committee. Middlesex, third in 1960, had a good team spirit and the main question mark for them in 1961 was the gamble of bringing Ian Bedford in as captain. He had not played in Championship cricket for nearly ten years.

Hampshire began their fixtures at Bournemouth with Worcestershire as the visitors. The rain that had affected so many matches in 1960 seemed destined to continue. 'This is where we came in', commented one disgruntled member of the eleven, when the second day of the match was entirely rained off. Only a fine innings by Martin Horton prevented a complete collapse by Worcestershire – he made 115 out of 208, only three other players reaching double figures. On the other hand Marshall and Gray began Hampshire's innings in contrast to the weather, their 117 first-wicket stand coming at a run a minute, and this was vital under the system of awarding points then in operation. Counties received only two points for first-innings lead, but a further two if, when obtaining that lead, they scored their runs at a faster rate.

The wet weather followed Hampshire to the little ground at Frome and on the Saturday, the first day of the match with Somerset, very little play was possible. Latham, making his first-class debut for Somerset, surprised even his admirers by clean bowling Marshall for nine and then Horton for a duck before the players disappeared into the pavilion. On Monday Hampshire struggled to 157 all out, but Somerset were confused by Burden, who in a devastating spell of 31 balls dismissed five batsmen for a single run conceded. Burden ended with the best figures of his career – eight for 38 – and on a wicket not given to runs Hampshire were in the happy position of a first innings lead of 55. Wickets continued to tumble when Hampshire began their second innings, and with Palmer picking up five for 19, Somerset required 172 for victory. Burden and Sainsbury soon had the visitors on the way to victory, but the young Latham was quite determined to set his mark on this match and, arriving at No 11, refused to bow to the Hampshire off-spin. He and Langford added 42 – the largest stand Somerset managed in either innings – before Ingleby-Mackenzie decided that spin was not enough and brought back White to remove Langford.

This first victory was followed by much good fortune at The Oval, allied to the generosity of the urbane Peter May. On the first day Surrey's batting was seen at its best, with the England players, Edrich and Barrington, each hitting hundreds. Barrington was not his more usual steady-stop self, but cruised to 151 in 210 minutes with 21 fours and not a single false stroke. May was able to declare the innings closed at 356 for four and then watch Hampshire, on the same bland pitch, battle against Loader and Gibson, only Horton with an unbeaten 85 being in control – he stayed for 230 minutes. Owing to a strange experimental law, May was not allowed to enforce the follow-on (Hampshire were 166 in arrears) and so was forced to bat a second time and gamble on a sporting declaration. He gave his opponents 330 minutes to make 308 – Hampshire's 190 had occupied 285 minutes in the first innings.

Gibson dismissed Gray for a single, but Marshall and Horton were in top form. The West Indian attacked from the word go and his 153 with 22 fours came in 135 minutes out of 280. Horton made 84 and Hampshire won with five wickets and an hour to spare. An incredible reversal of fortune!

The third successive away match took place on the County Ground at Northampton. Gray timed the ball sweetly on the first day and his innings of 136 came in 270 minutes, allowing Ingleby-Mackenzie to close at 350 for seven. All the bowlers troubled the Northants batsmen and Hampshire appeared to be heading for a commanding lead when the eighth wicket fell for 194. Then a little-known fast bowler from Norton-on-Tees played the same trick as Latham had tried in the first match, only this time with much more success. John

Williamson and the wicket-keeper, Keith Andrew, added 97 for the ninth wicket. Hampshire's lead was thus only 59, but Marshall and Gray hurried the score along in the second innings and a second declaration set 270, 168 runs having come before lunch on the last morning. All the Hampshire bowlers again had a hand in reducing Northants to 110 for six. Williamson then marched to the crease and for 45 minutes, in combination with the disabled Lightfoot, he gave no sign of budging, and Ingleby-Mackenzie surrendered, not even bothering with the extra half-hour.

Back home again – or at least just down the road in the United Services Ground – Hampshire opposed Lancashire, a side who had yet to win a match and were without their star bowler, Brian Statham. Ken Higgs managed to dismiss Marshall for nought, but Lancashire's joy was short-lived as Gray and Horton went for the bowling. Their partnership was worth 170 in 160 minutes. Gray went on to his hundred and Hampshire reached 300 comfortably. Shackleton and White put the Lancashire batsmen on the defensive, only Marner making a decent score. In the second innings, Hampshire tried too hard to go for the runs and the middle order fell to Greenhough's leg breaks, so Lancashire had the whole of Friday in which to score 251. The wicket was still in good condition, but the batting mirrored the first innings, with Marner playing well and no one else making much headway. Hampshire won by 47 runs and collected the maximum 14 points.

Hampshire had won three out of five matches at this stage, but the table was being headed by Yorkshire, who had won both games they had played – in 1961 the teams did not all play the same number of matches and thus the table was worked on an average basis.

The first match on the County Ground at Southampton saw Hampshire's first defeat. A declaration set Hampshire 375 to win at about 70 runs an hour. Horton hit a brilliant hundred, Marshall and Ingleby-Mackenzie made fifties and the side went for the runs even to the last man, but Sayer took the final wicket with the first ball of the last possible over and Kent won by 28 runs.

Whilst Hampshire were losing, Yorkshire clocked up their third win at the expense of Lancashire in the Whitsun Roses match, so the visit of Hampshire to Headingley was of crucial important if Hampshire were going to prevent Yorkshire obtaining a commanding lead in the title race.

Yorkshire made a very competent start with Stott and Bolus putting together 137 for the first wicket. Yorkshire scored 279 at 2.47 an over and on the first evening Hampshire had a few minutes' batting, losing night-watchman Harrison for a duck. On Thursday they could make only slow progress against Trueman and Cowan and when they were all out, nearly 100 in arrears, the run rate was less than two per over. Padgett batted well in the second innings and Wilson was able to set Hampshire 290 in 240 minutes. Marshall and Gray began briskly, but when four wickets were down before the hundred was hoisted, Ingleby-Mackenzie decided to settle for a draw and batted out time with Sainsbury.

Across the Pennines to Old Trafford and a shock. For the return with Lancashire Statham was fit and this fact won the match for his side. Hampshire batted first and Statham removed both openers for ten runs. Horton remained firm but could find no one to assist him and the side were all out for 152, with Horton having made 66. Lancashire just achieved first-innings points, but then some fine bowling by Statham, Higgs and Hilton skittled out the visiting side for 77 and Lancashire hit off the 54 runs they wanted with no difficulty. Unfortunately for Hampshire, Yorkshire at the same time were beating Leicestershire out of sight.

Hampshire went to Dean Park for their return with Somerset and collapsed again, with Langford taking six wickets. Somerset gained a first innings lead of 102. Marshall, who had not scored many runs in his last few visits to the wicket, then exploded. He hit a double century for the first time in his career and reached 212 in 260 minutes. Included in the innings were seven sixes and 21 fours. Of the first wicket partnership, Gray made just 38 out of 155. Ingleby-Mackenzie found himself in the happy position of being able to set Somerset 262 in 222 minutes, and after an opening stand of 73 between Atkinson and Lomax had been broken Burden ran through the side with little trouble, picking up seven for 72 in the process and gaining victory by 63 runs.

Hampshire had a much easier time at Swansea, where Sainsbury batted four hours and reached the then highest score of his career, 125 not out. This, together with Shackleton's six for 90, gave Hampshire a good lead on first innings, including the extra points for faster run rate. Unfortunately Harrison was injured and unable to keep wicket, so the captain stood behind and took four catches in the match. Hampshire hit out in their second innings and were able to set Glamorgan 257 in just over three hours. Their final innings was a repetition of the Somerset match, with the opening pair, Alan Jones and Hedges batting well – 102 for the first wicket – followed by a collapse and Wassell, in his first match of the summer took four for 22, as Hampshire won by 73 runs, with 30 minutes in hand.

At the other end of England, as it were, Yorkshire continued on their winning ways and won six out of seven matches. Hampshire kept up the pressure by some astute manoeuvring by their captain in the match at Portsmouth against Gloucestershire. Rain interrupted play three times on the first day as the western county were dismissed for 176 between the showers. No play at all was possible on the

Danny Livingstone from Antigua played over 500 innings for Hampshire between 1959 and 1972, averaging nearly 28.

second day. On the last morning Marshall and Gray hit 96 without loss in 70 minutes. Ingleby-Mackenzie declared. Gloucestershire found Shackleton too accurate and lost eight wickets, before closing their innings, which left Hampshire needing 199 in 137 minutes. Horton and the captain both made fifties, but the match was won by White, who struck some mighty blows, scoring 33 out of the 37 added for the ninth wicket and bringing success with two minutes left on the clock.

A maiden first-class hundred by Danny Livingstone allowed a declaration to be made just before the close of the first day in the Northants game at Southampton. On the second day Northants put up little resistance to White and their first innings deficit approached 200, but the experimental law again prevented Hampshire from enforcing the follow-on. So Hampshire hit out wildly in their second innings and Northants were left in the impossible position of making 301 – or at least very improbable judged on the relative batting and bowling strengths. they were all out for 128, giving Hampshire victory by 172 runs. For once Yorkshire, on the same dates, lost. It was their first defeat of 1961 and gave Hampshire an opportunity to close the gap.

Ingleby-Mackenzie put the backbone into Hampshire's innings at Dudley with 98 in 95 minutes on a wicket which always helped the bowlers. Shackleton and White then dismissed Worcestershire for 68, giving their side a lead of 209. Hampshire hit out in their second innings and the home side required 401 in eight hours for victory. The only resistance came in a two-and-a-half-hour partnership between Derek Richardson and Booth; they added 102, but Shackleton took another five wickets and the win was by 185 runs. Meanwhile Yorkshire were held to a draw at The Oval.

The team moved from Dudley to Hinckley, where Willie Watson won the toss and decided to bat – he hit a fine 79, but none of the other Leicestershire batsmen settled in and the total only reached 140. Mainstay of the Hampshire innings was Horton, who batted 255 minutes making 134, and the tail added 70, mainly due to 42 from Shackleton. Leicester could do little better in their second essay and Hampshire won by ten wickets. Yorkshire suffered their second defeat of the season and Hampshire moved to the head of the table. Breathing hard down Hampshire's neck, however, were the rejuvenated Middlesex, who had won three matches in succession and had no match during this period.

ALEXANDER COLIN DAVID INGLEBY-MACKENZIE

Appointed as captain of the County in 1958 at the age of 24, Ingleby-Mackenzie immediately became a personality to be reckoned with in county cricket. In that first year as captain he took Hampshire to second place in the Championship, hit the fastest hundred of the season and was voted 'Best Young Cricketer of the Year'. A swashbuckling left-handed batsman, his only rule as captain was said to be: 'Be in bed by breakfast time'; yet was a first-rate tactician and an acute judge of men. His inspiring leadership helped Hampshire to their first Championship title in 1961, while his gift of being able to diffuse a potential quarrel saved many dressing-room arguments from getting out of hand.

On occasion he might have appeared more concerned with the racing results than a change in the bowling, but he could decide to a minute the best time to declare and by dedicated practice turned himself into an excellent fieldsman. His affability made him essential to any 'friendly' touring team and he went with E. W. Swanton's side to the West Indies and India, with the Duke of Norfolk's to Jamaica and with the Cavaliers to South Africa and the West Indies.

Hampshire themselves then had three days' rest, while Middlesex beat Notts, and so to Lord's, for the vital game between Middlesex and Hampshire. The Hampshire seam bowlers looked completely in control as seven wickets went down for 84, but Titmus arrived and nearly doubled the score for the eighth wicket. When Hampshire batted the innings ended with slide rules much in evidence to calculate the run rate for two bonus batting points. Hampshire scored 196 to Middlesex's 190 and the run rate was 2.51 to 2.50 in Hampshire's favour. Gale batted well for Middlesex in the second innings and Hampshire were left requiring 281 in 150 minutes. It was a target they never looked like approaching and Titmus and Bedford took Middlesex to a 131-run win.

Hampshire seemed to be losing their grip, and the first half of the match at Cowes, where Essex were the opponents, did nothing to improve Hampshire's image. Essex found little to worry them in the home attack and hit 321 for nine on the first day, whereas Hampshire in reply could muster only 231, though they were handicapped by an injury to Marshall, who came in at No 7. Essex then knocked up 150 in their second innings before declaring, setting Hampshire 241 in 215 minutes. Bailey and Preston soon had wickets tumbling and the scoreboard looked a sorry sight at 35 for four. Ingleby-Mackenzie joined Livingstone and raised the total to 121 before the fifth wicket – Livingstone's – fell. Wassell arrived and survived 47 minutes, making 11, but adding with his captain a further 50 to the total. Another 72 runs were now required and Marshall arrived on one leg aided by a runner. In 44 minutes those runs were knocked off without another wicket falling. Ingleby-Mackenzie was undefeated on 132 and Marshall 36 – there were 15 minutes remaining.

Hampshire went to Edgbaston without the injured Marshall and the captain was still acting as wicket-keeper in the continued absence of Harrison. The first two days of the game with Warwickshire were tame affairs, with neither side's batsmen able to score with any certainty and Warwickshire just managing to gain a first-innings lead. Bannister caused problems for most of the Hampshire batsmen in the second innings and in the last phase of the game Warwickshire required 177 at 82 runs an hour. Hitchcock and Horner put on 58 in 48 minutes for the second wicket, but then wickets began to fall and Warwickshire settled for a draw.

Runs came even slower in the match with Notts at

Southampton – Notts gained a first-innings lead but could only just manage a rate of two runs an over. Baldry cheered up spectators in the second innings with 61 in half-an-hour and this allowed Hampshire to set Notts 196 in 125 minutes. Millman and Maurice Hill added 122 in an hour and only 19 runs were needed with nine minutes in hand, but Baldry and Sainsbury then won the game for Hampshire by two splendid throws which ran out Forbes and Morgan.

The Bournemouth wicket did not make run-getting any easier, when Hampshire went there for their next game against Glamorgan. The Welshmen could make only 211, but in reply Hampshire's score reached just 134. Glamorgan passed 200 in their second innings, which left Hampshire requiring 285, but the wicket was tailor-made for Shepherd's cutters and the best score a Hampshire batsman could manage was 21 by Henry Horton – Shepherd took seven for 41 and Glamorgan won by 183 runs. Meanwhile at The Oval Middlesex had beaten Surrey and, achieving maximum points, moved above Hampshire in the Championship.

The defeated Surrey then came to Bournemouth. The match clashed with the Gentlemen v Players fixture and so neither May or Lock were in the visiting party – and the days were now passed when Surrey could win despite the absence of leading players; Alec Bedser and Jim Laker were no longer at Kennington. On the first day Hampshire did more or less what they liked with the Surrey bowlers, and though John Edrich and Tindall each made fifty, Surrey had a first-innings deficit of 94. The last day belonged to Wassell, whose spin picked up seven wickets and a total of 12 in the match, his best career figures.

One curiosity of the next match at Hove was that Harrison, acting as 12th man for Hampshire, was allowed to act as substitute wicket-keeper when Ingleby-Mackenzie broke his finger. That apart, this was one of the few occasions in 1961 when Hampshire were comprehensively outplayed. Sussex gained a first-innings lead with six wickets down and immediately declared; Bates and Bell then dismissed Hampshire cheaply a second time and Alan Oakman and Richard Langridge had no difficulty in adding 100 of the 160 required for victory, even before the first wicket fell. Sussex won by eight wickets. Fortunately Yorkshire drew with Surrey, and Middlesex were busy losing to the Australians, so neither could take immediate advantage of Hampshire's lapse.

Off to Bristol, with Marshall as captain and Harrison

returning to the wicket-keeping slot. In the 1950s Bristol had been a spinners' paradise. Now it was made for seam and Shackleton and Heath bustled out Gloucestershire for 141. With Marshall at his entertaining best, Hampshire gained a first-innings lead with only three wickets gone. White's pace was too much for the home batsmen in their second innings and Hampshire needed only 50 to win when the final innings began.

With counties not playing the same number of matches it was difficult at a glance to decide who needed what to head the table, when Middlesex came to Portsmouth for the last match of July. There was nothing very exciting about the cricket during the first two innings. Livingstone made 91 and for Middlesex Parfitt scored 70. Some solid batting in Hampshire's second innings allowed Marshall to set a target of 319 in 240 minutes. Marshall dangled no carrots and Middlesex were content to bat out time. The positions at the top of the Championship after this drawn game were:

	P	W	L	D	NR	Bonus Pts	Pts	Avge
Hampshire	23	13	5	5	0	24	188	8.17
Middlesex	20	12	4	3	1	14	160	8.00
Yorkshire	23	13	3	7	0	22	184	8.00

Middlesex had eight more matches to play and Yorkshire and Hampshire nine. It was still very much an open race, but fourth-placed Sussex were way behind.

A second successive game at Portsmouth found Sussex as the visitors, and they were the victims of a remarkable piece of cricket. Hampshire had gained a first innings lead of 38 and Sussex seemed quite comfortably placed at 179 for four in their second innings, Dexter and Parks being the not out batsmen. It was a vile day with half a gale blowing and the ground almost deserted. White started his 21st over at 6.53 p.m. and bowled Parks with the first ball, then had night-watchman Thomson caught with his second and bowled Smith with his third. Gray then dropped Cooper off the fourth, but White had Cooper caught off the final ball – it was the first post-war Hampshire Championship hat-trick. Play then ended for the day. On the last morning the final two wickets could only muster a leg bye and Hampshire had no difficulty in knocking off the runs. In the same game Shackleton took his 100th wicket of the season for the 12th time.

Rain prevented any play before the middle of the afternoon on the first day of the game against Kent at Canterbury. Marshall ignored the damp wicket and outfield and hit his hundred in less than two hours. The Kent captain, Colin Cowdrey, replied with an equally distinguished three-figure innings and from then on the game was destined for a draw. It was the August Bank Holiday weekend and the traditional rain forced draws at Bramall Lane and Hove, the venues for Yorkshire and Middlesex, so again neither of Hampshire's rivals could make up leeway.

Ingleby-Mackenzie returned to the side for the match with Essex at Leyton, no doubt enforcing his strict code of discipline which meant that during matches every player had to be back in the team's hotel by breakfast time! Trevor Bailey caused a serious collapse by reducing Hampshire to 38 for four before Sainsbury came to the rescue with a stout innings of 74 which spanned some four hours. Hampshire's total reached 237, but Essex had little trouble in gaining a first-innings lead and then Bailey struck a second time. The England all-rounder took seven for 40 in 28.2 overs as Hampshire were dismissed for 120, leaving Essex needing just 44 to win, a task they accomplished with the loss of two wickets. It was fortunate that Middlesex also suffered defeat on the same days, though Yorkshire beat Notts by 207 runs. It was essential that Hampshire won their next game, which took place on the Racecourse Ground, Derby.

Marshall opened the batting in tremendous form, hitting 72 out of 95, whereas Horton remained over five hours for 141 – the highest score of his career to date. On the second day, due to some magnificent bowling by Shackleton, Derbyshire were dismissed for 262, giving Hampshire a first-innings lead of 88. Hampshire went for quick runs in their second innings and left Derbyshire needing 263 in 208 minutes. Johnson and Carr hit 65 in 50 minutes, but after this partnership was broken wickets began to fall, and though the home batsmen put up the shutters, the last wicket fell with five minutes left. Hampshire secured 14 points.

Shackleton and White won the next two Championship matches, each taking a total of 17 wickets in the two fixtures. In the Warwickshire game at Southampton, the Midland side appeared to be in a secure position when they made 343 for nine declared in the first innings, but in the second Shackleton and White dismissed them for 125 and Hampshire had an easy task on the last afternoon.

DEREK SHACKLETON

For 20 consecutive seasons, Shackleton captured an annual haul of 100 or more wickets, a record which is unlikely ever to be surpassed, yet he appeared in only seven Tests. His Test debut was at Trent Bridge in 1950, when, batting at No 8, he made England's highest score in their first innings, 42 out of 69 in 70 minutes. Then Weekes and Worrell tore the England bowling apart and Shackleton took one for 128. The selectors dropped eight of the side, including the Hampshire bowler, for the next Test. He was given one chance in 1951, but was not again selected until 1963.

During those 12 missing years he was in great form for Hampshire, usually ending the season in the top ten bowlers in the country. In 1955 was the best bowler of the year.

Shackleton was discovered by the Hampshire coach in 1947 when playing in Army cricket, and was given a trial as a batsman, then had a spell bowling leg-breaks and finally settled on his brand of seam bowling. He bowled a little above medium pace and his success was due to his control, which enabled him to swing the ball either way and vary his pace without a noticeable change of action. His run up and delivery were smooth and his high action served well as a model for others when he took up coaching at the close of his county career. It was this action which allowed him to bowl so many overs with so few injuries.

A hard-hitting batsman, Shackleton never reached a hundred in first-class cricket, his highest being 87 not out against Essex in 1949, but he compiled many useful fifties.

DEAN PARK: BOURNEMOUTH

It was at Dean Park on 1 September 1961 that Hampshire secured the County Championship for the first time. The ground thus holds a special place in the hearts of Hampshire supporters.

Laid out in 1869 for the members of Bournemouth Cricket Club, it was not until 1875 that a pavilion was erected and in 1897 that a cricket week was instituted, involving two County fixtures, though in that year the fixtures were only a two-day game against MCC and a three-day one against the Philadelphians.

Two attempts by the local municipal authority to run a cricket festival involving representative teams were financial failures. In September 1903, the Gentlemen of the South, under W. G. Grace, played the Players of the South, but the weather was unkind. The second festival was in 1928 when a most exciting contest between Gentlemen and Players was staged – the match ended with the former having one wicket left and needing 12 to win. A. W. Carr's batting – he made 71 and 63 – was the feature of the match. This game was followed by a match between North and South. R. W. V. Robins and P. G. H. Fender came in at Nos 6 and 7, both hit 90s and then both bowled well, taking 12 wickets between them and in effect winning the match for their side.

The outstanding innings on the ground remains R. H. Moore's 316 for Hampshire against Warwickshire in 1937.

In the following game against Leicestershire the two opening bowlers found the Leicester batsmen easy meat, dismissing them for 95 and 175, thus producing a win by 152 runs. These two victories ought to have pushed Hampshire clear of their rivals, but Yorkshire also won two matches on the same dates.

Hampshire went to Trent Bridge needing to win and at the same time hoping that Middlesex and Yorkshire would not be successful in their matches. Hampshire batted first and runs came freely. Marshall and Gray put on 132 in 95 minutes for the first wicket; Horton and Barnard hit 114 in 87 minutes. Ingleby-Mackenzie declared at 358 fox six. Norman Hill and Poole batted well for the home side and the Notts total reached 299 – Forbes was run out attempting a third run from an overthrow, when Marshall's shy at the wicket scored a direct hit. Hampshire's runs came quickly in their second innings, with Marshall once more to the fore, and Notts found themselves facing a target of 334 in 263 minutes. Only Poole responded to the challenge and Hampshire won by 128 runs; Yorkshire lost and Middlesex drew.

Hampshire leaving the Bournemouth field in triumph after beating Derbyshire and clinching the County Championship in 1961. Derek Shackleton, with his hand over his face, leads the way. Captain Colin Ingleby-Mackenzie has stopped to shake hands.

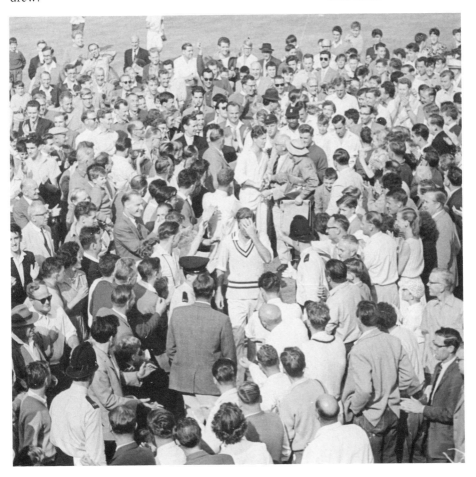

HAMPSHIRE *v* DERBYSHIRE

Played at Dean Park, Bournemouth, 30 and 31 August and 1 September 1961
HAMPSHIRE WON BY 140 RUNS

HAMPSHIRE	FIRST INNINGS		SECOND INNINGS	
R. E. Marshall	c Lee b Smith	76	c Lee b Morgan	86
J. R. Gray	run out	78	b Rhodes	4
H. Horton	c Taylor b Jackson	13	lbw b Rhodes	0
D. A. Livingstone	c Lee b Smith	7	c Johnson b Smith	11
P. J. Sainsbury	c Rhodes b Smith	1	c Lee b Smith	73
H. M. Barnard	c Rhodes b Morgan	19	c Taylor b Smith	61
*Mr A. C. D. Ingleby-Mackenzie	b Richardson	30	st Taylor b Smith	5
†L. Harrison	lbw b Morgan	35	b Jackson	0
A. R. Wassell	c Taylor b Jackson	13		
D. Shackleton	not out	27	not out	2
D. W. White	b Morgan	0	(9) not out	13
Extras	b 1, lb 4, w 1, nb 1	7	b 4, lb 3, w 1	8
Total		306	(for 8 wkts dec)	263

1st inns: 1-120, 2-145, 3-160, 4-166, 5-182, 6-229, 7-230, 8-256, 9-304
2nd inns: 1-8, 2-16, 3-40, 4-141, 5-240, 6-247, 7-248, 8-250

BOWLING	O	M	R	W	O	M	R	W
Jackson	24	9	44	2	14	5	25	1
Rhodes	22	4	48	0	15	8	19	2
Richardson	11	1	35	1	9	2	34	0
Lee	8	2	30	0				
Morgan	20.3	3	79	3	21	5	59	1
Smith	28	8	63	3	25	3	87	4
Oates					2	0	18	0
Gibson					2	0	13	0

DERBYSHIRE	FIRST INNINGS		SECOND INNINGS	
C. Lee	run out	5	c Harrison b Shackleton	4
Dr I. Gibson	b Sainsbury	46	lbw b Shackleton	3
H. L. Johnson	c Gray b Wassell	112	b Shackleton	14
W. F. Oates	c Harrison b Shackleton	89	b Shackleton	2
D. Millner	b Shackleton	14	c and b Wassell	17
D. C. Morgan	b Wassell	13	c Gray b Wassell	3
E. Smith	c Barnard b Shackleton	0	b Shackleton	9
*Mr G. W. Richardson	c Horton b Wassell	6	b Shackleton	0
†R. W. Taylor	not out	12	c Livingstone b Sainsbury	48
H. J. Rhodes	b Wassell	9	c and b Sainsbury	11
H. L. Jackson	c Ingleby-Mackenzie b Wassell	4	not out	0
Extras	b 4, lb 4	8		
Total		318		111

1st inns: 1-9, 2-102, 3-212, 4-248, 5-273, 6-274, 7-285, 8-297, 9-314
2nd inns: 1-4, 2-17, 3-23, 4-24, 5-35, 6-48, 7-52, 8-52, 9-104

BOWLING	O	M	R	W	O	M	R	W
Shackleton	39	15	70	3	24	10	39	6
White	10	3	22	0	3	1	5	0
Gray	7	2	19	0				
Wassell	42.1	13	132	5	24	10	62	2
Sainsbury	14	3	67	1	3.2	0	5	2

Umpires: H. Yarnold and A. E. G. Rhodes.
Hampshire won the toss. Close of play: 2nd day: Hampshire 306 and 101-3, Derbyshire 318.
*Captain; †Wicket-keeper.

Two Championship matches remained for Hampshire. The first was against Derbyshire and the second against Yorkshire. Middlesex also had two more fixtures, whilst Yorkshire had three, but Hampshire, due to their run of success, required only one victory to secure the title. Before anything could be decided however, Hampshire had a fixture against the Australian touring side.

Hants v Derbys:
Bournemouth, August 30, 31, September 1 1961
Taking 12 points, Hampshire made certain of the Championship, winning the game with about an hour to spare on the third afternoon.

Hampshire took the precaution of resting both Shackleton and White for this match, which was played in a somewhat light-hearted manner and won by the Australians by five wickets.

The penultimate Championship game took place at Bournemouth against Derbyshire. Marshall and Gray gave Hampshire a good start with 120 in 108 minutes, but the rest of the batsmen responded only in patches, and the total came to 306. Derbyshire lost one wicket before close of play, Lee being run out by Ingleby-Mackenzie. On the second day Laurie Johnson hit a fine hundred to give Derbyshire a first innings lead of 12. The Derbyshire fast bowler, Rhodes had two Hampshire second innings wickets down for 16, then a third wicket went at 40 and it was left to Marshall to stamp his authority on the innings. He hit 86 and was out at the beginning of the third day. Sainsbury and Barnard continued the good work, adding 99 in 68 minutes. Derbyshire were set 252 in 192 minutes. Shackleton broke the back of the home side's innings in the half-hour after lunch, when he took four wickets for eight runs, including that of Johnson. Bob Taylor and Harold Rhodes added 52 for the ninth wicket, but Sainsbury had both caught and the Championship was Hampshire's. The captain presented his team to the cheering

The County Champions, 1961. Back row, left to right: A. G. Holt (coach),
D. O. Baldry, D. W. White, M. Heath, A. Wassell, D. A. Livingstone,
H. M. Barnard, N. Drake (scorer). Front row: P. J. Sainsbury,

M. D. Burden, D. Shackleton, R. E. Marshall, A. C. D. Ingleby-
Mackenzie, L. Harrison, J. R. Gray, H. Horton. On ground:
B. S. V. Timms, B. R. S. Harrrison.

crowd from the pavilion balcony. To a storm of applause, Ingleby-Mackenzie told the Hampshire supporters: 'This is the most wonderful occasion of all time. I would like to toast the luckiest captain, and the great men who have made this possible. I am too excited to say much more. I just hope I won't wake up tomorrow morning and find that we are 12th in the table.'

The last Championship match was somewhat of an anticlimax. Yorkshire, who had been the 1960 champions and who had fought hard to retain their title came to Bournemouth. They, or rather Ray Illingworth, comprehensively outplayed the new Champions. In the first innings the England off-spinner took seven for 39 and in the second five for 63 – Marshall alone batted well, but was run out for 109. Yorkshire won by 58 runs. The fixture list contained a match between the County Champions and the runners-up, so the two sides met again. This time Illingworth did not dictate the terms. Hampshire, batting first, made 340 for six, with Horton 160 not out – a new personal record. Yorkshire batted in a painstaking manner, until Illingworth and Wilson joined forces in a sixth wicket stand of 109. Marshall hit a second-innings 100 in 98 minutes and this allowed Ingleby-Mackenzie to set Yorkshire 299 in 177 minutes. Rain however, permitted only 20 overs to be bowled and the match was drawn.

Marshall hit 2,455 Championship runs and Shackleton took 153 wickets. They were statistically the outstanding players of 1961, but all the regular members of the eleven pulled their weight. Horton reached 2,000 Championship runs and Gray failed by only 50 to do the same. Sainsbury, Ingleby-Mackenzie and Livingstone completed 1,000. White took 117 wickets and, as a statistical oddity, Wassell, Sainsbury and Heath each took 54 wickets, and together with Burden provided more than adequate support for the two opening bowlers. Ingleby-Mackenzie, a jester on the surface, took the tactics of captaincy very seriously and his studied declarations, especially in view of the experimental law banning 'follow-ons', went a long way to winning vital Championship points. The final table reads:

		P	W	L	DNR	First Inns Points Lost	Drawn	Bonus Pts	Pts	Avge
1	Hampshire	32	19	7	6	0	1	3	32	268	8.37
2	Yorkshire	32	17	5	10	0	1	5	34	250	7.81
3	Middlesex	28	15	6	6	1	3	1	26	214	7.64
4	Worcestershire	32	16	9	7	0	2	3	24	226	7.06
5	Gloucestershire	28	11	11	5	1	2	2	18	158	5.64
6	Essex	28	10	8	10	0	2	4	26	158	5.64
7	Derbyshire	28	10	9	9	0	3	3	22	154	5.50
8	Sussex	32	11	10	11	0	1	8	20	170	5.31
9	Leicestershire	28	9	13	5	1	2	4	26	146	5.21
10	Somerset	32	10	15	7	0	6	3	24	162	5.06
11	Kent	28	8	8	12	0	1	7	20	132	4.71
12	Warwickshire	32	9	10	13	0	1	7	26	150	4.68
13	Lancashire	32	9	7	15	1	1	7	18	142	4.43
14	Glamorgan	32	9	12	11	0	1	4	10	128	4.00
15	Surrey	28	4	13	11	0	6	8	24	100	3.57
16	Northants	28	5	13	10	0	1	5	10	82	2.92
17	Nottinghamshire	28	4	20	4	0	6	2	12	76	2.71

RICHARDS AND GREENIDGE ARRIVE

FIELDING THE SAME SIDE as that which proved triumphant in 1961, Hampshire appeared to have a good chance of retaining their title in the following season. On paper the record shows that they did not lose a single game up to the end of May, but an inspection of the scores soon reveals that the County were no longer the all-conquering combination of twelve months before.

In the first two games they were fortunate not to be defeated: at Edgbaston, with two wickets remaining, they still needed 20 runs to avoid an innings defeat when stumps were finally drawn, and at Bristol, in a very low scoring game, they again had two wickets in hand and wanted 36 to win when rain ended the match.

As the season progressed the Hampshire batting became firmer, but the bowling and fielding were not up to standard. The result: 20 draws out of the 32 Championship matches.

The first four in the batting order, Gray, Marshall, Horton and Livingstone, all averaged above 34 runs per innings and exceeded 1,500 Championship runs, with Gray leading the table and scoring more runs than ever. He also hit the only double-century of his career, taking advantage of a perfect wicket at Portsmouth to make 213 not out against Derbyshire. In the previous match he had hit 123 off the Glamorgan attack, and both these innings came at a most opportune time since Roy Marshall was laid low with measles.

Apart from the four principal run-getters, Sainsbury and Barnard both reached the 1,000-run mark in Championship games, while the captain reached 976. The most remarkable batting feat of the summer came, however, with the help of young Castell, the 19-year-old who had made his debut the previous season. Brought into the Championship team only for the last three games, he went to the wicket at No 10 against Surrey, when Hampshire were 128 for eight in reply to Surrey's 363 for nine declared and assisted Danny Livingstone in a record-breaking ninth-wicket stand of 230. Castell made 76 and Livingstone 200 – the highest innings of his career.

The season's bowling was not so happy. The veteran Shackleton sent down more than twice the number of overs bowled by any of his colleagues: 1,595.1, the next most being 723.3, and he returned almost identical figures to those of 1961. In all first-class matches Shackleton took more wickets than any other English bowler; but Shackleton's opening partner, White, never seemed fully fit. He missed eight Championship games and his figures bore little resemblance to those he achieved in 1961.

The spin attack, which consisted as before of the left-armers Wassell and Sainsbury and Burden's off-breaks, was also more expensive – fine at keeping batsmen quiet, but on most occasions not good enough to obtain the wickets of major batsmen. Hampshire were in need of a new recruit to bolster the attack.

The one immediate change at the start of the 1963 summer was the installation of Timms as the regular wicket-keeper, replacing Leo Harrison, the last remaining player from the pre-war Hampshire staff.

In view of the results obtained in 1962, the performance of Hampshire in 1963 was a distinctly curious affair: the batting failed to come up to standard. Gray, the prolific scorer of the previous year, lost his touch entirely and averaged less than 20 over 48 Championship innings. Livingstone, and to a lesser extent Horton, also lacked consistency and this threw an immense burden on Roy Marshall. Of course the weather must take some of the blame – Hampshire suffered more than most from the rain, three matches being abandoned, the one at Bournemouth against Warwickshire having no play whatsoever.

The two talking points in the County during the year had little to do with the team's results. After England were completely overwhelmed by West Indies in the First Test (West Indies hit 501 for six and won by ten wickets) the selectors called up Shackleton for the Second Test. He had not appeared for his country for 11 years, but did well enough to retain his place for the remaining three matches.

The 1963 season marked also the centenary of the Hampshire County Cricket Club. To celebrate the event, an England team chosen by MCC played the County after the final Championship match was over. This historic event caused a minor controversy. The Centenary Match was played on 11 September, the date of the first public meeting of the County Club, but the first meeting to form the Club had taken place on 12 August which therefore, argued historians, ought to have been the day of the Centenary Match.

To return to the 1963 Championship, Shackleton, as indicated by his Test selection, had an outstanding season, the cost of his wickets falling considerably, but Hampshire lost his services for eight matches. Happily White recovered his form and his 90 Championship wickets cost 22.04 runs each. A new face appeared: Bob Cottam, an 18-year-old from Lincolnshire. A fast bowler, he captured nine wickets in his second match, enabling the County to beat Middlesex at Lord's. The young leg-spinner, Castell, was tried in eight matches and his 23 Championship wickets cost less than 20 runs apiece. Of the two left-arm spinners, Wassell had a much better year than Sainsbury, but the latter, batting at No 5, scored some useful runs, including a century against Lancashire at Portsmouth. This innings was, however, overshadowed by Ingleby-Mackenzie, who hit a hundred in 90 minutes. The retirement of Leo Harrison lengthened the tail, which grew even longer when Cottam gained his place, and thus the general decline in the performance of the major batsmen was more apparent than it might have been. The County ended the season in tenth place, as in 1962. They failed to make any impression in the inaugural season of the Gillette Cup, being defeated in the first round by Derbyshire.

The two bright prospects of 1963 showed no improvement in the season which followed. The fast bowling of Cottam took only 18 Championship wickets at over 30 runs each and Castell's one wicket cost 127 runs. Sainsbury's record showed improvement both in batting and bowling, but Wassell was very expensive. The attack thus fell heavily on the shoulders of Shackleton and White – Shackleton in fact took more wickets than anyone else in England, but his continued success was not enough to improve Hampshire's standing in the Championship, and with five victories they fell two places to 12th.

Of the batsmen, Roy Marshall suffered from no less than three separate injuries, two broken fingers and a broken toe, and missed six matches. Gray announced before the season's start that his duties as assistant headmaster would mean missing the first eight matches, though when he did re-appear he was in much better form than in 1963. Danny Livingstone played in every Championship match and had his best season so far, topping the County's batting table,

PETER JAMES SAINSBURY

An all-round sportsman whilst at school, Sainsbury captained Bitterne Park at both cricket and soccer, though he was born at Chandler's Ford. He was only just 16 when he joined the Hampshire ground-staff in 1950 as a slow left-arm bowler who was also a brilliant field. He spent nearly three seasons with the County second eleven before he was called up for National Service. In 1954, Sainsbury made a great impression when he turned out for the Army against the RAF at Lord's. His County Championship debut came in the same summer.

His first full summer of County cricket was 1955 and so successful did it prove that he was chosen for the MCC team for Pakistan that winter. He learnt a great deal from Tony Lock during that tour, but on his return to England he had altered his bowling style, changing from flight to spin and henceforth he became a batsman who could bowl, rather than vice versa. This alteration meant that his prospects as a Test player declined, for whilst as a bowler it appeared he might develop into an international player, he has never approached that standard as a batsman. As a fielder, however, he had few equals at backward short leg.

By the time he retired in 1976 he had played in 593 matches for Hampshire, and in all matches hit over 20,000 runs as well as taking 1,300 wickets. He is now the County coach at Southampton.

whilst Henry Horton, in his benefit summer, was as reliable as ever.

Geoff Keith, a local player from Portsmouth, who had been given a couple of games the previous summer, looked a most promising recruit to the batting line-up and appeared in 15 Championship games.

Despite their poor overall record the County managed to defeat the two leading counties of the year, Worcestershire and Warwickshire, and in beating the latter in late August ruined their title prospects. Although the victory was by only 17 runs, the moral margin was much greater, since Hampshire declared both their innings closed, losing six and two wickets respectively, whilst Warwickshire were bowled out twice.

In the game with Worcestershire at New Road, it was the resolute batting of Henry Horton, once of Worcestershire, which gave Hampshire a commanding first innings lead: 280 to 109. Despite some good batting by Don Kenyon in the last innings, Worcester could not make up the large deficit and Hampshire won by 135 runs.

Hampshire again fared poorly in the Gillette Cup. Wiltshire proved no problem at Chippenham, though the Hampshire batsmen found more problems than they anticipated in the Minors' bowling. Cottam however took four wickets for nine runs and Sainsbury returned an analysis of 3.4-2-1-3, as Wiltshire collapsed for only 81. In the Second Round, M. J. K. Smith and the hard-hitting Jameson, whose hundred came in 90 minutes, allowed Warwickshire to set Hampshire a target over 300 and they never looked like approaching this figure.

One minor bright spot was the wicket-keeping of Timms, who claimed 77 victims, and his batting showed much improvement, though a large number of incompleted innings produced an average which was rather flattering.

It was the same again in 1965: five wins and 12th place. There was a great day at Middlesbrough in the middle of May, when the Yorkshire side were dismissed for a paltry 23, the lowest in the County's history. White was the chief perpetrator of this debacle, returning figures of 10-7-10-6. Hampshire won the game by ten wickets, the teams having been very close on first innings.

The batting during the summer looked decidedly patchy. Gray more or less retired, appearing in only four matches. Livingstone had a quite dramatic fall from grace, and his

DAVID WILLIAM WHITE

A great-hearted cricketer, 'Butch' White learnt his cricket in the Birmingham League playing for Aston Unity, and was invited to appear for Warwickshire 2nd XI as an amateur. He also played a lot of cricket during his National Service, when he served in the RASC as a driving instructor.

His debut for Hampshire came in 1957 at the age of 21, and after Cannings retired White gained a regular place in the County team, taking 124 wickets in his first full season in 1960. His fast bowling went a long way to capturing the Championship for Hampshire in 1961, when he topped 100 wickets for a second time. His reward was a place in the MCC team to India and Pakistan. He pulled a muscle in the Second Test in Karachi and this injury plus the slow pace of the wickets meant that he did not have a very successful tour. He was awarded a benefit by Hampshire in 1969, at which time he spent his winter evenings running the Indoor Cricket School at Southampton. His bowling seemed to lose its effectiveness in 1971 – he took only 14 wickets in his 11 County Championship matches – and at the end of the season, Hampshire did not renew his contract.

In 1972, White played for Glamorgan mainly in the limited-overs matches – in fact his only Championship game for his new county was against Gloucester at Swansea, when he took one for 32. After retiring from county cricket he was the cricket coach at Christ's Hospital.

'Butch' White bowling against Somerset at Southampton, 1969.

LANCASHIRE *v* HAMPSHIRE

Played at Old Trafford, 9, 10 and 11 June 1965

HAMPSHIRE WON BY 13 RUNS

HAMPSHIRE	FIRST INNINGS		SECOND INNINGS	
R. E. Marshall	c Knox b Higgs	3	c Statham b Higgs	7
H. M. Barnard	c Knox b Higgs	15	hit wkt b Statham	30
H. Horton	b Statham	30	b Higgs	11
D. A. Livingstone	c Goodwin b Statham	27	c Howard b Higgs	0
P. J. Sainsbury	c Goodwin b Higgs	11	c Beddow b Statham	2
★A. C. D. Ingleby-Mackenzie	b Howard	22	b Higgs	0
G. L. Keith	c Pullar b Statham	41	not out	13
†B. S. V. Timms	run out	14	lbw b Statham	6
D. Shackleton	not out	8	lbw b Higgs	0
D. W. White	c Beddow b Statham	0	b Statham	8
R. M. H. Cottam	lbw b Statham	0	lbw b Higgs	0
Extras	leg byes	3		
Total		174		77

1st inns: 1-10, 2-23, 3-75, 4-76, 5-108, 6-110, 7-158, 8-172, 9-174
2nd inns: 1-11, 2-40, 3-40, 4-43, 5-44, 6-52, 7-62, 8-63, 9-76

BOWLING	O	M	R	W		O	M	R	W
Statham	24.1	5	41	5		16	4	41	4
Higgs	27	9	49	3		15.3	4	33	6
Howard	24	5	48	1		1	0	3	0
Greenhough	21	8	33	0					

LANCASHIRE	FIRST INNINGS		SECOND INNINGS		
D. M. Green	b Cottam	61		c Marshall b Shackleton	53
G. K. Knox	c Ingleby-Mackenzie b Shackleton	10		c Barnard b Shackleton	25
G. Pullar	c Livingstone b Cottam	37		lbw b White	0
J. D. Bond	b Cottam	4		lbw b White	1
J. Sullivan	c Sainsbury b Cottam	2		c Livingstone b White	0
A. M. Beddow	c Sainsbury b Cottam	3		c Timms b Shackleton	1
K. Howard	hit wkt b Cottam	11	(8)	c Ingleby-Mackenzie b Shackleton	4
K. Higgs	c Keith b Cottam	0	(9)	c Shackleton b White	12
★J. B. Statham	c Timms b Cottam	0	(10)	c Livingstone b White	1
T. Greenhough	c Timms b Cottam	4	(11)	not out	1
†K. Goodwin	not out	1	(7)	b White	1
Extras	lb 1, nb 2	3		lb 2, nb 1	3
Total		136			102

1st inns: 1-34, 2-102, 3-115, 4-116, 5-117, 6-125, 7-125, 8-125, 9-133
2nd inns: 1-67, 2-67, 3-69, 4-69, 5-72, 6-83, 7-87, 8-91, 9-99

BOWLING	O	M	R	W		O	M	R	W
Shackleton	16	6	38	1		12	8	15	4
White	15	3	70	0		22.3	2	48	6
Cottam	11.1	4	25	9		13	4	36	0

Umpires: J. S. Buller and W. H. Copson.
Hampshire won the toss. Close of play: 1st day: Hampshire 174, Lancashire 60-1; 2nd day: Hampshire 174 and 136, Lancashire 136 and 92-8.
*Captain; †Wicket-keeper.

average failed to reach 20. Marshall was free of injury but had, for him, only a modest year, which in reality left Henry Horton holding the fort. In the whole summer only two County Championship hundreds were hoisted, one each by Marshall and Horton, and the lower order also fell away.

Too much bowling again rested on the County's workhorse, Shackleton, but Cottam played in 20 matches and rose to second place in the bowling table. The trio of seamers, Shackleton, White and Cottam, was as good as most County attacks, but the spin department was almost threadbare, only Sainsbury making any impact. Castell disappeared entirely and Wassell claimed only 18 Championship wickets. Keith's off-breaks were tried, but his six wickets cost over 40 runs each.

The flamboyant Ingleby-Mackenzie decided to leave cricket in favour of other ventures and announced his retirement from the captaincy, which meant the end of an era for Hampshire cricket, which lost another much more erudite figure just before the season began in H. S. Altham. The cricket master at Winchester for some 20 years, Altham was the inspiration for several generations of Wykehamists and a formidable figure behind the scenes at Lord's. He had appeared in 24 matches for Hampshire immediately after the First World War and at the time of his death was the County's President.

In the Gillette Cup Hampshire had their first victory over a first-class County. They had beaten Norfolk in the first round, though a certain Henry Blofeld opened Norfolk's batting and scored 60 – Sainsbury, however, baffled the rest. Sainsbury then enabled his County to beat the Kent side at Portsmouth. He hit the highest score of the day and then took three for 45, which produced a win by 23 runs. As in 1964, the County came unstuck against Warwickshire, due to a fine all-round performance by Ibadulla, with 75 and six for 32. Only Barnard, who survived two and a half hours, mastered the Pakistani's off breaks.

Hants v Lancs: Old Trafford, June 9, 10, 11 1965 Batting first, Hampshire could make only slow progress against some keen seam bowling by Statham and Higgs. In contrast, Lancashire opened brightly, Green being in fine form. The score reached 102 for one, but Cottam then produced an outstanding spell, nine wickets going down for the addition of 34 runs, all nine being victims of Cottam. Higgs and Statham in their turn dismissed Hampshire cheaply and by the end of the second day, Lancashire required 17 to win with two wickets in hand – they could only manage three singles on the Friday morning, thus giving Hampshire victory by 13 runs. Cottam's first-innings bowling analysis was a new Hampshire record.

There was a fine match in mid-August against the South African tourists, when Shackleton had an opening spell of 12-8-12-5 and the tourists' powerful batting side was dismissed for 133. Hampshire required 202 to win in 150 minutes, but failed to make a decent start and in the end were thankful to settle for a draw.

In 1966, Roy Marshall became the first contracted player to be appointed Hampshire's captain. His first problem was to solve the question of his opening partner. Since the departure of Gray from full-time cricket, Barnard had been given the place, but the results he achieved in 1965 were unspectacular, and Barry Reed, who had topped the Winchester averages back in 1955 and had since played on occasion for Hampshire in both first and second elevens, was brought in and in fact was Marshall's regular partner nearly all summer. Marshall and Horton, however, remained the leading batsmen, whilst Danny Livingstone recovered some of his form, which had eluded him in 1965. The lower-order batting was still brittle. Keith fell right away and lost his place. Wicket-keeper Timms hit a maiden hundred against Oxford, but his highest in the Championship was only 36. The fact that he commanded the eighth position in the order and indeed sometimes higher clearly highlighted Hampshire's weakness.

In the bowling department, Castell reappeared, abandoning his leg-breaks in favour of medium-pace seam and picking up 29 wickets at a reasonable cost; but this meant the spin attack was almost non-existent – Sainsbury's 21 wickets cost 40 runs each. Shackleton, Cottam and White formed practically the whole attack and the result was only five victories in the 28 Championship games.

At least Hampshire broke the jinx which had settled on Dean Park, Bournemouth, for after 24 matches on the ground without a single win, they beat Middlesex quite decisively. After an even first innings – it was one of those games when each first innings was restricted to 65 overs – Horton and Livingstone added 272 for the third wicket, both batsmen hitting hundreds, then Cottam and Shackleton, with Middlesex having 330 minutes to make 312, bowled the visitors out for 231. It was the only Hampshire win in the ten matches played from the beginning of August.

The County actually moved up one place in the Championship, to 11th, but there was virtually nothing separating them from the three counties immediately below.

In the Gillette Cup Lincolnshire came a little too close to victory, Hampshire winning in the end by only 31 runs. Danny Livingstone with 92 saved the side and won the Man of the Match award. Ingleby-Mackenzie was co-opted as emergency wicket-keeper for the Gillette second round and then stole the show by hitting Hampshire's highest score of 59 as well as claiming two victims behind the stumps – Hampshire beat Kent by 54 runs. A splendid innings by the captain enabled the County to win their third-round game against Surrey. Marshall and Reed, in reply to Surrey's 173, added 128 before the first wicket fell.

Marshall and Reed also gave Hampshire a sound start when they batted second in the semi-finals at Worcester, but the middle order collapsed and Ingleby-Mackenzie was unable to perform his miracle. Thus Worcester won by 99 runs.

The wet weather of May 1967 produced slow wickets and run-getting became very difficult. The Hampshire batsmen seemed more affected than most and only Sainsbury, with a liberal helping of incomplete innings, managed an average above 30. Three times the side retreated in utter confusion: against Kent at Maidstone they replied to the home side's total of 296 with scores of 95 and 31, Underwood being the cause; against Lancashire, the team went down for 39; and against Warwickshire they were dismissed for 44. Despite these upsets, Hampshire did fairly well for most of the season, but a very poor last month – they failed to win a single one of their nine matches from 2 August to the season's end – pushed them down one place to 12th.

Sainsbury, Marshall, Livingstone and Reed all topped 1,000 runs, but the old dependable Horton lost his place through injury and decided to retire at the season's close.

Richard Gilliat, the 1966 Oxford University captain, joined the side in July and played regularly at No 3 – he had played in a few games the previous season. He was appointed Assistant Secretary to Desmond Eagar.

As in the past the bowling relied almost entirely on seam. Shackleton took 100 wickets for the 19th consecutive season and overtook Kennedy's record total of wickets for the County. Cottam reached 100 wickets in all first-class matches and his progress was the most heartening feature of the season. White, the third seamer, also had a good summer, but the rest of the bowling was hardly worth noting. Keith Wheatley, who had appeared on and off since 1965 was given

18 Championship matches and averaged 20 with the bat, but his off-breaks did not mature. Castell's 12 wickets cost 42 runs each and Sainsbury's 31 cost 34 runs apiece. The most promising youngster was David Turner from Wiltshire; an 18-year-old left-hander, he won the County's single-wicket competition.

The most exciting match of the summer was the Middlesex game at Portsmouth. Hampshire required three runs to win with one wicket to fall at the start of the final over. Cottam was bowled by the last ball, which resulted in the game being tied.

Marshall hit a hundred in the first round of the Gillette Cup to enable Hampshire to obtain an easy win over Lincolnshire and the captain was also in good form in the second round against Glamorgan at Portsmouth, when he and Reed began the match with an opening stand of 110. Surprisingly, Reed, who made 47 against 61 by Marshall and 55 by Livingstone, was given the Man of Match award, his fielding tipping the balance in his favour. The opponents put up a good fight but Hampshire won by 16 runs. The third-round match was even closer. Sussex batted first and reached 233 off 60 overs. Hampshire did not seem to have much chance of winning until Timms hit out, scoring 55. When last man Cottam arrived, 11 were required, but with only a single added Tony Buss took the final wicket.

The season of 1968 saw the face of English county cricket altered dramatically – the decision to allow the instant registration of overseas players is still a controversial talking point. The Hampshire authorities set their sights on Clive Lloyd, but he backed down and elected to join Lancashire, and so Hampshire had to settle for the relatively unknown 22-year-old South African, Barry Richards. Interviewed on his arrival in England Richards announced that he was determined to hit 2,000 runs in the season. This was regarded by the cynics as highly optimistic, but the Natalian soon proved them wrong. It would not be a slur on the remainder of the County team to state that Richards alone was responsible for moving the Club up from 12th to fifth place in the Championship. In inter-county matches he scored 2,039 runs – no other Hampshire batsman even reached 1,000. His average was 48.54, the next best being 27.15. In the national averages Richards came second only to Boycott. He was chosen as one of *Wisden's* 'Cricketers of the Year' and the writer ended his note with: 'Richards' horizons seem

limitless, and it will be fascinating to see how far his talents
will take him. Few, anywhere in the world, have his
possibilities.'

The fact that only one Championship hundred was scored
by Hampshire's remaining batsmen (Richards made five),
illustrates the mediocrity of the rest. Marshall had a dismal
season, and Livingstone played in only half the matches.
Reed did not progress. Gilliat's highest innings in 17 matches
was only 64. Richard Lewis was tried in ten Championship
games, following a hundred at the expense of Oxford, and
seemed worthy of further trials, as did the 20-year-old
Trevor Jesty, who scored well in the second eleven.

The only alteration in the bowling was that the 44-year-
old Shackleton had to concede top place in the bowling table
to Cottam, but both took over 100 wickets and continued to
be well supported by White, with the left arm of Sainsbury
providing the only credible alternative. At the end of the year
Shackleton announced his retirement, though he seemed
almost as good as ever. Cottam went abroad with England in
1968–69 and gained two Test caps.

*Bob Cottam has the best
innings analysis of all
Hampshire bowlers: nine for
25 against Lancashire at Old
Trafford on 9 and 10 June
1965. He is pictured here
bowling against Somerset at
Southampton in 1969.*

Three vital catches went down in the second-round Gillette Cup game at Bournemouth against Warwickshire, and these resulted in Hampshire's defeat by 27 runs. Of the eight Championship victories, three came in succession in mid-July and were the highlight of the season, particularly the match at Westcliff, when Essex were dismissed by Shackleton for 95 and then Richards hit 176 to enable Marshall to declare at 301 for four. Essex did better in their second innings but it was unnecessary for Hampshire to bat a second time.

No less than seven of the first team players suffered injuries in 1969, including both Richards (missing six Championship games) and Marshall (missing five) that several of the young players were given much more opportunity than they expected. David Turner hit a splendid undefeated 181 against Surrey and Jesty secured a regular place as an all-rounder. So well did the younger element do that Hampshire, despite the accidents, maintained their fifth place in the Championship table and rather surprised the press by coming second in the new Sunday League competition, winning 12 matches and being only one point behind the winners, Lancashire, at the end.

The month of June belonged to Richard Gilliat – he hit four Championship hundreds for Hampshire, culminating in an innings of 223* against Warwickshire on the final day of the month. Against Essex he hit the fastest century of the Championship season in 101 minutes, despite being forced to retire early in his innings after being hit on the head. He came second to Richards in the batting table, nearly doubling the average he had achieved in 1968. In addition, he captained the side with aplomb when Marshall was absent injured.

The wicket-keeper, Timms, unexpectedly left the Hampshire staff after the 1968 season and the County specially registered Taylor's Derbyshire understudy, Bob Stephenson. He immediately gained a first-team place and appeared in every Championship match, becoming an integral part of the County side for the next decade.

With Shackleton gone – actually he reappeared against Sussex, picking up five for 58 in the second innings and ensuring a Hampshire victory – the effective attack was reduced to White and Cottam, with a little help from Sainsbury, Castell and Jesty. Too much therefore rested with the opening bowlers, but in the circumstances they were on many occasions equal to the demands and both had good seasons. Castell played much more often than he had done in 1968 and his wicket bag increased from 15 to 45; more important, the cost of each wicket dropped substantially.

The two Championship victories against Leicestershire and Sussex in the first week of August pushed the County into second place in the table, but they then failed to win any of the remaining six matches. In the two games which ended in defeat during this period, Richards batted almost alone. Against Northants he carried his bat undefeated through the first innings, making 127 not out from 192, and against Notts, when Halfyard took six for 14, the South African made 56 out of the all out total of 101. It must be added, however, that in the first of these matches, Marshall twisted his ankle and was unable to bat and also missed the second game as a result.

Although the toll of injury for 1970 was not as great as it had been 12 months before, two key figures were missing for much of the year. Gilliat broke his thumb in the first match, and then broke it a second time when he attempted to return. His County Championship season consisted of two matches. White played in nearly half the matches before succumbing to a cartilage injury. John Holder, the medium-fast bowler from Barbados, was a fairly effective replacement for White and by the end of the year had taken 51 Championship wickets and stood second in the bowling averages. Another Barbadian who came into the side was the 19-year-old opening bat, Gordon Greenidge, who, when qualified in July, not only made up for the absent Gilliat, but was some compensation for the fact that Barry Richards was called up for the Rest of the World in their five-match series with England.

The captain, Marshall, after his barren years of 1968 and 1969, was in much better form. He played in every Championship game and averaged just under 40. Demands of business prevented Reed from playing regularly, but David Turner completed his 1,000 runs and the notorious tail was substantially shortened. Lewis could do little right and appeared in only ten matches, but Wheatley's off-breaks were more accurate and both he and Jesty continued their progress as all-rounders.

In the Gillette Cup, Hampshire had little problem removing Bucks at Chesham, but were then unfortunate enough to be drawn against the eventual winners, Lancashire. The Southerners suffered the traumatic blow of losing their opening bat, Wheatley, run out off the first ball – a few moments later the total read 10 for three and that was more or less that.

The Sunday League was not the happy stamping ground it had been in 1969. Hampshire ended in the bottom half of the League, but Barry Richards had a great day at Hull, when he hit 155 not out, the highest innings then scored in the Sunday competition. Incredibly the next highest scorer in the Hampshire innings was Livingstone with 18. Obviously cowed into subservience, Yorkshire were then reduced to scoring 74 for nine off their statutory 40 overs, White taking four for 16.

Hampshire's position in the Championship, tenth as against fifth in 1969, looks much worse than it was, since there were only a few bonus points separating them from the four sides immediately above. However, 1971 seemed to confirm the County's decline, since they moved up just one place, and again won only four matches. The cares of captaincy were removed from Marshall and given to Gilliat, who managed to avoid breaking his thumb. However the cartilage operation on White was not completely successful and though he appeared in 11 Championship games he lost his sting and took only 14 expensive wickets.

With Richards and Greenidge as the openers, and Gilliat at No 3 followed by Marshall, the Hampshire batting, since all four had good seasons, was adequate. More important, the infamous tail seemed at last permanently reduced. Sainsbury had the best year of his career, which now spanned 18 summers. He topped the bowling averages, taking 101 Championship wickets at 18.15 runs each, and had a batting average of 33.82, missing the 'double' by only 41 runs.

Turner was left out of the first few matches, but then took over Livingstone's place and went on to complete 1,000 runs at an average above 30. The County found a useful off-spinner to help Sainsbury in Lawrence Worrell, a cousin of the West Indian captain. He took 44 wickets at a reasonable cost and like Jesty looked as if he would develop into a good all-rounder.

The weakness in the attack was now the seam bowling. Only Cottam, of the great trio of Shackleton, White and Cottam, remained as an effective force and his efficiency was quite clearly impaired by the lack of an adequate partner. John Holder, yet another Barbadian, opened the bowling in a few matches, but back trouble meant that his appearances were very limited. Castell was tried, but, as often before, was found wanting. The medium-pace John Rice had been signed at the beginning of the year, but was too inexperienced to achieve much.

Three of Hampshire's four victories were gained at the end of the summer, largely due to the bowling of Sainsbury, who took 11 wickets (including six for 14) against Yorkshire and another 11 in the other two games – *v* Somerset and Surrey.

Nine wins were recorded in the Sunday League, placing Hampshire sixth in the table. In the game against Gloucestershire, Hampshire's defeat was in part due to the bowling of Julian Shackleton – son of Derek. He dismissed both Marshall and Gilliat.

Warwickshire dispatched Hampshire in the Gillette Cup.

John Rice, from Chandlers Ford, played from 1971 to 1982 as an opening batsman and medium-pace bowler.

Jameson and Kanhai ran out of control, adding 134 for the second wicket, and Hampshire never approached the daunting target of 282, being subdued by Lance Gibbs.

Season 1972 seemed on paper a carbon copy of its predecessor. Hampshire again won four Championship matches and remained ninth in the table – in the Player League they repeated their sixth place and in the Gillette Cup were once more bundled out in the third round. The team, however, experienced various upheavals, so the results could be regarded with a certain satisfaction.

Cottam decided he needed a change and went off to Northants; White had gone, as had Livingstone, whilst a shoulder injury forced Castell into retirement. The County brought in two major recruits, the New Zealander David O'Sullivan, who bowled left-arm slows, and Bob Herman, son of the old Hampshire professional, O. W. Herman. Bob had been in and out of the Middlesex side since 1965 and in 1971 had been finally dropped from the staff of that county. The county of his birth therefore decided to give the fast-medium seam bowler a second chance.

Herman surprised Middlesex, himself and his new county by being their most successful bowler, with 75 Championship wickets at 21 runs each – no one else managed fifty. Holder, who ought to have been Herman's partner, lost his run-up and his direction. Rice was substituted, but remained expensive. Tom Mottram made his Championship debut against Worcestershire at Portsmouth in August and his medium pace took eight wickets, including five for 45 in the second innings, and won the match for Hampshire. Both Mottram and Rice were bowlers of the peg-away type, when Herman wanted someone with fire at the other end.

Richards, Marshall and Greenidge batted well throughout the year, with the South African particularly volatile in the one-day competitions – he hit two Sunday League hundreds and a quite brilliant 129 against Lancashire in the Gillette Cup, when everyone else failed. Greenidge, who reached a thousand runs in Championship matches, caught the eye of the West Indian selectors and was asked to return to his native Barbados – he had come to Britain at the age of 14. Turner, batting at No 3, hit a most convincing hundred in May against the Australian attack, which included Lillee, and the pundits were forecasting a possible Test place for him, but in the first home Championship game, he attempted to hook Tony Brown and the ball flew into his face. His left eye was damaged and though he returned to the team later in the season, he was not the same man.

Sainsbury's bowling was not so deadly as in 1971, and he shared the spin attack alternately with O'Sullivan and Worrell. Jesty showed some progress in both batting and bowling, but he usually went in too low in the order.

Gilliat found runs difficult to acquire and by the end of the season left himself out of the side for several matches, Sainsbury taking on the leadership. At the end of the year Marshall announced his retirement. It had been his 20th year in county cricket and he demonstrated that he was still one of the best batsmen in county cricket by hitting a coruscating 203 in mid-August against Derbyshire. He was 69 not out when play ended in Hampshire's final match of the year, against Yorkshire at Southampton – a fitting finale to a fine and often glittering career.

COWES, ISLE OF WIGHT

It was not until 1956 that Hampshire returned to the Isle of Wight for a first-class match and this time the venue was Cowes and the opponents, Worcester. The home county dominated the first half of the match. Ingleby-Mackenzie hit a well-judged hundred, Shackleton picked up four wickets and Worcestershire were forced to follow on 174 runs in arrears. Outschoorn thwarted the bowlers on the last day, opening the Worcestershire innings and carrying out his bat for an undefeated 154 in a stay of $6\frac{1}{2}$ hours.

The financial success of this match meant that Hampshire returned to Cowes for county fixtures until 1962, when the final Championship game to date was staged against Worcestershire. Marshall and Gray got Hampshire off to a fine start in this game with an opening partnership of 125 in 102 minutes, with Marshall going on to 99. Shackleton later took five wickets and Worcester were 168 behind on first innings. Unfortunately for Hampshire an experimental law in operation in 1962 prevented the follow-on being enforced and in the end Hampshire declared their second innings closed, setting the visitors 291 to win at a run per minute. Worcestershire never looked like getting the runs and Hampshire had dismissed eight batsmen when rain saved the visitors.

TOP OF THE TABLE AGAIN

AFTER THE YEARS OF MODEST ACHIEVEMENT, the prospects for 1973 did not appear much brighter. Both O'Sullivan and Greenidge were in the probables list for the New Zealand and West Indies teams which shared the English season. Marshall had gone, as had John Holder. The only new face was the 30-year-old Mike Taylor, who had soldiered on with Notts for nine summers, without becoming more than a run-of-the-mill all-rounder.

The first good news – from the County's selfish view – was that neither Greenidge or O'Sullivan were called to the colours. The Championship programme began at Grace Road. After a fairly even first innings, Richards and Greenidge opened the second with a sparkling partnership of 135 and Gilliat was able to declare, setting Leicestershire 261 in 210 minutes. Balderstone and Davison responded well, the former making his highest score in first-class cricket, but Bob Herman then dismissed them both, as well as removing Illingworth, and the home team's objective switched from trying to win to avoiding defeat – they accomplished the second.

In the season's first game at Southampton, the weather was thoroughly miserable, but the pitch suited Sainsbury, who ran through the Sussex batsmen, picking up six for 29, the only slight hiccup being with the tail, the last two wickets being allowed to increase the total from 73 for eight to 124 all out. Curiously, the Hampshire lower order also revived the patient – Bob Herman coming in last made the second highest score – 20 – whilst newcomer Mike Taylor at No 8 was the highest contributor with 33. In Sussex's second knock Geoffrey Greenidge (no relation to Gordon) opened the innings and carried his bat out for exactly 100, his chief support coming from Joshi at No 11, the last wicket adding 58 priceless runs. On this difficult wicket Hampshire began the fourth innings requiring 143. Fortunately there was plenty of time and with all the first five in the order playing a responsible role victory was gained off the last ball before tea.

A visit to St Helen's, Swansea for a Benson & Hedges game – this competition was now in its second year – resulted in a defeat; then the side moved on to Headingley for their third Championship game. A seamers' wicket on the first day enabled Herman and Mottram to remove Yorkshire

– save for Boycott, who made 73 out of their 168 – and then Chris Old had Richards leg before for two. Unfortunately for Yorkshire their star bowler broke down after six overs and did not deliver another ball during the match. Greenidge took full advantage of this, carrying out his bat for 196, including 33 boundaries, and giving Hampshire a commanding lead on first innings. At stumps on the second day Yorkshire were 78 for four and still required nearly a hundred runs to avoid defeat by an innings. The home batsmen displayed their traditional grit on the final day, which meant Hampshire needed 87 runs in 150 minutes to win. The victory was achieved without any crises.

There was another break in the Championship programme as Gloucester came to Southampton for a Benson & Hedges game. Some tight bowling by Mike Taylor, who also captured the vital wicket of Procter, meant that the western county could reach only 211 off their 55 overs. Rain ended play when Hampshire still required 129 to win off 35 overs with Richards out. Continued rain meant no play was possible on the second day, but on the third, Turner, Jesty and Greenidge made certain of victory. Gloucestershire were handicapped by the fact that Procter was forced to retire with back trouble and therefore could not complete his allowance of overs.

Mike Taylor bowls against Somerset at Taunton, while his brother Derek backs up. Mike is now the club's Marketing Manager.

The two teams moved from Southampton to Bristol and began a Championship match, with Gloucester and Procter quite determined to avenge the Cup defeat. The South African all-rounder hit a cavalier 147, Sadiq knocked up 109 and a declaration was made at 326 for eight. Davey and Tony Brown then shot out Hampshire for 82. The follow-on was enforced and apart from Turner all the principal batsmen again went cheaply. The lower order however fought a splendid rearguard action, in which Herman and Stephenson took the chief honours. This ninth-wicket pair came together at 183 a few minutes before tea − 61 more runs were required to avoid an innings defeat − and they remained unbeaten until close of play and made certain of a draw.

The St Helen's Ground at Swansea was Hampshire's next port of call. Trevor Jesty produced his best bowling performance to date, taking five for 27, as the Welshmen were dismissed for 110. Hampshire in their turn struggled and could obtain a lead of only 49, but this proved crucial when rain made the wicket even more unreliable as Glamorgan began their second innings. Sainsbury and O'Sullivan were all but unplayable − the highest scorer was Llewellyn with 22 and Glamorgan were all out for 98. Greenidge decided that all-out attack was the best way to success and hit 35 of the 50 Hampshire needed for victory, his runs including five fours.

The Glamorgan game completed the Championship matches for May, and Hampshire, with a total of 61 points and three wins out of five, were second to Essex in the League table, Essex having just two more points. No other county had as many as three wins.

June commenced with the final matches in the preliminary section of the Benson & Hedges Cup. Hampshire met Somerset at Bournemouth. The home side failed to make full use of an easy paced wicket when batting first, and were lucky that their highest scorer, Jesty, was dropped at mid-wicket off Close early in his innings. Somerset's main batsmen also failed, but Cartwright and Moseley, coming together for the ninth wicket, threatened to turn the game Somerset's way, scoring 59 in 39 balls. Cartwright then ran himself out and Hampshire moved into the knock-out section of the Competition, obtaining victory by 22 runs.

Barry Richards, who had missed two Championship games, treated the people of Coventry to an outstanding exhibition of batting when Hampshire came to the Courtauld's Ground for their sixth Championship fixture. Richards and Greenidge began with an opening stand of 119 and then Richards went on his merry way almost alone. He was at the crease 270 minutes and amassed 240 runs, of which 170 came in boundaries. Gilliat was able to declare with 396 runs on the board. None of the Warwickshire batsmen reached 40 and the follow on was enforced. The West Indian wicket-keeper, Murray, and McVicker put up some fight in the second innings, adding 77 for the sixth wicket, but Mottram – that tall lanky beanpole, as Greenidge later described him – took six for 63 and Hampshire required 35 to win. Young Bob Willis caused a slight hiatus by picking up three wickets very cheaply, but Hampshire won with seven wickets in hand.

Having entertained Midland cricket fans, Richards went to the Services Ground at Portsmouth and gave his home supporters something about which to cheer. A large crowd gathered on the first day, but were sent to sleep by Surrey, who could muster only 204 runs off 90 overs; Herman had a fine spell of 11 overs, picking up three for seven. At the close on Saturday, Hampshire were making slow progress with Richards and Greenidge still undefeated and the score 24 for no wicket. Those spectators who decided to return on Monday morning watched a completely different game. In the two hours prior to lunch Richards and Greenidge hit 183. Richards made 97 in 90 minutes. Both batsmen were out soon after the resumption, but Hampshire still managed a lead of 163. On the final day Surrey put up the shutters and the game gently subsided to a draw.

Hampshire met Kent in the quarter finals of the Benson & Hedges. A clear blue sky and another large crowd gathered at Southampton. Kent were the favourites and batted first, the major partnership of their innings being the fourth wicket stand of 82 by Asif and Julien. The total, however, reached only 206 and with Richards and Greenidge in such good form it was by no means an impossible target. But both these run machines failed and the score was 83 for five when the injured Gilliat struggled to the crease. He made 55 valuable runs and was launching a final assault – he had just hit Asif for six – when he slightly mistimed his stroke and was caught on the square leg boundary. Kent won the match by 11 runs, but the valiant captain obtained the 'Gold Award' from Ken

Roy Virgin of Northants is caught by Greenidge off O'Sullivan during the Championship-winning season of 1973. Mushtaq Mohammad is the non-striker.

Barrington. Kent went on to win the Benson & Hedges Trophy.

Gilliat's injury meant that Sainsbury took the eleven along the coast to Hove. The Sussex Greenidge, partnered by Jeremy Morley, opened the game with a cascade of runs, 77 coming off the first 15 overs. Thereafter Sainsbury decided to put himself and the brake on. John Snow, who found himself Sussex captain on the second day when Greig was injured in the intervening Sunday League match, had a useful burst of three for three in eight overs and gained a slender first innings lead for his side. Mike Buss briefly enlivened the proceedings with 47 at about two per minute, but most of the third day's play was given over to practice.

Hampshire proceeded to Tunbridge Wells for their next fixture. Gilliat returned to the side, but when the first day was entirely washed out, even the application of three strange declarations failed to provide the match with a positive conclusion. Gilliat closed the Hampshire first innings 75 runs behind Kent and then Brian Luckhurst left Hampshire 85 minutes plus 20 overs in which to score 225. Three wickets, including Richards and Greenidge, went for 25 runs, after which it was more a question of survival than run scoring. When the umpires decided to pack it all in, Hampshire were 84 for six.

This match ended Hampshire's Championship programme for June and indeed until 7 July. In the interval the West Indies came to Southampton. The County went into the field without Gilliat, Mottram, Richards and Stephenson and left again with a heavy defeat. Fredericks and Kanhai both hit hundreds; Clive Lloyd was run out for 81 in the first innings and made 86 not out in the second. A 22-year-old fast bowler from the Leeward Islands, called Andy Roberts, was Herman's opening partner. The unknown trialist took one wicket for 144 runs.

Apart from this match the Hampshire players were occupied by two Gillette Cup games. In the first they had a very easy win over Wiltshire, O'Sullivan taking four for 13, as the minor county were dismissed for 82, but in the second they bumped into Kent again and retired with a bloody nose. Greenidge played a quite outstanding innings to reach 100 in about three hours, but no one else could manage 25. Greenidge's innings was all the more meritorious because, after a lengthy journey from Taunton, the Hampshire team found their hotel accommodation double-booked, and did not find an alternative until about 3.00 am, when local police helped them get some rest 30 miles away. Luckhurst also hit a century – he, however, received the aid of Denness and Kent won by the large margin of eight wickets with 7.1 overs unbowled.

With the season now at the halfway stage the experts began to study form and predict the 1973 Champions. Hampshire had momentarily been at the top of the table, when they beat Warwickshire at Coventry, but Essex then returned to the head with a win over Sussex. Three counties were still undefeated – Hampshire, Essex and, lying in fourth place, Kent. Kent were the most fancied side. They possessed good reserves, while Hampshire relied too much on Richards and Greenidge. Their bowling line-up was also frail-looking. Warwickshire, who were third in the table, were discounted on the grounds that their stars. Kanhai, Kallicharran, Gibbs and Murray, had all been called up for the West Indies who toured England during the second half of the season.

The first three matches of July did nothing to enhance Hampshire's chances of the title. It was fortunate indeed that Kent also failed to win in the same period; nor in fact did Warwickshire.

The first July match was at Taunton, where Sainsbury came to the rescue of Hampshire. Coming in with the total

41 for four, he remained for five and a quarter hours and, aided by O'Sullivan, put on 107 for the eighth wicket. Sainsbury was 120 not out when the last wicket went down. Somerset put up a better batting display, but did not score quickly enough to allow much chance of a definite result. In Hampshire's second innings Richards hit 43 in 55 minutes, but after that the tempo moderated, and though Greenidge helped himself to a hundred, Gilliat in the end set Somerset the rather unrealistic target of 200 in 90 minutes. This token was deemed impossible by the redoubtable Close and the score stood at 40 for three when the cricketers went off to meet Kent and, as previously noted, search for hotel rooms.

Rain played an important part in the match at Portsmouth against Glamorgan, though it probably only prevented a Welsh victory. Richards was absent and the home batting looked thin without him. The best cricket of the game was the batting of Eifion Jones, Cordle and Lloyd. The last two added 106 for Glamorgan's eighth wicket and thus removed the initial advantage which had been gained by the Hampshire seam bowlers. Thereafter Hampshire were always at a disadvantage.

The rain followed Hampshire to May's Bounty at Basingstoke, where the County play one Championship match a year. The pitch helped the faster bowlers on the first morning, Mike Selvey obtaining two cheap wickets. Gilliat joined Greenidge and the pair raised the score by 126 runs. Fred Titmus then managed to dismiss both batsmen and the County were all out for 256, Titmus taking five for 51. Rain prevented any play on the second day and though the match restarted on the third morning, the drizzle thickened and the players gave up.

The last two July matches heartened Hampshire's supporters as the County acquired 41 points from two decisive victories. The first win put them back at the top of the Championship table and the margin was an innings and 74 runs. The ground was at Southport and the opponents, Lancashire. The Red Rose county, though experts at the one-day game, were not noted for their success in first-class matches and when put in to bat they collapsed on a slow pitch after Pilling and Snellgrove had added 128 for the third wicket – the last eight wickets went down for 60. Not long after tea, Richards and Greenidge were relishing conditions that had seemed to favour the bowlers before the adjournment. By stumps the total had risen to 74 without loss. On

BARRY ANDERSON RICHARDS

The hallmark of Barry Richards' batting was his cover drive, which the experts agreed equalled Hammond's. Modelling his technique on that of Len Hutton, Richards also possessed a brilliant knack of square cutting anything short of a length. Signed by Hampshire in 1968, he was an immediate success, and until he tired of the county circuit he was perhaps the best batsman in English cricket.

He made his first-class debut for Natal in 1964–65, and spent 1965 in England playing for Gloucestershire second eleven, but instead of staying to qualify for that county returned to Natal and did not return to county cricket until 1968.

He appeared in four Tests for South Africa in 1969–70, when he hit 508 runs at an average of 72.57, scoring two hundreds. The following winter he went to play for South Australia and was largely responsible for that state winning the Sheffield Shield, averaging 109.86 for the season.

He returned to Australia for Packer's World Series Cricket. Playing for the World XI he hit 207 against Australia at Perth in 1977–78 and was one of the leading batsmen for the World side. He left Hampshire rather abruptly in 1978, but continued to play for Natal with success until 1982–83. Peter Sainsbury once stated: 'If I wanted a batsman to make a hundred for my life, it would be Barry Richards.'

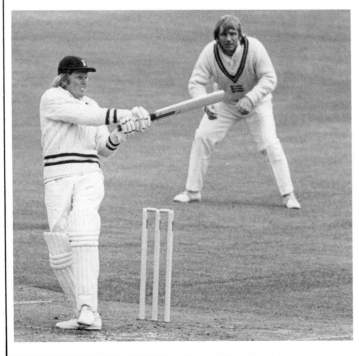

the second morning Richards broke loose. In all he was at the crease about 185 minutes for his 128 with three sixes and 19 fours. The opening pair had put on exactly 200. Greenidge went on to 153 and by the time Gilliat thought it worthwhile to declare the total had risen to 388 – a lead of 174. Jesty made certain the game was over before lunch on the third day by picking up five for 24, the Lancashire batsmen being distinctly uncomfortable.

At New Road not everything went Hampshire's way, though Gifford sprang a surprise by asking the visitors to bat and Hampshire responded with 342. Worcestershire in their turn found runs coming easily and they had the added advantage that both Sainsbury and Jesty were suddenly indisposed and unable to bowl for much of the innings. The run glut continued through Hampshire's second innings, the scoreboard moving so fast at one stage that 219 runs came in 110 minutes – Greenidge hit another hundred. So Gilliat could declare, setting Worcester 316 in four hours. Sainsbury, recovered, removed the danger man, Glenn Turner, after which Taylor sorted out most of the minnows and ended with figures of 7.4-3-17-4 as Hampshire won by 191 runs with 74 minutes to spare.

Hampshire now had six Championship matches still to play – curiously all at home. They began August 11 points clear at the top of the table, but had played one game more than second-placed Northants.

County champions, 1973. Back row, left to right: R. V. Lewis, D. R. O'Sullivan, M. N. S. Taylor, T. J. Mottram, R. S. Herman, C. G. Greenidge, A. J. Murtagh, T. E. Jesty. Front row: D. R. Turner, P. J. Sainsbury, R. M. C. Gilliat, B. A. Richards, G. R. Stephenson.

Rain struck them at Portsmouth on 6 August, the second day of their game with Essex, and what proved to be a vital hour was also lost on the last day. Essex decided to bat on a green wicket and quickly regretted their decision. Only Fletcher survived long as they were all out for 180. A life-saving stand by Turner and Gilliat provided Hampshire with a first innings lead of 73: Gilliat made 110, Turner 98 and the only other double-figure man was wicket-keeper Stephenson with 11. Acfield's off-spin was rather too much for the majority. O'Sullivan made the most of the turning wicket when Essex took their second innings and the side was 113 for nine when the end came – the New Zealander took six for 35.

A second match at Portsmouth followed immediately – Northants had also drawn their game and thus failed to take advantage of the Portsmouth rain. Derbyshire were the visitors. O'Sullivan continued where he had left off and the Midlanders wre removed on the first day for 176. For once both Greenidge and Richards failed, but the captain played another great innings and was very well supported by his crew, so that a lead in excess of 200 was hoisted. Brian Bolus, the Derbyshire skipper, aided by Geoff Miller put up much sterner resistance in the second innings, but once Sainsbury had baffled the old England opener the wickets fell like ninepins, the last five disappearing in 30 minutes for just 22 runs. Hampshire batted again needing four, and Stephenson did the deed from the first ball, delivered, unusually, by Bob Taylor.

There was a gap of a week in Hampshire's fixtures, due in part to the semi-final round of the Gillette Cup. The County had no interest in this, but their minds were fixed on the school ground at Wellingborough, where Northants played Glamorgan in a vital Championship game. The Welshmen were beaten and Northants collected 21 points. This meant that Hampshire and Northants were not only neck and neck, but they each had four matches left.

It was thus not surprising that the biggest crowd in years turned up at the County Ground, Southampton on 18 August to watch Hampshire play Northants. Northants decided to bat first, but soon regretted the decision as the home seam bowlers exploited the pitch and by lunch the score was 56 for eight. Only Bishen Bedi, the turbaned spinner, enabled his team to reach three figures. He hit 32, the highest score of the innings, coming in at No 10 and the ninth

RICHARD MICHAEL CHARLES GILLIAT

A brilliant left-hand bat at school, Gilliat captained the Charterhouse eleven for two seasons and crowned his school career by leading the Public Schools against the Combined Services at Lord's in 1963. Going up to Christ Church, Gilliat immediately found a place in the Oxford side as a middle-order batsman and was awarded his blue in his first season. In his second year – 1965 – he was appointed Hon Secretary of the University Cricket Club and in 1966 he captained the University when they achieved a resounding innings victory against Cambridge. His leadership was recognised by the authorities when he was invited to captain the MCC President's XI against the West Indies.

In the 1966 vacation he made his first-class debut for Hampshire. His best season in county cricket with the bat was 1969 when he hit 1,386 runs, average 39.60 and scored the highest innings of his career, 223 not out against Warwickshire at Southampton. In the winter of 1969 he went on tour with the MCC team to Ceylon.

He was appointed Hampshire's captain in 1971 and in 1973 led the County to its second Championship title. He continued to lead Hampshire until the end of the 1978 season, when he retired from first-class cricket. Although he compiled over 10,000 runs in first-class cricket it cannot be said that he fulfilled the hopes which his admirers held out for him. Apart from cricket he was a more than useful soccer player, and led Oxford in the University match of 1964.

wicket put on 36 and the last wicket a further 16. In contrast to the early Northants batsmen, Richards and Greenidge batted in style and by tea, with the score 72 for none off 20 overs, it appeared that a good lead would be obtained by the close. Bedi however had other plans. Directly after the interval he had Richards stumped, then removed Greenidge in a similar manner. Bob Cottam, enjoying success against his former teammates, disposed of Turner and Gilliat, the latter before he had scored, and with Bedi clean bowling Jesty, the score fell to 127 for 5. In the end, with Bedi still at his best, Hampshire were all out for 167. The game was still in favour of the home side, but at least Northants had a chance if their batsmen – and it must be remembered that the first four were Roy Virgin, Colin Milburn, David Steele and Mushtaq- – could improve on the first innings. Mottram and O'Sullivan, however, dismissed the quartet with little difficulty and Hampshire were left needing 90. Three wickets went down for 49, two of them to Bedi, but Richards played quite brilliantly, mastering both the spin of the Indian and the fast bowling of Cottam. Hampshire won inside two days by seven wickets. The win put Hampshire in high spirits for their next game and at the same time knocked the fight out of Northants, so while Notts were beaten at Bournemouth, Northants narrowly clung on to a draw against Leicestershire.

In the Dean Park match, Hampshire batted solidly, everyone but Jesty reaching double figures but no one making fifty, and the total of 263 was not very impressive considering that Notts had only won one match all summer. The old Middlesex pair, Pasty Harris and Bob White, opened the batting for Notts and took the total to 65, but the less said about the remainder of the visitors' batting the better – O'Sullivan returned figures of 16.5-5-9-26-6. Hampshire batted out time on the second afternoon, so that when Gilliat declared first thing on Tuesday morning, Notts required 345 runs to win and all day to do it. A hundred minutes later the match was all over. Notts were out for 49 in 32.3 overs. O'Sullivan was again the most successful bowler, bringing his match analysis to 28.5-16-41-11.

Gloucestershire arrived at Bournemouth for the second match of the week. Having collected 21 points from the Notts game, the team were virtually certain of the Championship, needing only 13 points to clinch the title and having two matches to play. Because of the batting and

HAMPSHIRE *v* GLOUCESTERSHIRE

Played at Dean Park, Bournemouth, 29, 30 and 31 August 1973

HAMPSHIRE WON BY 5 WICKETS

GLOUCESTERSHIRE	FIRST INNINGS		SECOND INNINGS	
Sadiq Mohammad	c Mottram b Taylor	47	c Greenidge b O'Sullivan	170
R. D. V. Knight	c Stephenson b Taylor	23	c Stephenson b Mottram	10
Zaheer Abbas	c Stephenson b Taylor	4	c Stephenson b O'Sullivan	20
M. J. Procter	b Taylor	0	c Herman b Sainsbury	27
D. R. Shepherd	b Taylor	51	b Sainsbury	0
†A. W. Stovold	c Stephenson b Taylor	0	c Stephenson b Sainsbury	10
R. B. Nicholls	c Richards b Herman	7	c Greenidge b O'Sullivan	13
J. C. Foat	c Sainsbury b Mottram	39	c Stephenson b Herman	19
*A. S. Brown	c Sainsbury b Taylor	2	c Stephenson b Herman	1
D. A. Graveney	b O'Sullivan	16	not out	11
J. B. Mortimore	not out	0	not out	1
Extras	lb 7, w 3, nb 5	15	lb 2, nb 6	8
Total		204	(for 9 wkts dec)	290

1st inns: 1-74, 2-75, 3-75, 4-84, 5-84, 6-107, 7-167, 8-169, 9-204
2nd inns: 1-17, 2-56, 3-115, 4-117, 5-147, 6-168, 7-223, 8-230, 9-288

BOWLING	O	M	R	W	O	M	R	W
Herman	21	4	59	1	18	4	45	2
Mottram	18	3	55	1	15	3	43	1
Taylor	25	9	53	7	4	0	16	0
O'Sullivan	8.5	5	15	1	33.2	6	75	3
Jesty	6	2	7	0	3	0	9	0
Richards					15	4	48	0
Sainsbury					26	6	46	3

HAMPSHIRE	FIRST INNINGS		SECOND INNINGS	
B. A. Richards	b Knight	26	b Brown	13
C. G. Greenidge	c Brown b Mortimore	96	b Brown	65
D. R. Turner	c Brown b Graveney	9	run out	19
*R. M. C. Gilliat	c Stovold b Mortimore	26	lbw b Knight	48
T. E. Jesty	b Mortimore	4	not out	33
P. J. Sainsbury	c Procter b Mortimore	41	lbw b Knight	1
M. N. S. Taylor	c Brown b Mortimore	30	not out	0
†G. R. Stephenson	not out	14		
D. R. O'Sullivan	st Stovold b Graveney	39		
R. S. Herman	b Graveney	4		
T. J. Mottram	st Stovold b Mortimore	10		
Extras	b 1, lb 7	8	b 4, lb 4, nb 3	11
Total		307	(5 wkts)	190

1st inns: 1-48, 2-65, 3-128, 4-167, 5-177, 6-229, 7-264, 8-278, 9-284
2nd inns: 1-29, 2-90, 3-108, 4-184, 5-186

BOWLING	O	M	R	W		O	M	R	W
Procter	4	1	24	0		9	1	44	0
Brown	3	0	15	0		10	1	46	2
Graveney	30	7	118	3		7.1	1	45	0
Knight	4	0	13	1		3	0	21	2
Mortimore	32	5	103	6		3	0	23	0
Sadiq Mohammad	6	1	26	0					

Umpires: R. Julian and T. W. Spencer.
*Captain; †Wicket-keeper.

bowling bonus system then in vogue, it was almost impossible not to pick up 13 bonus points in two games unless the rains returned.

Gloucestershire had already secured themselves a place in the 1973 Gillette Cup Final and were in the top half dozen both in the Championship and Player League. In Sadiq Mohammad, Zaheer Abbas and Mike Procter they possessed a quite excellent trio of mercenaries. Gloucestershire won the toss and reached 74 without loss, then unexpectedly Taylor took three wickets for one run and the score was 75 for three. The dreaded rain arrived. In fact there were no fewer than three interruptions which did little for Gloucestershire's concentration, and with Taylor ending with figures of seven for 53, Hampshire faced a total of 205. More importantly, they picked up five bowling bonus points.

Greenidge then decided to capture the Championship on his own, hitting 96 in 130 minutes, and with the aid of Sainsbury, Taylor and O'Sullivan the total reached 307, providing eight batting points and in effect securing the Championship, since no other county could exceed the Hampshire points total.

Sadiq Mohammad caused problems in Gloucester's second innings; he remained at the crease 315 minutes and scored 170 out of the total of 290 for nine. Tony Brown declared to set Hampshire 188 in 120 minutes. Greenidge was again in good form and hit a rapid 65, Gilliat made 48 and the target was reached with 3.5 overs to spare.

The rest was somewhat of an anti-climax, as the Gillette Cup Final intervened before the final round of Championship games, though these were mainly academic, the major interest being whether Hampshire could avoid defeat in their

Hants v Gloucs:
Bournemouth, August 29, 30, 31 1973
Rain made batting on the first day progressively more difficult, and in between showers Gloucestershire were dismissed for 204, bringing Hampshire five bowling bonus points. Taylor bowled with superb control and accuracy. On the second day, with Greenidge hitting 96 in 130 minutes, the home side collected eight batting bonus points and this harvest meant that they took the Championship title. Sadiq batted 5¼ hours in the second innings and Brown eventually declared, giving Hampshire two hours in which to make 188, a task they accomplished with 3.5 overs to spare.

last match and become one of the few counties to go through a summer undefeated in the Championship.

Kent were the visitors to Southampton for the last game. The first day, played in glorious weather (for September) was dominated by Asif Iqbal, who arrived with the score at 14 for two, found his partner disappearing without any addition, then proceeded to knock the bowling all over the field and complete his hundred before lunch. Kent were all out for 322, but Hampshire's openers celebrated the winning of the title in style putting on 241 before Richards mistimed a hook off a ball from Elms and fractured his cheekbone, thus retiring on 143. Greenidge sailed on to his own century and Kent did not in fact take the first wicket until the total had soared to 334. Gilliat was happy to declare at 471 for eight, Hampshire's highest total of the year, and O'Sullivan had Kent on the ropes at 107 for seven. The tenacious Knott, however, was still undefeated and carried out his bat for 84 with the aid of Bob Woolmer and Derek Underwood. The last wicket scraped together 61 runs and brought the game to an honourable conclusion for the visitors.

The factors which brought the title to Hampshire were the brilliant batting of Richards and Greenidge and the great team spirit which was greatly assisted by the ability to field the same team week in, week out. Only 14 players appeared in the 20 Championship games and six were ever-present, whilst the captain only missed a single game. The bowlers,

The 1973 Championship trophy being presented to Richard Gilliat by HRH the Duke of Edinburgh, with members of the team and club looking on appreciatively.

who looked nothing exceptional on paper – two of the six principal bowlers, Taylor and Herman, were other counties' rejects and another, young Mottram, was in his first full season – all pulled together and provided a nicely balanced machine. Above everything else was the fielding. Richards and Greenidge pouched virtually everything in the slips, Stephenson let little escape behind the stumps and Gilliat set a fine example, usually at mid-off.

The final Championship table read:

		P	W	L	D	T	Bns Pts Bat	Bwl	Pts
1	Hampshire	20	10	0	10	0	84	81	265
2	Surrey	20	9	3	8	0	71	73	234
3	Northants	20	8	4	8	0	53	75	208
4	Kent	20	4	3	13	0	98	59	197
5	Gloucestershire	19	6	4	9	0	63	70	193
6	Worcestershire	20	6	4	10	0	56	75	191
7	Warwickshire	20	5	5	10	0	74	62	186
8	Essex	20	6	5	9	0	46	72	178
9	Leicestershire	19	4	3	12	0	66	60	166
10	Somerset	20	7	2	11	0	29	60	159
11	Glamorgan	20	4	8	8	0	44	68	152
12	Lancashire	20	4	6	10	0	44	67	151
13	Middlesex	20	4	5	10	1	49	54	148
14	Yorkshire	20	3	5	11	1	28	69	132
15	Sussex	20	2	10	8	0	42	67	129
16	Derbyshire	20	2	10	8	0	15	67	102
17	Nottinghamshire	20	1	8	11	0	28	63	101

The Gloucestershire v Leicestershire match at Bristol was washed out and thus is not included in the above

THE WEST INDIAN INFLUENCE

WITH THE WEST INDIAN FAST BOWLER ANDY ROBERTS available for Championship matches in 1974, Hampshire seemed to have strengthened their Championship-winning side of the previous summer and thus were favourites for the 1974 title. They made a hash of the opening match against Middlesex at Lord's, but won the other three May matches so convincingly that the odds on their ultimate title shortened considerably. Kent, Essex and Notts were all beaten by an innings, the last two away from home.

The first match of June brought a fourth successive innings victory, this time at the expense of Sussex, and the County were now 11 points clear at the top of the table. Barry Richards, in prolific form, hit 609 runs in seven innings and averaged above a hundred. His most dominating innings was 225 not out at Trent Bridge, when eight of his colleagues failed even to reach double figures.

By the mid-point of the Championship programme, Hampshire had won seven out of ten matches and still lost just the one against Middlesex. They were now 16 points clear of Worcestershire, but the latter had a game in hand. On July 19, Sussex beat them fair and square at Hove, when John Snow returned figures of 11.4-4-14-6, dismissing Hampshire for 74 and giving his team a lead of 137. Though Gilliat and Stephenson fought hard in the final innings, they were unable to pull the game round and the margin of defeat was 64 runs. However Hampshire's rivals of the previous year, Northants, were disposed of in two days, with Richards and Greenidge hitting off the necessary 88 runs without loss. An innings victory at Portsmouth over Warwickshire boosted Hampshire's points total and in effect only Worcestershire looked like possible challengers, though even they were 19 points behind, each county having six matches to play. The race seemed over two days later, for Worcester came to Portsmouth and were trounced. Worcester were dismissed for 94 and 98 – Roberts took seven for 46 and Herman five for 32 – whilst Hampshire hit 236 in their only innings.

Rain saved Lancashire at Dean Park and Hampshire then travelled to Sophia Gardens. Everything seemed to be going

ANDERSON MONTGOMERY EVERTON ROBERTS

Andy Roberts appeared for Hampshire in 58 matches between 1973 and 1978. His most outstanding summer in England was 1974 – his first as a regular member of the Hampshire side. He took 119 first-class wickets at an average of 13.62 and 21 wickets at 10.76 in the Sunday League.

Up to this time he had appeared only once in a Test for the West Indies and then only as a last-minute replacement for Keith Boyce. However, the England captain in that initial Test, Mike Denness, expressed the opinion that Roberts was the fastest of the West Indian bowlers, and in 1974 Roberts soon impressed his Hampshire team-mate, Barry Richards.

Surprisingly Roberts did not take up cricket until he left school, but then made rapid progress until he made his first-class debut for the Leeward Islands in Tests for West Indies, retiring in 1983–84, but in 1978 severed his connection with county cricket and Hampshire. In 1981 he appeared in the ranks of Leicestershire and played with occasional success for that county for three seasons.

Roberts was a fast bowler who realised that speed was his strongest asset. He therefore did not take kindly to being overbowled in county matches and there were some differences of opinion between himself and the Hampshire captain on this question; but it was the cold English summers which finally persuaded Roberts to quit Hampshire.

NOTTINGHAMSHIRE *v* HAMPSHIRE

Played at Trent Bridge, 25 and 27 May 1974

HAMPSHIRE WON BY AN INNINGS AND 101 RUNS

NOTTINGHAMSHIRE	FIRST INNINGS		SECOND INNINGS	
P. A. Todd	b Herman	7(2)	c Jesty b Roberts	14
R. A. White	lbw b Roberts	3(1)	c Stephenson b Herman	14
D. W. Randall	lbw b Taylor	9	c Roberts b Sainsbury	29
G. St A. Sobers	b Taylor	11	c Sainsbury b Herman	2
M. J. Smedley	lbw b Roberts	9	b Sainsbury	46
S. B. Hassan	c Gilliat b Taylor	18	b Herman	21
*J. D. Bond	c Stephenson b Taylor	1	c Stephenson b Herman	0
H. C. Latchman	not out	23	lbw b Taylor	4
B. Stead	b Roberts	2	c Gilliat b Taylor	3
P. A. Wilkinson	b Taylor	9	not out	0
†D. A. Pullan	b Herman	1	b Sainsbury	6
Extras	lb 2, nb 3	5	b 1, w 2, nb 3	6
Total		98		145

1st inns: 1-10, 2-10, 3-30, 4-33, 5-46, 6-49, 7-70, 8-78, 9-91
2nd inns: 1-27, 2-31, 3-37, 4-66, 5-109, 6-109, 7-125, 8-137, 9-139

BOWLING	O	M	R	W		O	M	R	W
Roberts	18	5	36	3		15	6	39	1
Herman	19	10	22	2		19	7	34	4
Taylor	15	4	29	5		11	0	33	2
Jesty	5	1	6	0		4	2	4	0
Sainsbury	1	1	0	0		11	6	15	3
Richards						3	0	14	0

HAMPSHIRE	FIRST INNINGS	
B. A. Richards	not out	225
C. G. Greenidge	run out	14
D. R. Turner	lbw b Sobers	7
*R. M. C. Gilliat	lbw b Wilkinson	3
T. E. Jesty	c Pullan b Wilkinson	0
R. V. Lewis	c Pullan b White	7
P. J. Sainsbury	b White	1
M. N. S. Taylor	c and b White	68
†G. R. Stephenson	c Sobers b White	4
R. S. Herman	b Stead	8
A. M. E. Roberts	b White	1
Extras	b 1, lb 4, nb 1	6
Total		344

1st inns: 1-49, 2-74, 3-77, 4-77, 5-105, 6-113, 7-315, 8-319, 9-329

BOWLING	O	M	R	W
Stead	25.4	5	106	1
Wilkinson	23	8	68	2
Sobers	22	5	55	1
White	17	1	82	5
Latchman	6	0	27	0

Umpires: C. S. Elliott and D. L. Evans.
Notts won the toss. Close of play: Hampshire 152-6 (Richards 110, Taylor 9).
*Captain; †Wicket-keeper.

Hampshire's way. Although they scored only 234, Glamorgan were completely non-plussed by Roberts, who took eight for 47, and the Welshmen saved the follow-on by just ten runs. Richards batted well in Hampshire's second innings, but the rest were very inept with the result that Glamorgan needed 282 for victory. The Welsh county diligently fought their way to that required total. This astonishing reversal of fortunes was to cast its shadow over the whole summer.

Worcestershire meanwhile had won at home to Essex. Both counties had three matches to play and if Hampshire merely won one of the three and gained reasonable bonus points from all three, they would take the title, however brilliant Worcestershire's run-in might be. The weather then dealt the southern county a nasty blow. It began to rain in Hampshire – all three of the County's fixtures were at home. The return matches with Glamorgan and with Somerset were moral victories, but rain saved the visitors, which meant that the final game at Bournemouth against Yorkshire was absolutely crucial. Worcestershire were playing Essex at Chelmsford on the same days, and before the games began Hampshire were two points ahead. Worcestershire, after the start was delayed by rain, put Essex in, and bowling them all out for 84 picked up four bowling bonus points. By stumps Worcestershire were 126 for three in reply to Essex's 84. At Bournemouth no play was possible on the first day.

On the second day no play took place at either venue and when rain washed out play on the third day as well, the Championship title was Worcestershire's.

Hampshire won the same number of matches as in 1973 – ten – but since they lost three (as opposed to none) their record was hardly as impressive. They were most fortunate to be all but free of injury, no less than nine of the

Hants v Notts: Trent Bridge, May 25, 27 1974
Taylor, who had been released by Notts at the close of 1972 and joined Hampshire, took five for 29 and then hit 68, as Hampshire overwhelmed Notts in two days. Richards batted five hours to hit a magnificent 225, carrying his bat through the innings. Apart from the Notts captain, Smedley, the home eleven fared almost as badly in their second innings and Hampshire won inside two days by a large margin.

eleven appearing in every Championship fixture. The one change in the eleven was the replacement of Mottram by Roberts. Roberts took 111 Championship wickets at 13.45 each and was quite decisively the most deadly bowler in English cricket. Taylor also had his most productive summer with the ball and came sixth in the first-class averages, whilst Richards came second to Clive Lloyd in the batting table.

In the one-day competitions, Hampshire were knocked out in the second round of the Gillette Cup by Yorkshire, and knocked out of the Benson & Hedges in a thrilling quarter-final match with Somerset, a match in which the young Ian Botham first came to notice, winning the Gold Award with a swashbuckling and match-winning 45 not out, after being hit in the mouth by a Roberts bouncer. Hampshire came fifth in the Sunday League, so were not all that successful, even though the experts quoted them as an ideal 'one-day' team.

In 1975 they were to prove the experts right. Hampshire won the John Player Sunday League after a very keen struggle, being in the end two points ahead of second-placed Worcestershire. On 15 June Hampshire rose to the head of the table, only to lose the leadership to Essex, but in the second half of the year they were in tremendous form, winning all of their last seven games with relative ease – their rivals Worcestershire won six out of their seven, but were held to a tie by Lancashire at Old Trafford on 10 August and this lost them the two points which separated the counties in the end.

In the Championship, following two seasons without much distraction by injury or representative calls, Hampshire found themselves without Roberts and Greenidge (due to Prudential World Cup matches) and in the absence of their two West Indian stars, the County lost two matches. In addition Taylor was missing for eight weeks with injury problems and Roberts was missing for the three final matches, in two of which Hampshire's opponents had second-innings revivals, when they appeared beaten, leading to both matches being drawn. These factors meant that though the County still had ten Championship wins (as in 1973 and 1974) they not only lost six matches, but failed to win as many bonus points as in the previous seasons. Leicestershire took the title with 12 victories and a 16-point lead over second-placed Yorkshire, who managed just a single point more than Hampshire.

The County did well in the Benson & Hedges Competi-

tion, reaching the semi-finals for the first time when a crowd of 6,000 watched them beat Somerset at Southampton by 50 runs. Sainsbury, now the veteran of the side, won the Man of the Match award by taking the vital wickets of Rose, Denning and Close, though Viv Richards hit a forceful 62 not out, the highest score on either side.

The evergreen David Turner in full flight.
(Courtesy of Patrick Eagar)

The semi-final took Hampshire to Grace Road. The Australian fast bowler McKenzie dismissed Barry Richards in the first over of the match. Greenidge batted in excellent form, but could find little help and Hampshire were all out for 216, the West Indian making 111. When Hampshire fielded it was again a one-man effort. Roberts returned figures of 10.1-5-16-1 – everyone else conceded at least three runs per over, with Jesty conceding six. Balderstone scored 101 not out and Leicestershire won with the first ball of the last over.

HAMPSHIRE *v* GLAMORGAN (GILLETTE CUP)

Played on the County Ground, Southampton, 16 July 1975

HAMPSHIRE WON BY 164 RUNS

HAMPSHIRE

B. A. Richards	b Ellis	129
C. C. Greenidge	c Hopkins b Nash	177
D. R. Turner	lbw b Davis	19
T. E. Jesty	b Nash	12
*R. M. C. Gilliat	not out	5
A. M. E. Roberts	not out	14
P. J. Sainsbury		
A. J. Murtagh		
J. M. Rice		
†G. R. Stephenson		
R. S. Herman		
Extras	b 4, lb 6, nb 5	15
Total	(60 overs, 4 wkts)	371

Fall: 1-210, 2-284, 3-352, 4-353

BOWLING	O	M	R	W
Nash	12	1	84	2
Cordle	12	0	81	0
Solanky	12	1	57	0
Ellis	12	1	63	1
Armstrong	6	0	38	0
Davis	6	0	33	1

GLAMORGAN

A. Jones	lbw b Roberts	4
A. L. Jones	lbw b Roberts	11
R. C. Davis	st Stephenson b Sainsbury	25
*Majid J. Khan	c and b Sainsbury	29
J. A. Hopkins	hit wkt b Sainsbury	12
G. P. Ellis	c Stephenson b Jesty	25
J. W. Solanky	c Richards b Roberts	51
†E. W. Jones	c Stephenson b Rice	0
M. A. Nash	b Rice	0
A. E. Cordle	c Richards b Herman	8
G. D. Armstrong	not out	19
Extras	b 2, lb 16, w 2, nb 3	23
Total	(50.1 overs)	207

Fall: 1-19, 2-32, 3-78, 4-83, 5-98, 6-138, 7-142, 8-144, 9-163

BOWLING	O	M	R	W
Roberts	8.1	1	17	3
Herman	10	1	45	1
Rice	10	1	32	2
Jesty	12	2	37	1
Sainsbury	10	1	53	3

Umpires: R. Julian and K. E. Palmer.
Hampshire won the toss.
*Captain; †Wicket-keeper.

In the second round of the Gillette Cup Hampshire created an assortment of records at Glamorgan's expense. Richards and Greenidge put on 210 for the first wicket. Greenidge scored 177 and the total of 371 for four was not only the highest total in a Gillette Cup game, but the highest total ever recorded up to that date in a major limited-overs match anywhere in the world. This outstanding batting performance was in stark contrast to Hampshire's efforts in the next round, when 20,000 came to Old Trafford to see the new record breakers and saw them collapse in a heap – all out 98 in 43.1 overs, Barry Wood taking four for 17. Lancashire found Roberts difficult but still won by six wickets with only 31.5 overs bowled.

The value of Greenidge and Roberts to Hampshire became apparent in 1976 when their services were required by West Indies. In the Championship matters were not too critical until 20 July when the side were beaten by Gloucestershire at Bristol by 51 runs. This defeat signalled the start of one of the worst periods in the County's history when no less than eight successive matches ended in reverse. During this black period, the County's fortunes were not helped by the absence, in several matches, of Sainsbury, who was by far the most effective bowler over the season. Southern, a tall Londoner, who had a BSc in chemistry from Southampton University, played regularly as a second left-arm slow bowler and had some good spells. Another cricketer who had found a permanent place in the side the previous year and retained it in 1976 was locally born John Rice. Rice, a useful middle-order batsman and seam bowler, had been on the Surrey staff in 1970, but the following year had joined his native county. In 1975 he had achieved the hat-trick in the Sunday League game against Northants. Rice was promoted to open the innings with Richards for the last few matches – Lewis had begun the season as Greenidge's stand-in and failed; David Rock of Portsmouth Grammar School was then tried but scored only 69 runs in six innings; this led to the promotion of Rice. Mottram was resuscitated in the absence of Roberts, but his appearances were restricted by injury and Herman lost his control and eventually his place in the side.

Leaving the first-class game, Hampshire had moderate results in the Sunday League and Benson & Hedges, but in the Gillette they reached the semi-finals, meeting Northants at Southampton. Batting first they could score only 215 off the 60 overs and it looked all over when Northants had 180 for three on the board. At this point, Roy Virgin, who had made 82, was run out in the 51st over. Panic set in and four more wickets went down with only 31 runs added. Six runs were then required with two overs and also two wickets in hand, Sarfraz and Bedi however hit off the required half-dozen.

Two small crumbs of comfort for Hampshire were the winning of both the invitation limited-overs trophies – Fenner's and the new Tilcon Trophy.

The return of Roberts and Greenidge ought to have produced a revival in 1977, but when the summer was over, the County's record differed little from the year before. Injuries played their part in this unexpected turn of events, but the fact that Richards had been given a benefit probably contributed to his loss of form. Roberts was not the destroyer he had been. He missed eight Championship matches and though he headed the bowling table, took only 40 Championship wickets. Herman was scarcely seen, Mottram's efforts were confined to one-day matches, and in many matches R. B. Elms, the fast left-arm bowler, formerly with Kent, was Roberts' opening partner. Southern led the spin attack, though his wickets cost over 31 runs each. Nigel Cowley, an off-break bowler from Shaftesbury, bowled slightly quicker than in his previous matches and improved as a result, though his batting was the main reason for his inclusion in the side.

Greenidge improved even on his previous efforts and topped the batting table by a wide margin. He hit two double-centuries – 200 in 240 minutes at Guildford and 208 in 270 minutes at Headingley, when Roberts was also at his best and Hampshire had a most convincing victory. The County found the loss of Sainsbury, who had retired at the

CUTHBERT GORDON GREENIDGE

The unique statistic of Greenidge's batting with Hampshire is that at one time he held the individual record for the highest score in all three of the English limited-overs competitions: 177 *v* Glamorgan at Southampton in 1977 in the Gillette Cup; 173 not out *v* Minor Counties South at Amersham in 1973 in the Benson & Hedges Cup; 163 not out *v* Warwickshire at Edgbaston in 1972 in the Player Sunday League.

Of medium height, but very robust, Greenidge has been of recent years one of the hardest hitters of the ball in English cricket. He seemed to delight in the total destruction of the opposition bowling. Capable of driving the ball off either foot and possessing a brutal hook shot, his batting was reminiscent of Gary Sobers. One of his most famous innings was against the Pakistanis at Eastbourne in 1974 when he reached 273 not out in 255 minutes. The innings contained 13 sixes and 31 fours.

Since Barry Richards left Hampshire, Greenidge has shown more responsibility and this has made his wicket harder to take, even if the runs have not come in quite the same hurricane manner.

Coming to England as a teenager, he had the choice of playing for either his native West Indies or for England, but chose the former, making his Test debut in 1974. He has been a regular member of the West Indies side, as well as appearing in the Packer WSC 'Super-Tests'. For the West Indies *v* England in the Old Trafford Test of 1976 he had the distinction of scoring a century in each innings.

end of the previous season, a much greater blow than anticipated, and when Gilliat fractured a cheekbone in June a further shiver went through the supporters. Stephenson led the side in Gilliat's absence, and Richards, who had been the official vice-captain, resigned from that post.

In the Championship the County ended in 11th place, but there was little separating them from the three or four teams immediately above. In the one-day competitions the best results occurred in the Benson & Hedges Cup. The County were drawn at home in the semi-final against Gloucestershire. The western county batted first and though Stovold and Sadiq managed 106 for the first wicket, the remainder of the batting fell apart, so that Gloucestershire were all out for 180. Hampshire then seemed to have a very good chance of going to Lord's, but Mike Procter dismissed Richards, Greenidge, Jesty and Rice in five balls. The score was then 18 for four. Cowley joined Turner and the pair added 109 for the next wicket. Procter however picked up two more cheap wickets, his final analysis being 11-5-13-6, and Hampshire lost by seven runs.

Hampshire were involved indirectly in the race for the County Championship, for they met Gloucestershire again, this time at Bristol, in the final match of the season. Victory would have given Gloucestershire the title. Procter played brilliantly, hitting 115 out of 223 and then taking six for 68 in Hampshire's first innings of 229. In the final innings Hampshire needed 271 to win – and a dropped catch gave them the match. Greenidge survived to hit 94 in 95 minutes and with Turner add 123 in 65 minutes. Hampshire won by six wickets.

Four days after the season closed, Desmond Eagar, who had been captain and Secretary before his retirement in 1957, and had remained Secretary afterwards, died on holiday in Devon. He had had a serious operation earlier in the year, but had been able to resume his secretarial duties, and his death came as a shock to the cricket world.

In 1978 Hampshire won the Sunday League for a second time, but only because of their superior run-rate, since Somerset and Leicestershire also obtained an equal number of points. Hampshire, however, deserved the title in that they won four of their last five matches without Richards or Roberts, both of whom in effect walked out of the club in July. Richards had said at the beginning of the season: 'When I walk off a county ground for the last time, it will be with a

sense of relief.' His departure, since it was plain from his batting that his interest in county cricket was now non-existent, was hardly unexpected; but Roberts' abrupt departure was more of a surprise.

The captain, Gilliat, had a difficult task holding together his depleted eleven, a job made harder by the fact that it was his own benefit season and he also missed several matches through injury. The only ready-made recruit of 1978 was the Derbyshire seamer, Keith Stevenson, who played throughout the summer and took 47 Championship wickets, but the main burden of the attack fell on Southern and Cowley, for the other seamers who helped Stevenson (excluding Roberts) were not really match-winning bowlers – Taylor fell right away, his 19 wickets costing over 40 runs each (interestingly, his batting and bowling averages were virtually identical!) and Richard Elms hardly played and was released at the season's close. Tim Tremlett, son of the old Somerset pro, appeared in six Championship games and looked a promising all-rounder who could deliver a useful ball at medium pace.

Aside from their success in the Sunday League, Hampshire moved up three places in the County Championship, though they only won four matches, two of which were the last two

A one-day trophy for Hampshire. Richard Gilliat with their second John Player League trophy in 1978. (Courtesy of Patrick Eagar)

of the season. They made no impact in the Gillette or Benson & Hedges Competitions, however.

A. K. James, formerly the Secretary to Lancashire CCC, had succeeded to the post left vacant by the death of Desmond Eagar, but Hampshire faced two more vital decisions in the close season of 1978–79. A new overseas cricketer was required to fill the shoes of Richards or Roberts, while Gilliat had handed in his resignation, so a new captain was needed. Stephenson filled the latter position, and for the former the County chose a 20-year-old Barbadian, Malcolm Marshall. He had made his debut for his native island in 1977–78, and in 1978–79 had toured India and Sri Lanka with the West Indies. The Hampshire Secretary noted: 'He is an opening bowler and useful lower-order batsman and comes with a good reputation as a fielder. Although he may take a time to settle to English conditions, Hampshire have high hopes that he will develop quickly with experience.'

The 1979 season began with a series of embarrassments. All four Benson & Hedges preliminary matches were lost and the team were also bundled quickly out of the Gillette Cup. The batting simply failed. Greenidge was as brilliant as before but apart from Jesty he received no support. Two extreme examples were Taylor, whose average plummeted from 40 to 19 and the promising Tremlett from 22 to 4. Twelve times in Championship matches the team were dismissed for under 200 and they also suffered four innings defeats. With three Championship wins they ended in 12th place, and in the Player League they fell from first to tenth.

Both Greenidge and Marshall missed some games due to their World Cup commitments, though the latter was not in fact required by the West Indies. He topped the bowling averages, and with Stevenson also effective, the County at least possessed a good pair of opening bowlers. The spinners were not so successful, though to an extent the reason for this was the illness of Southern. Taylor and Rice, the medium-pace trundlers, could both point to fair records, but as with his batting, Tremlett had a lean time and Jesty almost ceased to bowl. Two boys from public schools, Mark Nicholas from Bradfield and Paul Terry from Millfield, looked most promising prospects, and the former hit a hundred off the Oxford attack.

With the West Indies touring England, 1980 was always going to be a difficult summer for Hampshire. The Old

Shrewsbury captain, Nick Pocock, was appointed to lead the County in place of Stephenson. Pocock had played in 27 first-class matches spread over the last four seasons and at 28 was unlikely to develop into more than a useful middle-order batsman. To fill in for Marshall, Shaun Graf, the Victorian fast bowler, was engaged, and Greenidge's replacement was the 21-year-old Natal batsman, Chris Smith, who had spent 1979 playing for Glamorgan second eleven. A third import was Steve Malone, the Essex medium pace bowler.

A blow to the County's slender resources was David Rock's announcement just before the season began that he was retiring. This threw a great responsibility on the only other (in the absence of Greenidge) experienced opening bat, Rice. In the event he just couldn't get going, and after several experiments, an unlikely opening partnership of Tremlett and Chris Smith evolved. The former, as opener, was mainly responsible for Hampshire's only Championship victory. Batting at No 2 he scored 76 out of 236 and 67 not out from 142 for six, when Worcester were beaten by four wickets. Both Tremlett and Chris Smith had good seasons, but the remaining batsmen were very erratic and it was unfortunate that neither Jesty nor Turner really shouldered the burden which had been thrust upon them. The old stager, Taylor, announced his intention to retire, as did the wicket-keeper, Stephenson, and the Committee omitted both from the later matches, in an attempt to blood some youngsters. Bobby Parks, son of the Sussex wicket-keeper-batsman, took over behind the stumps and looked likely to make some runs.

Neither Graf or Malone proved very penetrative and Stevenson took most Championship wickets, though at high cost.

Bottom of the Championship – their worst record since 1905 – Hampshire found no consolation in the one-day game and Hampshire supporters could only grit their teeth and await the return of Greenidge and Marshall. A financial loss of £5,717 did not make life any easier.

The weather made for a gloomy start to 1981. Hampshire's Championship game at The Oval was totally washed out and the fixtures with Somerset and Leicestershire were rain-affected, but in June a more cheerful state of affairs prevailed. The rank outsiders obtained three Championship victories and a fourth (in two days) at the beginning of July suddenly produced red faces in book-making circles by placing Hampshire at the head of the table. Derbyshire were

TREVOR EDWARD JESTY

Although he played little cricket at his secondary school, Jesty attracted enough attention in local matches to gain a place in the Hampshire Schools eleven and later the English Schools side. His brother had been offered a place on the Hampshire staff and though he did not accept he played a good standard of club cricket with Gosport Amateurs. Trevor himself played for the neighbouring side of Gosport CC, and whilst there was taken on the Hampshire ground-staff. His Championship debut was made at the age of 18 (in 1966), but his career did not run smoothly through the 1970s, perhaps because he was at times not in accord with Gilliat, the captain.

As a batsman he is an attacking front-foot player, appearing to model himself on Barry Richards. His seam bowling looks innocent enough, but he is quite capable of taking wickets at a moderate cost. Although he has never represented England in a Test Match, he has been selected for ten one-day internationals.

At the close of the 1984 season he left Hampshire over the question of the captaincy. He had been vice-captain to Pocock, but when Pocock retired the Committee decided to appoint Nicholas instead of Jesty. Since 1985 Jesty has played for Surrey where, ironically, he immediately took on the role as acting captain in the absence of Geoff Howarth.

then beaten by an innings at Portsmouth – young Parks picking up a Hampshire catching record with ten in the match – but there followed defeats at the hands of Surrey, Kent and Gloucestershire and the County's dream of moving in one season from bottom to top of the Championship faded.

In the end six wins put the side in seventh place which was certainly a most pleasant position after 1980. In the Sunday League they also moved upward and results in the other two limited-overs competitions were favourable.

The two West Indians topped the batting and bowling tables, but Jesty also had a fine season with the ball and was only marginally behind Marshall. In the batting Rice, who was recalled to the side when Tremlett broke his wrist, scored a maiden hundred – after ten years – and this gave him much needed confidence, so much so that he finished second to Greenidge in the averages. Chris Smith was a pillar of the second eleven and played well when he was able to appear in the first team. Richard Hayward, the former Buckingham-shire batsman, scored a century on his first-class debut for the County, against the Sri Lankans, but did little in six Championship games.

The outstanding feature of the 1982 season was the bowling of Malcolm Marshall. Although he came second to Hadlee in the overall averages, Marshall took twice as many wickets and was the only bowler in the country to reach the hundred mark. Twelve times he took five wickets in an innings for Hampshire – a figure not recorded in the County since the days of Shackleton – and batsmen on the county circuit had no doubts in proclaiming him the fastest bowler in England. If this was not enough, Marshall hit a century against Lancashire and came fourth in the Hampshire batting table. As Marshall's bowling partner, the County introduced Kevin Emery, a 21-year-old from Swindon; he played in the first match and immediately gained a permanent position in the side. No doubt the assistance of Marshall helped him, but even so 78 Championship wickets at 22 runs each is an impressive record for a debut summer. The other feature of the year was the all-round performance of Jesty, who even out-batted Greenidge, as well as coming second in the bowling table. Greenidge himself was not quite the player of 1981, but still a formidable striker of the ball.

The rest of the side, under the enterprising leadership of Pocock, may have played second fiddle to Marshall and Jesty, but they all made useful contributions at the right times and the result was eight Championship victories and a rise to third place in the table. Nine of the eleven played in at least 20 of the 22 games, which meant the continuity of a basic regular eleven, and this in itself was a contrast to a number of seasons in the immediate past.

Rather surprisingly Hampshire failed to make any impression in the one-day competitions and again had the miserable experience of failing to win a Benson & Hedges game.

Chris Smith, who had been largely confined to the second eleven in 1982, qualified for England in 1983, making him eligible for Hampshire as a 'home' player, and the depth of Hampshire's batting almost doubled overnight.

The South African hit six Championship hundreds and was actually selected for England for the last two Tests. He averaged over 60 and scored more runs than Greenidge on account of the fact that the West Indian was involved in the World Cup. Jesty had another good year with the bat and Paul Terry, who had been in and out of the Hampshire team for several seasons, gained a regular place and reached a thousand runs for the first time with the impressive average of 45.17. Terry was also a fine fieldsman, which proved an additional benefit to the team.

The bowling strength did not match the batting. Marshall was as potent as ever, but missed matches because of his World Cup appearances; Emery, the discovery of 1982, played in only five matches due to a combination of injury and lack of form. The left-arm spin of Southern proved less and less effective and he decided to retire at the end of the summer. The seam bowling of Tremlett, usually coming on as first change, was the bright spot of the attack. Marshall had either Malone or Stevenson as his opening partner, but Malone's wickets were costly.

In the Championship race, Hampshire were the early pace-setters, but when the World Cup depleted the side they were unable to sustain their winning streak and gained only one victory in June. Hampshire's most satisfactory game was against Essex, the eventual Champions, at Southend in July. After a low scoring first innings on both sides, Essex hit 340 for six declared and set Hampshire the awe-inspiring target of 410. Chris Smith made 163 and the enormous total was reached in the penultimate over.

With ten victories, the side came third in the table, but

CHRISTOPHER LYALL SMITH

A successful career as a batsman at Northlands High School, Durban, led to Chris Smith's selection for South African Schools in 1975–76 and from there to Natal 'B', for which team he made an unsuccessful debut in February 1978. In 1979 he came to England and played for Gorseinon in the South Wales League as well as appearing for Glamorgan Second Eleven. He won a place in the Glamorgan team against the Sri Lankans and, in contrast to his failure on his Natal debut, he hit the highest score for the Welsh county – 67.

In 1980 he switched his allegiance to Hampshire. Converted to an opening batsman, he was so successful that he not only topped the Hampshire averages, but was the only player to reach 1,000 runs for the County. After playing only occasionally in 1981 and 1982, he became qualified as an 'English' cricketer in 1983 and immediately demonstrated that the period of waiting had been worthwhile. He hit over 1,900 runs in the season, came 11th in the overall first-class averages and displaced Graeme Fowler as England's opening batsman in the third Test against New Zealand at Lord's.

He was included in the England touring team to New Zealand and Pakistan the following winter, played in five Tests on the tour and had his most impressive innings at Auckland, when he batted 459 minutes for 91 to force a draw.

Though he lost form in 1984, and with it his Test place, he had an outstanding year in 1985, completing 2,000 runs, and remains one of the most reliable batsmen in English county cricket.

HAMPSHIRE *v* SURREY
(JOHN PLAYER LEAGUE)

Played at United Services Ground, Portsmouth, 10 July 1983

HAMPSHIRE WON BY 104 RUNS

HAMPSHIRE

C. G. Greenidge	not out	108
C. L. Smith	b Thomas	5
T. E. Jesty	not out	166
V. P. Terry		
M. C. J. Nicholas		
*N. E. J. Pocock		
N. G. Cowley		
M. D. Marshall		
T. M. Tremlett		
†R. J. Parks		
S. J. Malone		
Extras	lb 5, w 1, nb 7	13
Total	(40 overs, 1 wkt)	292

Fall: 1-23

BOWLING	O	M	R	W
Thomas	7	0	47	1
Feltham	8	0	61	0
Knight	8	0	31	0
Clarke	8	0	57	0
Pocock	4	0	37	0
Payne	5	0	46	0

SURREY

A. R. Butcher	c Greenidge b Cowley	65
†C. J. Richards	b Cowley	43
D. M. Smith	st Parks b Cowley	20
M. A. Lynch	c Terry, b Malone	33
D. J. Thomas	b Cowley	0
*R. D. V. Knight	not out	11
I. R. Payne	not out	5
A. J. Stewart		
S. T. Clarke		
M. A. Feltham		
P. I. Pocock		
Extras	lb 5, w 4, nb 2	11
Total	(40 overs, 5 wkts)	188

Fall: 1-82, 2-126, 3-146, 4-146, 5-175

BOWLING	O	M	R	W
Marshall	7	2	14	0
Malone	7	0	26	1
Tremlett	8	0	39	0
Nicholas	8	0	51	0
Cowley	8	1	42	4
Greenidge	1	0	4	0
Pocock	1	0	1	0

Umpires: M. J. Kitchen and N. T. Plews.
Surrey won the toss.
*Captain; †Wicket-keeper.

instead of being 75 points behind the leaders, as in 1982, the gap was narrowed to 33.

Hampshire reached the quarter-finals of the Benson & Hedges Cup and the semi-finals of the NatWest Trophy (formerly Gillette Cup). In both cases they appeared to be in a winning position, but let the opportunity slip. The County were now in the unenvied position of being the only side not to appear in a Lord's one-day final. In the Sunday League, Greenidge lost his crown for the League's highest individual score to Trevor Jesty, but hit the most runs in 1983 Sunday matches. The side's best win was at Portsmouth when Greenidge and Jesty added an unbroken 269 for the second wicket, with the West Indian, in his benefit match, for once, outscored – Jesty 166, Greenidge 108. Surrey were beaten by 104 runs. Hampshire's final place in the League was fifth, with nine wins.

As in the past, the West Indian tour of England caused Hampshire headaches in 1984. Marshall and Greenidge were not seen all summer. To replace Marshall, the County signed Milton Small, only to find that Small was unexpectedly selected for the West Indies tour. Hampshire then signed Elvis Reifer, twin brother of the Barbadian cricketer, George Reifer. A second pace bowler to be recruited was Cardigan Connor, a West Indian-born cricketer, but with English qualifications. Neither had experience of first-class cricket, but the latter, who did not appear in the Championship until the last match of May was the most successful and ended with 60 Championship wickets, against Reifer's 38. Tremlett was top of the bowling, being both consistent and economical. Emery again failed as did Malone and both left the

Hants v Surrey: Player League 1983
Hampshire batsmen broke several records in this match. Greenidge and Jesty added 269* for the second wicket, which was a record for any partnership by the county in Sunday League cricket; Jesty's 166* was the highest Hampshire individual innings in the competition, beating Greenidge's 163 made in 1979, and at 59 Greenidge broke Barry Richards' Hampshire record for the most runs scored in a career in the Sunday League. Jesty became the first player to score 4,000 runs and take 200 wickets in the League. Surrey made a valiant attempt to score runs at the required rate, but after the opening stand of 82 was broken they gradually slipped further and further behind.

Hampshire staff at the season's end. To take Southern's place, a slow left-armer from Middlesex was signed – Rajesh Maru. He appeared in 15 Championship games and picked up 43 wickets.

The most alarming decline compared to 1983 was the batting of Chris Smith. His average halved in first-class matches, but in odd contrast he could do no wrong in the Sunday League. Terry began the summer in fine style and played for England in the Third and Fourth Tests, unfortunately suffering a broken arm in the latter and missing the last part of the season.

Weakness in the bowling meaht a worse record than in 1983. The County fell to 15th in the Championship, ninth in the Sunday League made little progress in the other two one-day competitions. Financially the County had had two bad years in 1982 and 1983, losing nearly £100,000 over the two-year period. For the 1984 season subscription rates were raised quite steeply from £25 to £35, though this bold step did not produce the exodus of members which some pessimists predicted.

The yo-yo Hampshire results continued in 1985. Marshall and Greenidge returned and the side ended as runners-up in the Championship. In a hard fought race they battled it out for the leadership with Middlesex and Gloucestershire through the whole summer. The County also had at least a theoretical chance of capturing the Sunday League title until the last set of matches, but they finished third behind Essex and Sussex.

Chris Smith recovered from his barrren patch of 1984 and topped the Championship batting averages. His powerfully built younger brother, Robin, qualified as an English player at the beginning of the summer and proved most successful, hitting 1,351 Championship runs at an average of 39.73. Another young batsman who caught the eye was Jon Hardy, a left-hander from Canford School, but he could not command a permanent place. Turner also found himself edged out of the Championship team, though he played on Sundays. Mark Nicholas was the full-time captain in 1985, having taken over from Pocock in August 1984.

Malcolm Marshall continued to vie with Hadlee for the best bowler in county cricket accolade. In 1985 he took 95 wickets at 17.68 runs apiece. Tremlett was Marshall's lieutenant, whilst the side's most fruitful spinner was Maru.

Marshall and Greenidge dominated the 1986 county scene.

MALCOLM DENZIL MARSHALL

Behind the laughter and the party-loving jaunty air hides a very serious cricketer. Marshall takes not only the match itself but the preliminary training and practice with the seriousness of a dedicated professional. He was 21 when he made his Hampshire debut in 1979, and by 1982 he had become much more than just another fast bowler from Barbados.

In 1982 Marshall captured 134 wickets, easily the highest total in English first-class cricket since the reduction in the number of three-day matches. In 1986 he again took 100 wickets in a season.

Unlike his West Indian partner, Joel Garner, Marshall does not have the advantage of height to make the ball bounce. Marshall is under six feet, but his whippy action and his co-ordination enable him to make the ball come off the pitch much faster than the batsman expects. He has been attacked in the press for intimidatory tactics, more especially since one of his deliveries broke Gatting's nose in the 1986 one-day international in Kingston, but Marshall does not need the fast West Indian pitches in order to succeed, and as his record for Hampshire shows he can adapt his style to the slower pitches often found in England and can swing the ball most effectively.

One of his ambitions is to score a century in Test cricket and against India at Kanpur in 1982 he did reach 92. His batting is attractive in style and if he could manage to curb a natural impetuosity, he might well achieve his ambition.

The former headed the first-class bowling table with 100 wickets and the latter headed the batting with 2,035 runs. In view of the two West Indians repeated successes – Greenidge hit no less than eight hundreds including 222 against Northants at Northampton and two three-figure innings at Derby – it was disappointing that the County managed to finish in only sixth place in the Championship.

Two weak links in the batting line-up were Terry and the captain, Nicholas, neither of whom managed an individual Championship hundred. Chris Smith twice broke a finger and missed six matches and his brother did not prove as productive as in his first full summer. In the bowling Cardigan Connor opened with Marshall, but his Championship wickets cost nearly 33 runs each. Maru and Tremlett failed to live up to the reputations they earned in the previous year, though aided by 'not outs' they both returned good batting figures.

All, however, was not gloom, for the County won the Sunday League for the third time. They caught up with the leaders in late June and had the advantage of a game in hand over their chief rivals for much of the rest of the year, actually being able to claim the title with a win in their penultimate match.

In the NatWest Trophy and the Benson & Hedges Cup they were unable to make much progress and the County's continued failure to reach a Lord's knock-out final is becoming one of the phenomena of county cricket.

Having won the Sunday League in 1986 and retaining all their staff, except Chris Goldie, for 1987, Hampshire looked forward to a prosperous summer. Greenidge had been in brilliant form for West Indies against New Zealand, scoring a double-hundred in the Second Test and making two hundreds in the one-day internationals. Paul Terry had been breaking records in District cricket in Australia and Steve Andrew had spent the winter improving his bowling.

When the final averages appeared at the end of 1987 virtually all Hampshire's cricketers could look at the figures with satisfaction. In the batting the captain, Nicholas, and Terry each more or less doubled their average. The veteran Turner had a splendid year, and only Greenidge and Chris Smith 'declined' in comparison with the previous year; but both still averaged over 45! Indeed, with four players (James, Greenidge, Turner and Robin Smith) in the top ten of the national averages, and seven players averaging over 40,

MARK CHARLES JEFFORD NICHOLAS

Appointed captain of Hampshire in 1985, Mark Nicholas was then given the task of leading the England 'B' side to Sri Lanka the following winter. On this tour his best innings were played in the third one-day international and the third unofficial Test, but like most of the English players he found the standard of cricket in Sri Lanka higher than expected; his selection for the tour is however an indication that he is regarded as a potential English Test cricketer.

An attractive right-hand batsman, Nicholas was three years in the eleven at Bradfield, being captain of the school side in 1976, and he led a Public Schools side to South Africa in 1976–77. In 1977 he played regularly for Hampshire Second Eleven and in 1978 he made his first-class debut, appearing in two County Championship games. He spent the winter of 1978–79 in Australia as captain of Southern Lakes CC, but 1979 saw him make little advance towards a permanent place in the County side. His confidence returned in 1980. His attacking stroke play was much admired and in the middle of June he found a regular place in the side. His maiden first-class hundred came off the Somerset attack at Bournemouth and his reward was a place in the MCC side to Bangladesh in 1980–81. He was awarded his Hampshire cap in 1982, in which season he hit a double-century at The Parks off Oxford University – this score of 206 not out remains his highest so far.

He had a very moderate summer in 1986, but 1987 saw him making 1626 runs at an average of 40.65. He should be one of Hampshire's leading batsmen for some years to come, and may yet win Test honours.

SURREY *v* HAMPSHIRE (JOHN PLAYER LEAGUE)

Played at The Oval, 7 September 1986

HAMPSHIRE WON BY 3 RUNS

HAMPSHIRE

C. G. Greenidge	c Richards b Gray	16
V. P. Terry	hit wkt b Thomas	2
R. A. Smith	lbw b Bicknell	21
*M. C. J. Nicholas	c Bullen b Gray	0
C. L. Smith	c Bullen b Butcher	16
K. D. James	not out	54
N. G. Cowley	c Richards b Butcher	0
M. D. Marshall	c Richards b Bicknell	1
T. M. Tremlett	run out	4
†R. J. Parks	not out	10
C. A. Connor		
Extras	b 6, lb 5, w 11, nb 3	25
Total	(40 overs, 8 wkts)	149

Fall: 1-13, 2-32, 3-32, 4-56, 5-94, 6-95, 7-95, 8-114

BOWLING	O	M	R	W
Gray	8	1	37	2
Thomas	8	1	41	1
Bullen	8	1	13	0
Bicknell	8	1	19	2
Needham	4	0	16	0
Butcher	4	0	12	2

SURREY

*A. R. Butcher	c Terry b Tremlett	44
G. S. Clinton	c R. A. Smith b Marshall	6
M. A. Lynch	c Parks, b Connor	0
†C. J. Richards	lbw b Tremlett	10
D. M. Ward	lbw b Tremlett	3
N. J. Falkner	b Marshall	31
D. J. Thomas	c James b Connor	34
A. Needham	run out	5
A. H. Gray	not out	2
C. K. Bullen	not out	0
M. P. Bicknell		
Extras	lb 4, nb 7	11
Total	(40 overs, 8 wkts)	146

Fall: 1-17, 2-17, 3-38, 4-45, 5-96, 6-117, 7-143, 8-145

BOWLING	O	M	R	W
Marshall	8	0	27	2
Connor	8	0	21	2
Tremlett	8	0	34	3
James	8	0	32	0
Cowley	8	1	28	0

Umpires: D. G. L. Evans and A. G. T. Whitehead.
Surrey won the toss.
★Captain; †Wicket-keeper.

Hampshire could fairly lay claim to having the strongest batting line-up in the country.

One worry at the start of the year was adequate support for Marshall in the seam bowling department, but both Andrew and Tremlett returned impressive statistics. Andrew took 46 wickets at 21.65 each, as against 10 at 33.10 in 1986, and Tremlett 66 at 18.95, against 40 at 29.37.

So what happened? Hampshire finished in fifth place in the County Championship, one up on 1986, but dropped to seventh in the Sunday League, were knocked out in the second round of the NatWest Trophy and in the quarter-finals of the Benson & Hedges Cup.

The nearest the County got to a trophy was in the Championship, when after a moderate first three months, they suddenly saw the light. A hundred from Nicholas enabled them to defeat Kent; Rajesh Maru produced his best bowling of the year (five for 45) to beat Somerset; Marshall, perhaps inspired by gaining the bowling prize in the MCC's 200th anniversary junket at Lord's, took four for 23 to beat Worcestershire unexpectedly; then Terry hit form with innings of 74 and 83 not out, which combined with nine wickets by Tremlett to produce a fourth successive victory. Within the space of a few days the County had been propelled upwards from the centre of the table to third place.

Anticlimax followed. The final two matches were drawn, so the team subsided to a comfortable fifth – of their total of seven victories, four had come in the last six matches.

The reverse pattern emerged in the Refuge Sunday League, when after nine matches, Hampshire stood second in the table to Derbyshire, only two points separating the two. Later, however, defeats at the hands of Worcestershire, Nottinghamshire and Somerset removed any hopes Hampshire entertained of retaining the title.

In the group C matches of the Benson & Hedges Cup,

Hants v Surrey: Player League 1986
Put in to bat by Butcher, Hampshire's main batsmen did not flourish, but the side was rescued by James, who came in at no. 6 and, as it turned out, shared a vital ninth-wicket stand of 35 with wicket-keeper Parks. Surrey lost four wickets for 45, but Falkner then joined Butcher and the score was doubled for the fifth wicket. Surrey then reached 143 for six, but, needing just seven runs, could only score three and lost two wickets in the process. This victory gave Hampshire the title.

Hampshire in 1987. Standing: V. Isaacs, scorer, C. L. Smith, K. D. James, T. M. Tremlett, S. J. W. Andrew, R. A. Smith, C. A. Connor, R. J. Parks, R. J. Maru. Seated: M. D. Marshall, N. G. Cowley, M. C. J. Nicholas, capt., V. P. Terry, D. R. Turner. Inset: C. G. Greenidge. (Courtesy of Bill Smith)

Greenidge hit 133 off the University attack to produce victory in the first game and Middlesex were overwhelmed by nien wickets in the second game, with Greenidge, Terry and Nicholas enjoying themselves. Martin Crowe, however, had the measure of the Hampshire bowlers in the Somerset fixture. The New Zealander hit 155 not out and his captain, Roebuck made 110, as Somerset reached an unbeatable 319 for two.

Andrew and Marshall struck back in the final Group match, the former taking five for 24 and the latter four for 33 as Essex were removed for 100 and Hampshire made their way into the knock-out section with victory by 86 runs. In the quarter-final, the County met Yorkshire and were demoralised when Greenidge struggled for runs and after 11 overs was run out. Yorkshire won by nine wickets, Metcalfe making 93 not out.

Looking to the immediate future, one bright point of 1987 was the fact that the County did not rely so heavily on Greenidge and Marshall. The former, through knee injury and back trouble, missed about half the matches and the latter was not so fearsome as in 1986. Thus when in 1988 both these Test players are absent due to West Indian commitments, the County will still have batsmen and bowlers capable of holding their own in the highest company.

The Hampshire outlook for 1988 was summed up by Tony Baker, the Club's Chief Executive:

To many people, the prospects for Hampshire for 1988 will seem to be relatively moderate, taking into account that Gordon Greenidge and Malcolm Marshall will be unavailable for most of the season assuming their selection for the West Indies Tour.

Mark Nicholas will, however, lead a talented side determined to improve on the frustrating results of last year. The batting should be very strong, with a good deal of competition for a regular place seeming certain. Despite the loss of Marshall, the bowling attack should be varied and effective, particularly as further improvement still is expected from Stephen Andrew.

Many of the younger players are eagerly looking forward to having an opportunity in 1988 to stake a claim for a regular 1st XI place. If the talent that undoubtedly exists can be developed properly, then the prospects for 1988 and succeeding years will be very exciting.

BIOGRAPHICAL DETAILS OF HAMPSHIRE PLAYERS

NAME AND EXTENT OF CAREER	BIRTH-PLACE	DATE OF BIRTH	DATE OF DEATH
Anthony John Abdy *1881*		26. 4.1856	4. 7.1924
Cecil Halliday Abercrombie *1913*	Mozufferpore	12. 4.1886	31. 5.1916
J. Acton *1880–1882*			
Geoffrey Coker Arding Adams *1928–1930*	London	24. 5.1909	
Ronald Aird *1920–1938*	London	4. 5.1902	16. 8.1986
Robert Berkeley Airey *1911*	Southminster	21. 9.1874	23. 6.1933
Marmaduke Cecil Allenby *1900*	York	30. 8.1873	16. 4.1932
Harry Surtees Altham *1919–1923*	Camberley	30.11.1888	11. 3.1965
Steven John Walter Andrew *1984–*	London	27. 1.1966	
William Andrew *1897–1898*	Bournemouth	22. 3.1869	30. 3.1911
Arthur John Andrews *1880–1885*	Southampton	8.1856	26. 2.1943
Clifford Jack Andrews *1938–1948*	Swindon	6. 8.1912	
Francis Godfrey Bertram Arkwright *1923*	Bramdean	30. 1.1905	1. 7.1942
Edward Leathley Armitage *1919–1925*		1891	24.11.1957
H. H. Armstrong *1882–1885*			
Alban Charles Phidias Arnold *1912–1914*	Fareham	19.11.1892	7. 7.1916
John Arnold *1929–1950*	Cowley	30.11.1907	3. 4.1984
Adrian Nigel Aymes	Southampton	4. 6.1964	
Francis Hugh Bacon *1895–1911*	Colombo	24. 6.1869	31.10.1915
John Badcock *1906–1908*	Christchurch	4.10.1883	24. 8.1940
James Bailey *1927–1952*	Shawford	6. 4.1908	
Michael John Bailey *1979–1982*	Cheltenham	1. 8.1954	
W. P. Bailey *1864*			
Paul-Jan Bakker *1986–*	Vlaardingen	19. 8.1957	
William Stanford Baldock *1877–1882*	Chilworth	20. 1.1847	20. 8.1923
Dennis Oliver Baldry *1959–1962*	Acton	26.12.1931	
Henry Baldwin *1877–1905*	Wokingham	27.11.1860	12. 1.1935
Amyas Evelyn Michael Baring *1930–1939*	Roehampton	21. 1.1910	29. 8.1986
Henry Michael Barnard *1952–1966*	Portsmouth	18. 7.1933	
Edward Barrett *1885*		11. 6.1846	23.12.1923
Edward Ivo Medhurst Barrett *1896–1925*	Pitt	22. 6.1879	10. 7.1950
Peter Barrett *1975–1976*	Winchester	3. 6.1955	28.10.1983
Edward Leslie Dayrell Bartley *1931*	Clifton, Glos	2. 3.1896	7.10.1969
Charles Gerard Barton *1895–1896*	Romsey	26. 6.1860	3.11.1919
Harold George Mitford Barton *1910–1912*	Christchurch	10.10.1882	3. 7.1970
Victor Alexander Barton *1895–1902*	Netley	6.10.1867	23. 3.1906

Name	Place	Born	Died
Richard Bateman *1883*	Farnham	1849	5.11.1913
Frederick Stanley Bates *1920*	Lambourn	25. 2.1899	13. 8.1969
Sir Frederick Thomas Arthur Hervey Bathurst *1864–1866*	London	13. 3.1833	20. 5.1900
Lionel Hervey Bathurst *1875*	Clarendon Park	7. 7.1849	4. 5.1908
Sydney Wilford Beadle *1911*	Wadhwan, India	9.11.1885	24. 7.1937
H. Bedford *1882*			
Gordon Belcher *1905*	Brighton	26. 9.1885	16. 5.1915
Sir Henry William Russell Bencraft *1876–1896*	Southampton	4. 3.1858	25.12.1943
Richard Alexander Bennett *1896–1899*	Bournemouth	12.12.1872	16. 7.1953
Bernhard Walter Bentinck *1900–1902*	Hartley Wintney	16. 7.1877	27. 6.1931
Henry Beauclerk Bethune *1885–1897*	Horsham	16.11.1844	16. 4.1912
Guy Newcombe Bignell *1904–1925*	Mozufferpore	3.12.1886	10. 6.1965
Hugh Glennie Bignell *1901–1902*	Mozufferpore	4.10.1882	6. 5.1907
Percy John Bird *1900*	West Cowes	27. 5.1877	11.11.1942
Lennox Graham Black *1903–1919*		1880	1950
David Eustace Blake *1949–1958*	Havant	27. 4.1925	
John Philip Blake *1937–1939*	Portsmouth	17.11.1917	3. 6.1944
Frederick (John) Blundell *1880*	Romsey	1851	26. 4.1929
Cecil Herbert Bodington *1901–1902*	Suffield	20. 1.1880	11. 4.1917
Robert Henry Dundas Bolton *1913–1922*		13. 1.1893	30.10.1964
Lothian George Bonham-Carter *1880–1885*	Petersfield	29. 9.1858	13. 1.1927
Clement Booth *1875–1880*	Friskney	11. 5.1842	1. 7.1926
Horace Alexander William Bowell *1902–1927*	Oxford	27. 4.1880	28. 8.1957
Norman Henry Bowell *1924*	Oxford	2. 2.1904	5. 3.1943
Edward Ernest Bowen *1864*	Glenmore, Ireland	30. 3.1936	8. 4.1901
J. Bower *1897–1898*			
George Stuart Boyes *1921–1939*	Southampton	31. 3.1899	11. 2.1973
Sir Evelyn Ridley Bradford *1895–1905*	Goonah, India	16. 4.1869	14. 9.1914
Rev John Richard Bridger *1946–1954*	Dulwich	8. 4.1920	14. 7.1986
Charles Edward Briggs *1900*	Ashbourne	17. 9.1873	16.12.1949
Bernard Maynard Lucas Brodhurst *1897*	Benares, India	6. 8.1873	27. 4.1915
Sir Reginald Alexander Dallas Brooks *1919–1921*	Cambridge	2. 8.1896	22. 3.1966
George Brown *1908–1933*	Cowley	6.10.1887	3.12.1964
Charles Phipps Brutton *1921–1930*	Southsea	20. 1.1899	11. 5.1964
Septimus Brutton *1904*	Newcastle on Tyne	1869	30. 9.1933
William Dalton Buck *1969*	Southampton	30. 9.1946	

Edward Hastings Buckland *1895*	Laleham-on-Thames	20. 6.1864	10. 2.1906
William Lloyd Budd *1934–1946*	Hawkley	25.10.1913	23. 8.1986
Charles Budden *1900*	Fareham	18. 7.1879	26.11.1969
James Thomas W. F. Budden *1912*	Southampton	1882	1965
G. Bull *1900*			
Mervyn Derek Burden *1953–1963*	Southampton	4.10.1930	
Lindsay Bury *1877*	Withington	8. 7.1857	30.10.1935
Richard Dawson Busk *1919*	Marylebone	21. 6.1895	24.12.1961
Arthur Maitland Byng *1905*	Ireland	26. 9.1872	14. 9.1914
Alexander Richard Cadell *1923–1927*	Ferozepore	19. 8.1900	14. 5.1928
Edward Henry Cadogan *1933–1935*	Kasauli, India	11. 9.1908	
Henry Calder *1882–1885*	South Stoneham	14. 4.1858	19. 5.1938
Alistair Keyon Campbell *1908–1909*	South Stoneham	29. 5.1890	16. 6.1943
Victor Henry Douglas Cannings *1950–1959*	Brighton	3. 4.1919	
Robert Graham Caple *1961–1967*	Chiswick	8.12.1939	
George Carter *1869–1878*	Warbleton	4. 8.1846	unknown
Donald Colin Cartridge *1953*	Southampton	31.12.1933	
Richard Arthur Carty *1949–1954*	Southampton	28. 7.1922	4. 3.1984
George Henry Case *1864*	Fareham	4. 4.1839	21. 4.1911
Alan Terrance Castell *1961–1971*	Oxford	6. 8.1943	
Edward Postle Gwyn Causton *1919*	Fulham	1877	18. 4.1957
Aubrey Bruce Cooper Cecil *1876*	Toddington	10. 3.1847	unknown
Egerton Dodge Cooper Cecil *1875*		1853	25. 9.1928
Geoffrey Henry Barrington Chance *1913*	Burghfield	16.12.1893	11. 7.1987
G. Chandler *1865*			
Frank Henry Charters *1913*	Plymouth	1884	1953
Thomas Alexander Chignell *1901–1904*	Havant	31.10.1880	25. 8.1965
Ian James Chivers *1985–1987*	Southampton	5.11.1964	
George Lamount Cole *1909–1911*	Hastings	5. 9.1885	14.10.1964
Thomas Hugh Collins *1935*	Nottingham	4. 3.1895	19. 5.1964
Cardigan Adolphous Connor *1984–*	Anguilla, W. I.	26. 3.1961	
Oswald Wykeham Cornwallis *1921*	Linton	16. 3.1894	28. 1.1974
Robert Michael Henry Cottam *1963–1971*	Cleethorpes	16.10.1944	
Richard Charles Lucy Court *1937–1939*	Ambala, India	23.10.1916	10. 4.1974
Alexander Gordon Cowie *1910*	Lymington	27. 2.1889	7. 4.1916
Nigel George Cowley *1974–*	Shaftesbury	1. 3.1953	
Cosmo Stafford Crawley *1923*	Chelsea	27. 5.1904	
William Leonard Charles Creese *1928–1939*	Parktown, S Africa	28.12.1907	9. 3.1974
Edward Hugh Crofton *1881*	Plymouth	7. 9.1854	15. 5.1882
Edmund Sclater Crofts *1885*	Winchester	23. 1.1859	23.12.1939

John Edward Crookes *1920*	Horncastle	7. 3.1890	8. 9.1948
Rev James Gordon Crowdy *1875–1884*	Faringdon	2. 7.1847	16.12.1918
George Cull *1877*	Lymington	1856	9. 5.1898
Cecil Edmund Currie *1881–1885*	Brightwalton	4. 4.1861	2. 1.1937
Christopher Colin Curzon *1981*	Lenton	22.12.1958	
James Herbert Darby *1884–1897*	Fareham	26.10.1865	7.11.1943
Reginald Dare *1949–1954*	Blandford	26.11.1921	
Thomas Henry Knyvett Dashwood *1904*	Hitchin	3. 1.1876	24. 1.1929
Henry Gwyn Saunders Davies *1883*	Pembroke	2. 2.1865	4.12.1934
Gilbert Wilkinson Dawson *1947–1949*	Bradford	9.12.1916	24. 5.1969
Harold Dawson *1947–1948*	Todmorden	1. 9.1919	
Harold Lindsay Vernon Day *1922–1931*	Darjeeling	12. 8.1898	15. 6.1972
— Dean *1907*			
Thomas Arthur Dean *1939–1949*	Gosport	21.11.1920	
Marmaduke William Deane *1895*	Petersham	23. 5.1857	1936
Alexander Frederick Henry			
Debnam *1950–1951*	Belvedere	12.10.1922	
Arthur Henry Delme-Radcliffe *1896–1900*	South		
	Tidworth	23.11.1870	30. 6.1950
Harold Alfred Denham *1896*	Howrah, India	13.10.1872	25. 2.1946
William Guy Dible *1883–1885*	Southampton	5.11.1861	15. 8.1894
Cecil Egerton Dixon *1929*		21. 7.1903	3. 3.1973
William Thomas Francis Dodd *1931–1935*	Steep	8. 3.1908	
Lewis Hugh John Dorey *1925*	St Albans	23.10.1901	
J. H. Down *1914*			
H. R. Downer *1946*			
Edward Joseph Drake *1931–1936*	Southampton	16. 8.1912	
Horatio Norris Dumbleton *1884*	Ferozepore	23.10.1858	18.12.1935
Arthur James Duncan *1878–1883*	Southampton	1856	unknown
Dunbar Wilson Johnston			
Duncan *1875–1885*	Southampton	8. 7.1852	12.12.1919
Arthur Murray Duthie *1911*	Saharanpur	12. 6.1881	3. 6.1973
Henry John Dutton *1875*	Kensington	17. 1.1847	1. 1.1935
Edward Desmond Russell Eagar *1946–1957*	Cheltenham	8.12.1917	13. 9.1977
Charles Vernon Eccles *1870–1875*	Davenham	20. 8.1843	21. 2.1890
Edward Lee Ede *1864–1870*	Southampton	22. 2.1834	7. 7.1908
Edward Murray Charles Ede *1902–1906*	Southampton	24. 4.1881	unknown
George Matthew Ede *1864–1869*	Southampton	22. 2.1834	13. 3.1870
John Drennan Eggar *1938*	Nowshera	1.12.1916	3. 5.1983
Richard Burtenshaw Elms *1977–1978*	Sutton, Surrey	5. 4.1949	
Kevin St John Dennis Emery *1982–1983*	Swindon	28. 2.1960	
Edward Apsey English *1898–1901*	Dorking	1. 1.1864	8. 9.1966
Alfred Englefield Evans *1919–1920*	South Africa	30. 1.1884	29.12.1944
Alfred Henry Evans *1885*	Madras	14. 6.1858	26. 3.1934

Name	Place of birth	Born	Died
Alfred John Evans *1908–1920*	Newtown, Berks	1. 5.1889	18. 9.1960
Bertram Sutton Evans *1900–1909*	Guildford	17.12.1872	2. 3.1919
Dudley MacNeil Evans *1904–1911*	South Africa	11.12.1886	18.12.1972
James Evans *1913–1921*		14. 7.1891	26. 8.1973
Ralph du Boulay Evans *1912*	Newtown, Berks	1.10.1891	27. 7.1929
William Henry Brereton Evans *1902–1910*	South Africa	29. 1.1883	7. 8.1913
Rodney Noel Exton *1946*	Bournemouth	28.12.1927	
James Fellowes *1883–1885*	Cape of Good Hope	25. 8.1841	3. 5.1916
Walter George Feltham *1884*	Ringwood	1864	23. 9.1904
Stanley Fenley *1935*	Kingston-on-Thames	4. 1.1896	2. 9.1972
Albert Edward Fielder *1911–1913*	Sarisbury Green	3. 4.18890	29. 4.1947
Walter George Fielder *1923*	Fareham	1899	7. 1.1968
Reginald Wordsworth Cecil Fisher *1898*	Grantham	17. 4.1872	31.12.1939
Raymond David Flood *1956–1960*	Southampton	20.11.1935	
Harold Thomas Forster *1911*	Winchester	14.11.1878	29. 5.1918
Henry William Forster *1885–1895*	South End, Kent	31. 1.1866	15. 1.1936
Francis George Foster *1876*	Havant	6.11.1848	unknown
Robert St Leger Fowler *1924*	Enfield, Ireland	7. 4.1891	13. 6.1925
Thomas Colcott Fox *1875*	Broughton, Hants	1849	11. 4.1916
Sir Edward Boscawen Frederick *1903–1904*	Wem	29. 6.1880	26.10.1956
John St John Frederick *1864–1869*	London	6. 1.1846	10. 9.1907
Frederick William Freemantle *1900*	Whitchurch, Hants	1871	12. 9.1943
Henry Tobias Frere *1864–1866*	Odiham	27. 9.1830	15. 8.1881
Charles Anthony Fry *1960*	Henley-in-Arden	14. 1.1940	
Charles Burgess Fry *1909–1921*	West Croydon	25. 4.1872	7. 9.1956
Stephen Fry *1922–1931*	Portsmouth	23. 5.1899	26. 8.1976
Charles Garnet Fynn *1930–1931*	Marylebone	24. 4.1897	26. 8.1976
Henry Gale *1865–1866*	Winchester	11. 7.1836	3. 3.1898
John George Galpin *1875–1880*	Gosport	13. 1.1843	unknown
Christopher Henry Gandy *1900*	Bethnal Green	1867	18. 6.1907
Thomas Parry Garnier *1864*	Longford	22. 2.1841	18. 3.1898
Leslie Hewitt Gay *1900*	Brighton	24. 3.1871	1.11.1949
Jack Sydney Bates Gentry *1919*	Wanstead	4.10.1899	16. 4.1978
Herbert Gladstone Gibbons *1925–1928*	Bradfield, Berks	12. 3.1905	13. 1.1963
Richard Michael Charles Gilliat *1966–1978*	Ware	20. 5.1944	

Name	Place	Born	Died
Frederick Gladdon *1905*		9. 6.1881	unknown
John Frederick Godfrey *1939–1947*	Oxford	1917	
Christopher Frederick Evelyn Goldie *1983–1985*	Johannesburg	2.11.1960	
James Parrington Gornall *1923*	Farnborough, Hants	22. 9.1899	13.11.1983
Shaun Francis Graf *1980*	Melbourne, Austr	19. 5.1957	
Mark Gravett *1899–1900*	Milford, Surrey	11. 2.1865	8. 2.1938
James Roy Gray *1948–1966*	Southampton	19. 5.1926	
George Price Greenfield *1875*	Winchester	24. 1.1843	3. 9.1917
Hubert McLean Greenhill *1901*	Christchurch	18. 9.1881	22. 1.1926
Cuthbert Gordon Greenidge *1970–*	St Peter, Barbados	1. 5.1951	
Sir Granville George Greenwood *1875*	London	3. 1.1850	27.10.1928
John Thomas Gregory *1913*	Chesterfield	1887	27.10.1914
John Glennie Greig *1901–1922*	Mhow, India	24.10.1871	24. 5.1958
Frederick Albert Gross *1924–1929*	Southampton	17. 9.1902	11. 3.1975
David Radclyffe Guard *1946–1949*	Romsey	19. 5.1929	12.12.1978
Charles Richards Gunner *1878*	Bishops Waltham	7. 1.1853	4. 2.1934
John Hugh Gunner *1906–1907*	Bishops Waltham	17. 5.1884	9. 4.1918
George Gilbert Gutteres *1882*	Kensington	11.10.1859	2. 3.1898
Herbert Denys Hake *1920–1925*	Bournemouth	8.11.1894	12. 4.1975
Clifford Geoffrey Hall *1933–1935*	Breamore	19. 1.1902	
E. Hall *1880–1885*			
Patrick Martin Hall *1919–1926*	Portsmouth	14. 3.1894	5. 8.1941
Jonathan James Ean Hardy *1984–1985*	Nakuru, Kenya	2.10.1960	
Lewis Harfield *1925–1931*	Cheriton	16. 8.1905	19.11.1985
James Henry Hargreaves *1884–1885*		1859	11. 4.1922
Reginald Gervic Hargreaves *1875–1885*	Accrington	13.10.1852	13. 2.1926
Frederick Vere Harold *1909–1912*	New Forest	1888	17. 2.1964
George Woodrouffe Harris *1899*	Chelsea	6. 8.1880	10. 7.1954
Henry Edward Harris *1880*	Brighton	8. 6.1854	8.12.1923
Bernard Reginald Stanhope Harrison *1957–1962*	Worcester	28. 9.1934	
Gerald Cartmell Harrison *1914–1920*		8.10.1883	
Leonard Harrison *1939–1966*	Mudeford	5. 6.1922	
William Henry Harrison *1902*		1866	23.12.1936
Frank Northam Harvey *1899–1900*	Southampton	19.12.1864	10.11.1939
Peter Haslop *1962*	Midhurst	17. 9.1941	
Edward Brownlow Haygarth *1875*	Circencester	26. 4.1854	14. 4.1915
Ernest Hayter *1935–1937*	Poole	8. 9.1913	

Montague William Hayter *1904*	Ringwood	1871	6. 5.1948
A. J. Hayward *1925–1926*		12. 9.1906	
Richard Edward Hayward *1981–1982*	Hillingdon	15. 2.1954	
Edwin Hills Hazelton *1883*	Southampton	16.12.1861	25. 7.1916
Allan Borman Heath *1883–1885*	East Woodham	19. 1.1865	unknown
George Edward Mansell Heath *1937–1949*	Hong Kong	20. 2.1913	
Malcolm Heath *1954–1962*	Bournemouth	9. 3.1934	
Geoffrey George Lockwood Hebden *1937–1951*	London	14. 7.1918	
Walter Coote Hedley *1905*	Taunton	12.12.1865	27.12.1937
Edward Hemsted *1866–1869*	Whitchurch, Hants	10.10.1846	12. 3.1884
Anthony Alfred Henley *1866*	Sherbourne	1846	14.12.1916
Robert Henley *1875*	Sherborne	10. 6.1851	21. 3.1889
Oswald William Herman *1929–1948*	Cowley	18. 9.1907	24. 6.1987
Robert Stephen Herman *1972–1977*	Southampton	30.11.1946	
Christopher Heseltine *1895–1904*	London	26.11.1869	13. 6.1944
Hesketh Vernon Hesketh-Prichard *1900–1913*	Jhansi, India	17.11.1876	14. 6.1922
Anthony Ewart Ledger Hill *1920–1930*	Spurshot	14. 7.1901	25.10.1986
Arthur James Ledger Hill *1895–1921*	Bassett	26. 7.1871	6. 9.1950
Gerald Hill *1932–1954*	Brook, Hants	15. 4.1913	
Michael John Hill *1973–1976*	Harwell	1. 7.1951	
Basil Ferguson Burnett Hitchcock *1896*	Medway	3. 3.1877	23.11.1938
John Wakefield Holder *1968–1972*	St George, Barbados	19. 3.1945	
Thomas Vernon Hollingworth *1929*		27. 7.1907	2.10.1973
Henry Holmes *1864–1878*	Romsey	11.11.1833	6. 1.1913
Arthur George Holt *1935–1948*	Southampton	8. 4.1911	
Frank Jesse Hopkins *1906–1911*	Birmingham	20. 6.1875	16. 1.1930
Henry Horton *1953–1967*	Hereford	18. 4.1923	
Alexander Lindsay Hosie *1913–1935*	Wenchow, China	6. 8.1890	11. 6.1967
Sir Alan Geoffrey Hotham *1901*	Edinburgh	3.10.1876	10. 7.1965
William Humphrey *1864*	Mitcham	15. 9.1843	24. 2.1918
Walter Alexander Humphreys *1900*	Southsea	28.10.1849	23. 3.1924
Frederick James Hyland *1924*	Battle	1894	27. 2.1964
Hector Henry Hyslop *1876–1877*	Southampton	13.12.18400	11. 9.1920
Alexander Colin David Ingleby-Mackenzie *1951–1965*	Darmouth	15. 9.1933	
Lionel Charles Ramsbottom Isherwood *1919–1923*	Portsmouth	13. 4.1891	30. 9.1970
Frederick Jackman *1875–1877*	Fareham	15. 5.1841	1891
Kevan David James *1985–*	Lambeth	18. 3.1961	

Name	Place	Born	Died
Thomas George Cairnes Jameson *1930–1931*		1908	
Tom Ormsby Jameson *1919–1932*	Clonsila, Ireland	4. 4.1892	6. 2.1965
Arthur Jaques *1913–1914*	Shanghai	7. 3.1888	27. 9.1915
Arthur Frederick Jeffreys *1876–1878*	London	7. 4.1848	14. 2.1906
Frederick Gilbert Gardiner Jellicoe *1877–1880*	Southampton	24. 2.1858	29. 7.1927
William Vincent Jephson *1903–1919*	Ayot St Peter	6.10.1873	12.11.1956
Robert Wilfred Fairey Jesson *1907–1910*	Southampton	17. 6.1886	22. 2.1917
Gilbert Laird Osborne Jessop *1933*	Kensington	6. 9.1906	
Trevor Edward Jesty *1966–1984*	Gosport	2. 6.1948	
Guy Alonzo Frederick William Jewell *1952*	Axford	6.10.1916	23.12.1965
Alexander Colin Johnston *1902–1919*	Derby	26. 1.1884	27.12.1952
Henry James Jolliffe *1902*	Fordingbridge	1867	1909
George Leonard Jones *1937*	Lockerbie	11. 2.1909	6. 6.1944
Arthur Kenneth Judd *1925–1935*	Staines	1. 1.1904	
William George Judd *1878*	New Forest	23.10.1845	12. 3.1925
George Demetrius Katinakis *1904–1905*	London	25. 7.1873	15. 5.1943
Henry George Kay *1882*	Havant	3.10.1851	8. 9.1922
James Levett Kaye *1881*	Barnet	27.12.1861	17.11.1917
Geoffrey Leyden Keith *1962–1967*	Winchester	19.11.1937	26.12.1975
Charles Edward Compton Kendle *1899*	Amesbury	10. 2.1876	3. 1.1954
William James Kendle *1869–1878*	Romsey	9. 4.1847	30. 1.1920
John Adam Gaskell Kennard *1919*	Chelsea	8.11.1884	6. 4.1949
Alexander Stuart Kennedy *1907–1936*	Edinburgh	24. 1.1891	15.11.1959
Arthur Edwards Kimish *1946*	Southampton	5. 7.1917	
J. King *1882*			
Frederick George Kitchener *1896–1903*	Hartley Row	2. 7.1871	1948
Arthur Harry Kneller *1924–1926*	Kingsclere	28. 4.1894	19. 7.1969
Arthur Egerton Knight *1913–1923*	Godalming	7. 9.1887	10. 3.1956
Charles James Knott *1938–1954*	Southampton	26.11.1914	
Sir Francis Eden Lacey *1880–1897*	Wareham	10.10.1859	26. 5.1946
Bruce Lamb *1898–1901*	Andover	25. 8.1878	22. 3.1932
Walter Lancashire *1935–1937*	Hemsworth	28.10.1903	7. 7.1981
William Thomas Langford *1902–1908*	New Forest	5.10.1875	20. 2.1957
Percy Edward Lawrie *1921–1928*	London	12.12.1902	
Howard Maurice Lawson *1935–1937*	Bournemouth	22. 5.1914	
Maurice Bertie Lawson *1907–1919*	Christchurch	28. 2.1885	8. 8.1961
Charles William Leat *1878–1885*	Ringwood	6.12.1855	1937
Arthur Michael Lee *1933*	Liphook	22. 8.1913	14. 1.1983
Edward Cornwall Lee *1896–1909*	Torquay	18. 6.1877	16. 6.1942

Frederick Archibald Gresham Leveson-Gower *1899–1900*	Titsey	20. 2.1871	3.10.1946
Arthur Hamilton Lewis *1929*	Maseru, Basutoland	16. 9.1901	23. 8.1980
Richard Victor Lewis *1967–1976*	Winchester	6. 8.1947	
Elisha Edward Light *1898–1900*	Winchester	1. 9.1873	12. 3.1952
William Frederick Light *1897–1898*	St Faiths	1. 3.1880	10.11.1930
Edwin Lineham *1898*	Portsmouth	1879	12. 8.1949
Francis Wallis Lipscomb *1881–1882*		20. 7.1834	3.10.1906
William Henry Lipscomb *1866–1867*	Winchester	20.11.1846	9. 4.1918
Daintes Abbia Livingstone *1959–1972*	St John's, Antigua	21. 9.1933	
Walter Herbert Livsey *1913–1929*	Todmorden	23. 9.1893	12. 9.1978
Charles Bennett Llewellyn *1899–1910*	Pietermaritz-burg	26. 9.1876	7. 6.1964
Lewis Vaughan Lodge *1900*	Darlington	21.12.1872	21.10.1916
Okeover Butler Longcroft *1869–1870*	Havant	3.1850	7. 9.1871
George Henry Longman *1875–1885*	Farnborough	3. 8.1852	19. 8.1938
John Carr Lord *1864*	Hobart, Tasmania	17. 8,1844	25. 5.1911
Raymond Henry Arnold Davison Love *1923*	Chatham	11. 5.1888	12.10.1962
H. F. Lowe *1882*			
William Geoffrey Lowndes Frith Lowndes *1924–1935*	Wandsworth	24. 1.1898	23. 5.1982
Arthur John Hamilton Luard *1897*	Watlair, India	3. 9.1861	22. 5.1944
Charles Frank Lucas *1864–1880*	Stowe	25.11.1843	27. 9.1919
Verner Valentine Luckin *1910–1912*	Woking	14. 2.1892	28.11.1931
Algernon Hay Lushington *1870–1877*	Lyndhurst	29. .9.1847	13. 9.1930
Joseph Lynn *1875*	London	1856	1927
Sir George Hamilton D'Oyly Lyon *1907*	Bankipore, India	3.10.1883	20. 8.1947
Sydney Gratien Adair Maartensz *1919*	Colombo	14. 4.1882	10. 9.1967
Walter Nelson McBride *1925–1929*	Croydon	27.11.1904	30. 1.1974
Neil Thomas McCorkell *1932–1951*	Portsmouth	23. 3.1912	
Harold Clark McDonell *1908–1921*	Wimbledon	19. 9.1882	23. 7.1966
Charles Edward McGibbon *1919*	Portsmouth	1880	2. 4.1954
Richard Johnston McIlwaine *1969–1970*	Southsea	16. 3.1950	
Arthur Seymour McIntyre *1920–1923*	Hartley Wintney	29. 5.1889	14. 3.1945
Percy Alec Mackenzie *1938–1939*	Canterbury	5.10.1918	
Frederick Albert McLaren *1908*	Farnham	19. 8.1874	24. 9.1952
Alastair MacLeod *1914–1938*	Kensington	12.11.1894	24. 4.1982
Steven John Malone *1980–1984*	Chelmsford	19.10.1953	

Name	Place	Date	Date
John Errol Manners *1936–1948*	Exeter	25. 9.1914	
George Mannings *1864*	Downton	13.10.1843	28.11.1876
Robert Marsack Manser *1904*	Tunbridge	1880	15. 2.1955
Edward Charles Mariner *1896*	Winchester	1877	10. 5.1949
Malcolm Denzil Marshall *1979–1987*	St Michael, Barbados	18. 4.1958	
Roy Edwin Marshall *1953–1972*	St Thomas, Barbados	255. 4.1930	
Charles Martin *1869–1870*	Breamore	6. 8.1836	28. 3.1878
George Martin *1898–1899*		29.11.1875	unknown
J. Martin *1904*			
William Martin *1867*	Nursling	19. 2.1844	27. 5.1871
Rajesh Janan Maru *1984–1987*	Nairobi	28.10.1962	
Henry Maturin *1864–1882*	Fanetglebe, Ireland	5. 4.1842	24. 2.1920
William Herbert Maundrell *1900*	Nagasaki, Japan	5.11.1876	17. 6.1958
John May *1867–1870*	Southampton	26. 9.1845	unknown
Charles Philip Mead *1905–1936*	Battersea	9. 3.1887	26. 3.1958
H. J. B. Meaden *1881*			
Basil George von Brandis Melle *1914–1921*	Somerset, S Africa	31. 3.1891	8. 1.1966
Edward John Michell *1880*	Steyning	15. 6.1853	5. 5.1900
Tony Charles Middleton *1984–*	Winchester	1. 2.1964	
Sir Henry Paulet St John Mildmay *1881–1884*	London	28. 4.1853	24. 4.1916
Henry Misselbrook *1869*	Otterbourne	16.12.1832	11. 7.1895
John Cornelius Moberly *1877*	Winchester	22. 4.1848	29. 1.1928
William Moorcroft *1911*			
John William Moore *1910–1913*	Hartley Wintney	29. 4.1891	23. 6.1980
Richard Henry Moore *1931–1939*	Bournemouth	14.11.1913	
Henry John Mordaunt *1885*	London	12. 7.1867	15. 1.1939
Robert Harry Mornement *1906*	Wayland, Norfolk	15. 8.1873	16. 4.1948
Thomas James Mottram *1972–1976*	Liverpool	7. 9.1945	
Henry Murgatroyd *1883*	New Swindon	19. 9.1853	15. 3.1905
Andrew Joseph Murtagh *1973–1977*	Dublin	6. 5.1949	
John Alfred Newman *1906–1930*	Southsea	12.11.1884	21:12.1973
Edward Newton *1900*		31.10.1871	9. 5.1906
Mark Charles Jefford Nicholas *1978–1987*	London	29. 9.1957	
Duncan Victor Norbury *1905–1906*	New Forest	3. 8.1887	23.10.1972
Frank Henry Nugent *1904*	Basingstoke	5. 9.1880	12. 3.1942
Eric Olivier *1911*	Outschoorn, S Africa	24.11.1888	1. 6.1928

Name	Place		
Sidney Richard Olivier *1895*		1. 3.1870	21. 1.1932
Hugh James Orr *1902–1907*	Deniliquin, NSW	21. 1.1878	19. 4.1946
David Robert O'Sullivan *1971–1973*	Palmerston North	16.11.1944	
Thomas Heritage Page *1900*	Canterbury	28. 5.1872	7.12.1953
Cecil Howard Palmer *1899–1907*	Eastbourne	14. 7.1873	26. 7.1915
Rodney Howell Palmer *1930–1933*	Basingstoke	24.11.1907	
Cecil Gerard Alexander Paris *1933–1948*	Kirkee, India	20. 8.1911	
William Paris *1875–1881*	Old Alresford	29. 4.1840	12. 1.1915
Frederick Anthony Vivian Parker *1946*	London	11. 2.1913	
John Palmer Parker *1926–1933*	Portsmouth	29.11.1902	9. 8.1984
Robert James Parks *1980–*	Cuckfield	15. 6.1959	
Walter Dyett Parsons *1882*	Southampton	1861	24.12.1939
Alfred William Parvin *1885*	Southampton	1860	1916
George Passmore *1896*	Plympton	1852	8. 2.1935
Kenneth Edwin Paver *1925–1926*	Dover	4.10.1903	
Stanley Herbert Hicks Pearce *1885*	Totton	21. 9.1863	unknown
Walter Kennedy Pearce *1923–1926*	South Stoneham	2. 4.1893	31. 7.1960
Francis William Pember *1885*	Hatfield	16. 8.1862	19. 1.1954
Henry Wilfred Persse *1905–1909*	Southampton	19. 9.1885	28. 6.1918
Howard William Phillips *1899–1902*	Isle of Wight	20. 4.1872	17. 3.1960
James Daniel Piachaud *1960*	Colombo	1. 3.1937	
Albert Alexander Pillans *1896*		25. 2.1869	28.11.1901
Alfred Pink *1885*	Fratton Bridge	1. 6.1855	1931
Raymond Walter Charles Pitman *1954–1959*	Bartley	21. 2.1933	
Sir Henry Meredyth Plowden *1865*	Sylhet, India	16. 9.1840	8. 1.1920
Nicholas Edward Julien Pocock *1976–1984*	Maracaibo	15.12.1951	
Brig-Gen Robert Montagu Poore *1898–1906*	Carysfort, Ireland	20. 3.1866	14. 7.1938
Albert Lavington Porter *1895*	Croydon	21. 1.1864	14.12.1937
Arthur Ernest Pothecary *1927–1946*	Southampton	1. 3.1906	
Sidney George Pothecary *1912–1920*	Southampton	26. 9.1886	1976
Ernest Ormsby Powell *1884–1885*	Liverpool	19. 1.1861	29. 3.1928
Walter Norman Powys *1877–1878*	Titchmarsh	28. 7.1849	7. 1.1892
Rowland Edmund Prothero *1875–1883*	Clifton-upon-Teme	6. 9.1851	1. 7.1937
Roland Barton Proud *1938–1939*	Bishop Auckland	19. 9.1919	27.10.1961
Ralph Oliver Prouton *1949–1954*	Southampton	1. 3.1926	

Francis William Drummond			
Quinton *1895–1900*	Fyzabad	27.12.1865	5.11.1926
James Maurice Quinton *1895–1899*	Simla	12. 5.1874	22.12.1922
George Berkley Raikes *1900–1902*	Carleton-		
	Dorehoe	14. 3.1873	18.12.1966
Victor Joseph Ransom *1947–1950*	New Malden	17. 5.1917	
John Rooke Rawlence *1934*	Lymington	23. 9.1915	
Alan William Harrington			
Rayment *1949–1958*	Finchley	29. 5.1928	
Robert Raynbird *1878*	Whitchurch,		
	Hants	29. 6.1851	26.12.1920
Walter Raynbird *1880–1881*	Basingstoke	1. 6.1854	6. 5.1891
Ernest George Read *1903*	Portsmouth	8.10.1874	21. 3.1921
— Redhouse *1900*			
Barry Lindsay Reed *1958–1970*	Southsea	17. 9.1937	
Elvis Leroy Reifer *1984*	Barbados	21. 3.1961	
Ernest Richard Remnant *1908–1922*	Croydon	1. 5.1881	18. 3.1969
John Michael Rice *1971–1982*	Chandlers Ford	23.10.1949	
Arthur Carew Richards *1884–1904*	Grays	20. 2.1865	29.11.1930
Barry Anderson Richards *1968–1978*	Durban,		
	S Africa	21. 7.1945	
Cyril James Ridding Richards *1895*	Andover	14. 7.1870	27.10.1933
Charles Henry Ridding *1861–1864*	Winchester	26.11.1825	13. 3.1905
Alfred Bayley Ridley *1884–1885*	Hollington	14.12.1859	26. 3.1898
Arthur William Ridley *1875–1878*	Newbury	11. 9.1852	10. 8.1916
Anthony Geoffrey Jordan			
Rimell *1946–1950*	Kasauli, India	29. 8.1928	
Anderson Montgomery Everton			
Roberts *1973–1978*	Urlings Village	29. 1.1951	
Charles Robson *1895–1906*	Twickenham	20. 6.1859	27. 9.1943
David John Rock *1976–1979*	Southsea	20. 4.1957	
H. J. Rogers *1912–1914*			
Neville Hamilton Rogers *1946–1955*	Oxford	9. 3.1918	
Colin Roper *1957*	Dorchester	25. 7.1936	
Donald George B. Roper *1947*	Botley	1922	
H. Russell *1884*			
William Cecil Russell *1898*	Rokewood,		
	Austr	25. 4.1866	9. 5.1929
Arnold Page Rutherford *1912*	Highclere	2. 9.1892	23. 7.1980
John Seymour Rutherford *1913*	Highclere	27. 2.1890	14. 4.1943
Francis Peter Ryan *1919–1920*	New Jersey,		
	USA	14.11.1888	5. 1.1954
Peter James Sainsbury *1954–1976*	Southampton	13. 6.1934	

227

George Amelius Crawshay			
Sandeman *1913*	London	18. 4.1883	26. 4.1915
William Ernest Newnham Scott *1927*	Ryde	31. 5.1903	
Alfred Seymour *1870*		16. 2.1843	31. 1.1897
Charles Read Seymour *1880–1885*	Winchfield	6. 2.1855	6.11.1934
Derek Shackleton *1948–1969*	Todmorden	12. 8.1924	
Edgar Francis Talman Sheldrake *1884–1885*	Aldershot	18. 1.1864	1950
Thomas Winter Sheppard *1905*	Havant	4. 3.1873	7. 6.1954
Ian Noel Ridley Shield *1939*	Lymington	25.12.1914	
William Robert de la Cour			
Shirley *1922–1925*	London	13.10.1900	23. 4.1970
Alexander Campbell Shirreff *1946–1947*	Ealing	12. 2.1919	
Herbert Shutt *1906*	Chorlton	1879	1922
V. Simpson *1885*			
Christopher Lyall Smith *1980–1987*	Durban,		
	S Africa	15.10.1958	
Hamilton Augustus Haigh			
Smith *1909–1914*	Sandown	21.10.1884	28.10.1955
Robin Arnold Smith *1982–1987*	Durban,		
	S Africa	13. 9.1963	
Thomas Michael Smith *1923–1924*	Lambeth	15. 6.1899	17.11.1965
George Smoker *1885*	Winchester	1857	23. 5.1925
Henry George Smoker *1901–1907*	Alresford	1. 3.1881	7. 9.1966
Henry Soames *1867*	Brighton	18. 1.1843	30. 8.1913
Thomas Soar *1895–1904*	Whitemoor,		
	Notts	3. 9.1865	17. 5.1939
John William Southern *1975–1983*	Kings Cross	2. 9.1952	
James Southerton *1864–1867*	Petworth	16.11.1827	16. 6.1880
Adolphus James Sparrow *1902*	Alverstoke	1869	1946
Gilbert Joshua Spencer-Smith *1864*	Brooklands	17.12.1843	4. 2.1928
Orlando Spencer-Smith *1866*	Brooklands	17.12.1843	23.11.1920
James Spens *1884–1899*	Subathoo, India	30. 3.1853	19. 6.1934
Henry Robert James Sprinks *1925–1929*	Alexandria	19. 8.1905	
Edward Mark Sprot *1898–1914*	Edinburgh	4. 2.1872	8.10.1945
David Aubrey Steele *1895–1906*	Southampton	3. 6.1869	25. 3.1935
John William Jackson Steele *1938–1939*	Nantwich	30. 7.1905	
George Robert Stephenson *1969–1980*	Derby	19.11.1942	
Keith Stevenson *1978–1982*	Derby	6.10.1950	
Sir Herbert Stewart *1869*	Sparsholt	30. 6.1843	16. 2.1885
William Anthony Stewart *1869–1878*	Sparsholt	19. 5.1847	31. 7.1883
James Stone *1900–1914*	Southampton	29.11.1876	18.11.1942
Herbert William Studd *1898*	Tidworth	26.12.1870	8. 8.1947
Reginald Augustus Studd *1895*	Tidworth	18.12.1873	3. 2.1948
Sir William Henry Marsham Style *1865*	Bicester	3. 9.1826	13. 1.1904

Name	Place	Born	Died
James Frederick Sutcliffe *1911*	Medway	12.12.1876	14. 7.1915
Thomas Sutherland *1898–1899*		17. 2.1880	unknown
Ernest Castle Sykes *1896*	Sheffield	31. 5.1869	30.11.1925
Edward Tate *1898–1902*	Lyndhurst	30. 8.1877	4. 1.1953
Frederick Tate *1870–1876*	Lyndhurst	6. 6.1844	24. 4.1935
Henry William Tate *1869–1885*	Lyndhurst	10.1849	9. 5.1936
Robert Frederick Tayler *1866*	Hastings	17. 3.1836	1. 1.1888
George Rammell Taylor *1935–1939*	Havant	25.11.1909	31.10.1986
John Dennis Taylor *1947–1949*	Ipswich	18.12.1923	
Michael Norman Somerset Taylor *1973–1980*	Amersham	12.11.1942	
Hon Lionel Hallam Tennyson *1913–1935*	Westminster	7.11.1889	6. 6.1951
Vivian Paul Terry *1978–1987*	Osnabruck, Germany	14. 1.1959	
Hugh Reginald Patrick Thompson *1953–1954*	Scunthorpe	11. 4.1934	
Robert Thorne *1883*	Southampton	11. 2.1930	
Philip Thresher *1865–1869*	South Stoneham	1. 3.1844	11. 4.1883
Bryan Stanley Valentine Timms *1959–1968*	Ropley	17.12.1940	
Edward Tolfree *1906–1919*	Southampton	12. 7.1881	20. 3.1966
Geoffrey Percy Robert Toynbee *1912*	Paddington	18. 5.1885	15.11.1914
Stanley Mease Toyne *1905*	Bournemouth	13. 6.1881	22. 1.1962
Timothy Maurice Tremlett *1976–*	Wellington, Som	26. 7.1956	
Samson Tubb *1864–1867*	East Dean	1839	27. 1.1891
James Jeffry Tuck *1877–1882*	Ringwood	3. 6.1853	20. 1.1918
Derek Thomas Tulk *1956–1957*	Southampton	21. 4.1934	
David Roy Turner *1966–1987*	Chippenham	5. 2.1949	
Francis Gordon Turner *1912*	London	1. 3.1890	21.11.1979
George Ubsdell *1864–1870*	Southampton	4. 4.1844	15.10.1905
George Underdown *1882–1885*	Petersfield	1859	29. 5.1895
Richard Peter Hugh Utley *1927–1928*	Havant	11. 2.1906	28. 8.1968
Alan Noel Edwin Waldron *1948*	Portsmouth	23.12.1920	
Clifford Walker *1949–1954*	Huddersfield	27. 6.1920	
Donald Frederick Walker *1937–1939*	Wandsworth Common	15. 8.1912	18. 6.1941
Frank Walkinshaw *1885*		28. 2.1861	14. 7.1934
Nesbit Willoughby Wallace *1884*	Halifax, Nova Scotia	20. 4.1839	31. 7.1931
Francis Walton *1864–1866*		1832	14. 7.1871
Albert Paine Ward *1921*	Highgate	9.11.1896	5. 3.1979
Charles Gordon Ward *1897–1901*	Braughing	23. 9.1875	27. 6.1954
Herbert Foster Ward *1895–1897*	Hammersmith	24. 3.1873	6. 6.1897

John Ward *1877*			
Merrick de Sampajo Cecil			
Ward *1927–1929*	London	15. 7.1908	13. 2.1981
Alan Robert Wassell *1957–1966*	Fareham	15. 4.1940	
Arthur Lacon Watson *1885*	West Cowes	27. 8.1866	28. 6.1955
Ian Ronald Watson *1973*	Staines	9. 6.1947	
Alfred William Watts *1882*	South		
	Stoneham	1859	unknown
Philip Humphrey Peter Weaver *1938*	Kalimpong,		
	India	12. 3.1912	
Arthur Stuart Webb *1895–1904*	Bridge, Kent	6. 8.1868	3.12.1952
Hubert Eustace Webb *1954*	Tonk, India	30. 5.1927	
Edward Whalley-Tooker *1883–1885*	Wem	15. 1.1863	23.11.1940
Keith James Wheatley *1965–1970*	Guildford	20. 1.1946	
Walter Charles Wheeler *1878–1880*	Newport, IOW	30.12.1841	10.10.1907
William Whitcher *1864–1867*	Emsworth	1832	1910
David William White *1957–1971*	Warwick	14.12.1935	
William Nicholas White *1903–1914*	London	10. 9.1879	27.12.1951
T. Wild *1880*			
William Wild *1877*	Thorncombe	21. 2.1846	unknown
George Wilder *1909*	Emsworth	9. 6.1876	10. 6.1948
Edmund Henry Lacon Willes *1865*	Hythe, Hants	7. 7.1832	9. 9.1896
G. E. Williams *1904*			
Frederick George Willoughby *1885*	Edinburgh	25. 4.1862	1952
Thomas Henry Wilson *1870*		10. 6.1841	31. 1.1929
Alfred Herbert Wood *1901*	Portsmouth	23. 4.1866	19. 4.1941
Arthur Hardy Wood *1870–1885*	Theddon	25. 5.1844	10. 7.1933
Sir Matthew Wood *1876*	Isle of Wight	21. 9.1857	13. 7.1908
Maxmillian David Francis Wood *1907*	Kamptee, India	22. 2.1873	22. 8.1915
Kenneth Herbert Clayton			
Woodroffe *1912–1913*	Lewes	9.12.1892	9. 5.1915
James Wootton *1895–1900*	Sutton-at-Hone	9. 3.1860	21. 2.1941
Lawrence Roosevelt Worrell *1969–1972*	St Thomas,		
	Barbados	28. 8.1943	
H. W. Wright *1885*			
Francis Joseph Caldwell Wyatt *1905–1919*	Trichinopoly	10. 7.1882	5. 5.1971
Edward George Wynyard *1878–1908*	Saharanpur	1. 4.1861	30.10.1936
Charles Henry Yaldren *1912*	Southampton	1891	23.10.1916
Humphrey William Maghull			
Yates *1910–1913*	Eccles, Lancs	25. 3.1883	21. 8.1956
Charles Robertson Young *1867–1885*	Dharwar, India	2. 2.1852	unknown

CAREER RECORDS OF HAMPSHIRE PLAYERS 1864–1987

The following career records cover ALL First-class matches played by Hampshire since 1864, a sum total of 2,251 games. Fifteen matches, listed at the end of these statistics were abandoned without a ball being bowled, and are therefore excluded from this survey. The matches 1864–1885 are taken from the Association of Cricket Statisticians publication, 'British Isles First-class Guide'.

Name	Inns	NO	Runs	HS	Avge	100s	Runs	Wkts	Avge	Best	5wI
Abdy A. J.	2	0	30	23	15.00	—					
Abercrombie C. H.	25	1	920	165	38.33	3	166	1	166.00	1/81	—
Acton J.	3	0	41	31	13.66	—	12	0	—	—	—
Adams C. G. A.	33	2	421	42	13.58	—	162	4	40.50	1/0	—
Aird R.	175	13	3603	159	22.24	4	191	2	95.50	1/4	—
Airey R. B.	5	0	52	30	10.40	—					
Allenby M. C.	1	0	0	0	0.00	—					
Altham H. S.	38	6	713	141	22.28	1	11	0	—	—	—
Andrew S. J. W.	18	11	43	7	6.14	—	2963	103	28.76	7/92	3
Andrew W.	22	1	312	106	14.85	1	626	23	27.21	5/157	1
Andrews A. J.	12	1	236	62*	21.45	—	2	0	—	—	—
Andrews C. J.	10	1	127	29	14.11	—					
Arkwright F. G. B.	5	0	44	14	8.80	—					
Armitage E. L.	15	1	183	42	13.07	—					
Armstrong H. H.	42	7	502	68	14.34	—	1376	68	20.23	7/33	2
Arnold A. C. P.	23	1	542	76	24.63	—	0	0	—	—	—
Arnold J.	701	45	21596	227	32.92	36	1182	17	69.52	3/34	—
Aymes A. N.	1	0	58	58	58.00	—					
Bacon F. H.	132	11	1909	110	15.77	1	190	6	31.66	2/23	—
Badcock J.	102	19	1199	74	14.44	—	5414	212	25.53	8/44	12
Bailey J.	408	35	9301	133	24.93	5	12595	467	26.97	7/7	25
Bailey M. J.	29	9	228	24	11.40	—	996	18	55.33	5/89	1
Bailey W. P.	2	0	14	10	7.00	—					
Bakker P-J.	3	1	6	3*	3.00	—	469	18	26.05	7/31	1
Baldock W. S.	13	1	155	40	12.91	—	48	2	24.00	1/10	—
Baldry D. O.	148	13	3342	151	24.75	3	2574	70	36.77	7/76	1
Baldwin H.	240	65	1863	55*	10.64	—	14336	580	24.71	8/74	41
Baring A. E. G.	91	24	562	46	8.38	—	4837	176	27.48	9/26	10
Barnard H. M.	463	41	9314	128*	22.07	6	563	16	35.18	3/35	—
Barrett E.	4	2	22	13*	11.00	—	48	0	—	—	—
Barrett E. I. M.	122	14	3518	215	32.57	6	40	0	—	—	—

Name	Inns	NO	Runs	HS	Avge	100s	Runs	Wkts	Avge	Best	5wI
Barrett P.	11	0	138	26	12.54	—	4	0	—	—	—
Bartley E. L. D.	4	1	5	5★	1.66	—					
Barton C. G.	5	2	28	22	9.33	—	152	3	50.66	2/66	—
Barton H. G. M.	15	2	146	31	11.23	—					
Barton V. A.	261	13	6204	205	25.01	6	3819	130	29.37	6/28	3
Bateman R.	2	1	18	14★	18.00	—					
Bates F. S.	3	0	18	9	6.00	—					
Bathurst F. T. A. H.	4	1	53	30	17.66	—					
Bathurst L. H.	4	0	30	14	7.50	—	8	0	—	—	—
Beadle S. W.	2	0	22	16	11.00	—					
Bedford H.	1	0	3	3	3.00	—	5	1	5.00	1/5	—
Belcher G.	2	0	0	0	0.00	—	3	0	—	—	—
Bencraft H. W. R.	76	18	908	62★	15.65	—	185	5	37.00	2/15	—
Bennett R. A.	41	3	468	47	12.31	—					
Bentinck B. W.	4	0	26	15	6.50	—					
Bethune H. B.	4	1	26	9	8.66	—	27	1	27.00	1/27	—
Bignell G. N.	81	4	1582	109	20.54	1	722	17	42.47	3/67	—
Bignell H. G.	9	2	99	49★	14.14	—	29	0	—	—	—
Bird P. J.	2	0	37	28	18.50	—					
Black L. G.	5	0	36	21	7.20	—	229	1	229.00	1/27	—
Blake D. E.	89	6	1811	100	21.81	1					
Blake J. P.	25	1	328	48	13.66	—					
Blundell F.	1	0	2	2	2.00	—	22	2	11.00	2/22	—
Bodington C. H.	18	4	154	36	11.00	—	287	9	31.88	3/19	—
Bolton R. H. D.	12	0	121	24	10.08	—					
Bonham-Carter L. G.	15	0	260	67	17.33	—	63	2	31.50	2/22	—
Booth C.	37	2	620	77	17.71	—	143	2	71.50	1/13	—
Bowell H. A. W.	806	43	18466	204	24.20	25	1766	34	51.94	4/20	—
Bowell N. H.	2	0	8	6	4.00	—	56	0	—	—	—
Bowen E. E.	2	0	0	0	0.00	—					
Bower J.	4	1	14	8	4.66	—	166	8	20.75	4/43	—
Boyes G. S.	677	156	7515	104	14.42	2	33513	1415	23.68	9/57	71
Bradford E. R.	14	2	311	102	25.91	1	328	20	16.40	6/28	2
Bridger J. R.	66	4	1725	142	27.82	2	40	0	—	—	—
Briggs C. E.	10	0	158	58	15.80	—					
Brodhurst B. M. L.	1	0	9	9	9.00	—	23	0	—	—	—
Brooks R. A. D.	15	0	244	107	16.26	1					
Brown G.	900	46	22962	232★	26.88	37	17857	602	29.66	8/55	23
Brutton C. P.	127	12	2052	119★	17.84	1	125	0	—	—	—
Brutton S.	2	0	22	15	11.00	—					

Name	Inns	NO	Runs	HS	Avge	100s	Runs	Wkts	Avge	Best	5wI
Buck W. D.	did not bat						25	0	—	—	—
Buckland E. H.	8	0	116	73	14.50	—	211	9	23.44	5/30	1
Budd W. L.	98	16	941	77*	11.47	—	2506	64	39.15	4/22	—
Budden C.	3	1	35	32*	17.50	—	102	2	51.00	1/30	—
Budden J. T. W. F.	did not bat						46	0	—	—	—
Bull G.	3	1	12	10	6.00	—	25	0	—	—	—
Burden M. D.	191	59	901	51	6.82	—	12559	481	26.11	8/38	23
Bury L.	2	0	15	15	7.50	—	23	1	23.00	1/23	—
Busk, R. D.	3	2	0	0*	0.00	—	125	2	62.50	1/28	—
Byng A. M.	5	0	40	21	8.00	—	16	0	—	—	—
Cadell A. R.	3	1	8	6	4.00	—	25	2	12.50	1/7	—
Cadogan E. H.	9	2	53	27	7.57	—	405	17	23.82	5/52	1
Calder H.	9	0	128	44	14.22	—	118	5	23.60	3/24	—
Campbell A. K.	10	0	91	21	9.10	—					
Cannings V. H. D.	294	103	1888	43*	9.88	—	18091	834	21.69	7/52	39
Caple R. G.	99	15	1531	64*	18.22	—	1003	28	35.82	5/54	1
Carter G.	23	0	274	34	11.91	—	12	1	12.00	1/11	—
Cartridge D. C.	6	0	6	4	1.00	—					
Carty R. A.	79	25	798	53	14.77	—	4164	138	30.17	7/29	8
Case G. H.	3	0	85	48	28.33	—	21	0	—	—	—
Castell A. T.	138	38	1600	76	16.00	—	6903	225	30.68	6/22	8
Causton E. P. G.	1	0	21	21	21.00	—	4	0	—	—	—
Cecil A. B. C.	2	0	6	4	3.00	—					
Cecil E. D. C.	1	0	4	4	4.00	—	8	0	—	—	—
Chance G. H. B.	2	1	0	0	0.00	—	42	0	—	—	—
Chandler G.	2	0	16	16	8.00	—					
Charters F. H.	2	0	14	9	7.00	—					
Chignell T. A.	28	10	181	29*	10.05	—	1108	33	33.57	5/68	1
Chivers I. J.	1	1	20	20*	—	—	76	2	38.00	1/4	—
Cole G. L.	10	1	110	33	12.22	—					
Collins T. H.	4	0	31	13	7.75	—	22	1	22.00	1/22	—
Connor C. A.	54	23	202	36	6.51	—	6093	180	33.84	7/37	2
Cornwallis O. W.	did not bat										
Cottam R. M. H.	178	65	615	35	5.44	—	14354	693	20.71	9/25	38
Court R. C. L.	27	5	224	35	10.18	—	1228	33	37.21	4/53	—
Cowie A. G.	3	1	3	2	1.50	—	261	9	29.00	5/94	1
Cowley N. G.	349	55	6537	109*	22.23	2	13540	412	32.86	6/48	5
Crawley C. S.	2	0	22	14	11.00	—					
Creese W. L. C.	453	41	9894	241	24.01	6	11141	401	27.78	8/37	15
Crofton E. H.	5	0	32	23	6.40	—	42	1	42.00	1/21	—
Crofts E. S.	2	0	5	3	2.50	—					
Crookes J. E.	5	1	50	36*	12.50	—	6	0	—	—	—

233

Name	Inns	NO	Runs	HS	Avge	100s	Runs	Wkts	Avge	Best	5wI
Crowdy J. G.	11	0	101	21	9.18	—	31	1	31.00	1/31	—
Cull G.	4	0	14	7	3.50	—					
Currie C. E.	30	9	284	32	13.52	—	1225	56	21.87	8/57	2
Curzon C. C.	2	1	53	31★	53.00	—					
Darby J. H.	7	1	78	35	13.00	—	24	0	—	—	—
Dare R.	169	32	1679	109★	12.25	1	6479	185	35.02	6/28	5
Dashwood T. H. K.	4	0	34	12	8.50	—					
Davies H. G. S.	2	0	45	42	22.50	—					
Dawson G. W.	107	7	2643	158★	26.43	4	7	0	—	—	—
Dawson H.	19	1	236	37	13.11	—	8	0	—	—	—
Day H. L. V.	126	5	3047	142	25.18	4	46	0	—	—	—
Dean —	1	1	3	3★	—	—	52	2	26.00	2/52	—
Dean T. A.	44	13	283	26	9.12	—	1587	51	31.11	7/51	4
Deane M. W.	7	2	15	8	3.00	—					
Debnam A. F. H.	18	3	239	64	15.93	—	193	4	48.25	1/2	—
Delme-Ratcliffe A. H.	13	0	190	43	14.61	—					
Denham H. A.	2	0	8	7	4.00	—					
Dible W. G.	45	8	495	68	13.37	—	1991	90	22.12	7/60	5
Dixon C. E.	4	0	10	5	2.50	—					
Dodd W. T. F.	16	2	95	31	6.78	—	321	10	32.10	5/63	1
Dorey L. H. J.	2	0	0	0	0.00	—					
Down J. H.	2	1	32	31★	16.00	—	53	1	53.00	1/33	—
Downer H. R.	4	0	8	4	2.00	—					
Drake E. J.	27	0	219	45	8.11	—	171	4	42.75	2/37	—
Dumbleton H. N.	2	0	16	9	8.00	—	14	0	—	—	—
Duncan A. J.	4	0	28	26	7.00	—					
Duncan D. W. J.	29	3	581	87★	22.34	—	18	3	6.00	1/1	—
Duthie A. M.	2	0	6	5	3.00	—	141	5	28.20	3/85	—
Dutton H. J.	2	2	7	7★	—	—	8	0	—	—	—
Eagar E. D. R.	514	34	10091	158★	21.02	8	937	15	62.46	2/10	—
Eccles C. V.	4	0	36	23	9.00	—	44	0	—	—	—
Ede E. L.	30	4	260	49	10.00	—	382	15	25.46	4/79	—
Ede E. M. C.	25	7	218	43	12.11	—	1130	38	29.73	7/72	2
Ede G. M.	29	2	257	52	9.51	—	22	1	22.00	1/22	—
Eggar J. D.	3	0	38	28	12.66	—					
Elms R. B.	16	4	196	48	16.33	—	1015	27	37.59	4/83	—
Emery K. St. J. D.	27	15	45	18★	3.75	—	2154	84	25.64	6/51	3
English E. A.	32	2	565	98	18.83	—	101	1	101.00	1/11	—
Evans A. E.	8	0	84	47	10.50	—	407	14	29.07	4/74	—
Evans A. H.	6	0	82	33	13.66	—	178	10	17.80	4/47	—
Evans A. J.	11	0	307	51	27.90	—	207	5	41.40	3/92	—
Evans B. S.	8	2	67	18★	11.16	—					

Name	Inns	NO	Runs	HS	Avge	100s	Runs	Wkts	Avge	Best	5wI
Evans D. M.	27	3	361	64	15.04	—	1370	50	27.56	6/81	3
Evans J.	26	7	196	41	10.31	—	81	1	81.00	1/34	—
Evans R. du B.	1	1	4	4*	—	—					
Evans W. H. B.	35	0	940	115	26.85	1	1491	45	33.13	7/59	2
Exton R. N.	5	1	39	24*	9.75	—	40	0	—		
Fellowes J.	20	5	186	26	12.40	—	393	11	35.72	3/38	—
Feltham W. G.	5	1	1	1	0.25	—	254	12	21.16	3/41	—
Fenley S.	6	0	25	11	4.16	—	162	1	162.00	1/66	—
Fielder A. E.	4	1	38	35	12.66	—	255	6	37.50	5/128	1
Fielder W. G.	1	1	2	2*	—	—	26	0	—		
Fisher R. W. C.	1	0	3	3	3.00	—					
Flood R. D.	43	5	885	138*	23.28	1	9	0	—	—	—
Forster H. T.	8	3	33	13*	6.60	—	212	10	21.20	5/38	1
Forster H. W.	8	0	76	28	9.50	—	80	5	16.00	3/22	—
Foster F. G.	2	0	12	10	6.00	—					
Fowler R. St. L.	6	0	106	51	17.66	—	206	4	51.50	3/68	—
Fox T. C.	4	0	10	7	2.50	—	26	0	—	—	—
Frederick E. B.	9	4	32	11	6.40	—	331	9	36.77	3/41	—
Frederick J. St. J.	10	0	171	44	17.10	—	69	4	17.25	4/45	—
Freemantle F. W.	4	1	28	26	9.33	—	53	0	—	—	—
Frere H. T.	11	2	92	23	10.22	—	248	6	41.33	2/20	—
Fry C. A.	8	0	134	38	16.75	—	4	0	—	—	—
Fry C. B.	72	7	3829	258*	58.90	14	19	0	—	—	—
Fry S.	50	2	508	78*	10.58	—					
Fynn C. G.	12	5	45	21	6.42	—	446	11	40.54	3/92	—
Gale H.	8	0	144	44	18.00	—					
Galpin J. G.	14	5	100	27	11.11	—	462	28	16.50	6/68	2
Gandy C. H.	4	1	6	6*	2.00	—	117	3	39.00	2/84	—
Garnier T. P.	2	0	29	23	14.50	—					
Gay L. H.	17	1	164	34*	10.25	—					
Gentry J. S. B.	1	0	3	3	3.00	—	13	0	—	—	—
Gibbons H. G.	8	1	70	27	10.00	—	92	0	—	—	—
Gilliat R. M. C.	351	40	9358	223*	30.09	16	133	3	44.33	1/3	—
Gladdon F.	2	0	1	1	0.50	—	44	0	—	—	—
Godfrey J. F.	19	5	61	25*	4.35	—	753	15	50.20	4/116	—
Goldie C. F. E.	2	1	6	6	6.00	—					
Gornall J. P.	2	0	18	11	9.00	—					
Graf S. F.	19	5	284	57*	20.28	—	889	20	44.45	2/24	—
Gravett M.	7	1	41	17*	6.83	—	445	15	29.66	5/50	1
Gray J. R.	809	81	22450	213*	30.83	30	13543	451	30.02	7/52	11
Greenfield G. P.	1	0	0	0	0.00	—	32	0	—	—	—
Greenhill H. M.	3	0	15	6	5.00	—	77	3	25.66	3/39	—
Greenidge C. G.	472	35	19840	259	45.40	48	387	16	24.18	5/49	1
Greenwood G. G.	2	0	2	1	1.00	—					

Name	Inns	NO	Runs	HS	Avge	100s	Runs	Wkts	Avge	Best	5wI
Gregory J. T.	1	0	0	0	0.00	—	87	0	—	—	—
Greig J. G.	137	9	4375	249*	34.17	10	2050	64	32.03	6/38	4
Gross F. A.	44	16	202	32*	7.21	—	1850	50	37.00	5/53	1
Guard D. R.	27	1	405	89	15.57	—					
Gunner C. R.		did not bat				—					
Gunner J. H.	9	1	65	32	8.12	—					
Gutteres G. G.	2	0	52	28	26.00	—					
Hake H. D.	29	2	478	94	17.70	—	24	0	—	—	—
Hall C. G.	7	0	77	37	11.00	—					
Hall E.	21	2	198	22	10.42	—					
Hall P. M.	17	1	164	94*	10.25	—					
Hardy J. J. E.	45	10	1255	107*	35.85	1	3	0	—	—	—
Harfield L.	133	10	2460	89	20.00	—	649	14	46.35	3/35	—
Hargreaves J. H.	4	0	15	14	3.75	—					
Hargreaves R. G.	23	3	307	38*	15.35	—	376	14	26.85	4/55	—
Harold F. V.	2	0	16	16	8.00	—	15	0	—	—	—
Harris G. W.	2	0	10	10	5.00	—					
Harris H. E.	5	0	53	28	10.60	—					
Harrison B. R. S.	24	2	519	110	23.59	1	65	1	65.00	1/34	—
Harrison G. C.	37	2	991	111	28.31	1					
Harrison L.	593	100	8708	153	17.66	6	166	0	—	—	—
Harrison W. H.	2	1	12	12*	12.00	—					
Harvey F. N.	4	0	20	7	5.00	—					
Haslop P.	1	1	2	2*	—	—	82	2	41.00	2/82	—
Haygarth E. B.	2	0	10	6	5.00	—					
Hayter E.	6	1	36	17	7.20	—	29	0	—	—	—
Hayter M. W.	12	0	166	82	13.83	—					
Hayward A. J.	4	0	17	10	4.25	—					
Hayward R. E.	22	4	454	101*	25.22	1	5	0	—	—	—
Hazelton E. H.	5	0	83	50	16.60	—					
Heath A. B.	14	0	132	42	9.42	—	28	2	14.00	2/28	—
Heath G. E. M.	188	83	586	34*	5.58	—	11359	404	28.11	7/49	23
Heath M.	163	66	569	33	5.86	—	13237	527	25.11	8/43	18
Hebden G. G. L.	11	3	69	22*	8.62	—	172	3	57.33	1/11	—
Hedley W. C.	6	0	69	35	11.50	—	125	2	62.50	1/23	—
Hemsted E.	13	1	204	39	17.00	—	98	8	12.25	5/14	1
Henley A. A.	2	0	16	9	8.00	—					
Henley R.	1	0	14	14	14.00	—	14	0	—	—	—
Herman O. W.	495	105	4327	92	11.09	—	28137	1041	27.02	8/49	58
Herman R. S.	92	17	869	56	11.58	—	6768	270	25.06	8/42	8
Heseltine C.	81	5	1039	77	13.67	—	3185	116	27.45	7/106	5
Hesketh-Prichard H. V.	93	25	461	36	6.77	—	5464	233	23.45	8/32	15
Hill A. E. L.	28	2	193	24	7.42	—					

236

Name	Inns	NO	Runs	HS	Avge	100s	Runs	Wkts	Avge	Best	5wI
Hill A. J. L.	291	17	8381	199	30.58	17	6213	199	31.22	7/36	3
Hill G.	595	94	9085	161	18.13	4	18464	617	29.92	8/62	18
Hill M. J.	8	4	68	27*	17.00	—					
Hitchcock											
B. F. B.	3	0	33	21	11.00	—					
Holder J. W.	49	14	374	33	10.68	—	3415	139	24.56	7/79	5
Hollingworth											
T. V.	3	0	14	14	4.66	—	17	0	—	—	—
Holmes H.	50	4	692	71	15.04	—	658	22	29.90	5/57	1
Holt A. G.	140	13	2853	116	22.46	2	47	1	47.00	1/24	—
Hopkins F. J.	6	3	12	6*	4.00	—	175	4	43.75	2/66	—
Horton H.	723	80	21536	160*	33.49	32	162	3	54.00	2/0	—
Hosie A. L.	137	5	3542	155	26.83	5	315	4	78.75	2/35	—
Hotham A. G.	2	0	16	11	8.00	—	6	0	—	—	—
Humphrey W.	8	1	50	25	7.14	—	100	4	25.00	3/61	—
Humphreys W. A.	4	2	17	13*	8.50	—	246	9	27.33	5/71	1
Hyland F. J.	did not bat										
Hyslop H. H.	13	1	106	34	8.83	—	31	2	15.50	2/12	—
Ingleby-											
Mackenzie											
A. C. D.	513	60	11140	132*	24.59	10	22	0	—	—	—
Isherwood											
L. C. R.	42	4	627	61*	16.50	—					
Jackman F.	4	2	26	16	13.00	—	42	1	42.00	1/21	—
James K. D.	40	12	1163	142*	41.53	3	2084	55	37.89	6/22	3
Jameson T. G. C.	4	1	44	23*	14.66	—	11	0	—	—	—
Jameson T. O.	89	8	2013	105*	24.87	2	2557	77	33.20	7/92	3
Jaques A.	80	16	864	68	13.50	—	3617	168	21.52	8/21	10
Jeffreys A. F.	18	1	203	51	11.94	—					
Jellicoe F. G. G.	6	2	37	12	9.25	—	243	23	10.56	7/23	2
Jephson W. V.	99	6	1571	90	16.89	—	13	1	13.00	1/13	—
Jesson R. W. F.	26	4	191	38	8.68	—	513	21	24.42	5/42	1
Jessop G. L. O	5	0	47	25	9.40	—	47	1	47.00	1/16	—
Jesty T. E.	538	74	14753	248	31.79	26	13596	475	28.62	7/75	14
Jewell											
G. A. F. W.	2	0	1	1	0.50	—	52	1	52.00	1/38	—
Johnston A. C.	190	13	5442	175	30.74	10	805	18	44.72	4/21	—
Jolliff H. J.	2	0	1	1	0.50	—					
Jones G. L.	16	4	169	37*	14.08	—					
Judd A. K.	106	13	1625	119	17.47	1	926	28	33.07	6/65	1
Judd W. G.	2	0	8	7	4.00	—	50	1	50.00	1/22	—
Katinakis G. D.	6	1	46	16*	9.20	—	27	0	—	—	—
Kay H. G.	2	0	0	0	0.00	—	20	0	—	—	—
Kaye J. L.	2	0	14	11	7.00	—					

Name	Inns	NO	Runs	HS	Avge	100s	Runs	Wkts	Avge	Best	5wI
Keith G. L.	95	12	1775	101*	21.38	1	552	12	46.00	4/49	—
Kendle C. E. C.	4	1	27	11	9.00	—					
Kendle W. J.	9	0	66	29	7.33	—					
Kennard J. A. G.	3	1	46	18	23.00	—	17	0	—	—	—
Kennedy A. S.	916	110	14925	163*	18.51	10	53950	2549	21.16	9/33	205
Kimish A. E.	4	1	18	12*	6.00	—					
King J.	2	0	13	9	6.50	—	93	5	18.60	4/64	—
Kitchener F. G.	19	3	80	16	5.00	—	630	28	22.50	6/59	2
Kneller A. H.	11	2	76	25*	8.44	—					
Knight A. E.	7	0	41	29	5.85	—	17	1	17.00	1/17	—
Knott C. J.	235	94	1003	27	7.11	—	15224	647	23.53	8/26	44
Lacey F. E.	59	8	2028	211	39.76	4	942	45	20.93	7/149	3
Lamb B.	7	0	29	8	4.14	—					
Lancashire W.	29	1	471	66	16.82	—	357	7	51.00	2/49	—
Langford W. T.	153	23	1663	62*	12.99	—	5781	215	26.88	8/82	5
Lawrie P. E.	44	1	959	107	22.30	1					
Lawson H. M.	68	12	527	53	9.41	—	2494	69	36.14	5/91	2
Lawson M. B.	11	1	122	36	12.20	—	170	5	34.00	2/45	—
Leat C. W.	29	1	323	63	11.53	—	49	2	24.50	2/10	—
Lee A. M.	1	0	0	0	0.00	—					
Lee E. C.	79	11	994	54*	14.61	—	673	9	74.72	2/0	—
Levenson-Gower F. A. G.	4	0	45	20	11.25	—	22	0	—	—	—
Lewis A. H.	1	0	20	20	20.00	—					
Lewis R. V.	186	13	3282	136	18.97	2	104	1	104.00	1/59	—
Light E. E.	22	6	168	35	10.50	—	263	5	52.60	2/22	—
Light W. F.	19	2	101	41	5.94	—	343	10	34.30	3/32	—
Lineham E.	2	1	0	0*	0.00	—					
Lipscomb F. W.	5	0	92	53	18.40	—	103	2	51.50	2/46	—
Lipscomb W. H.	7	0	99	34	14.14	—	19	0	—	—	—
Livingstone D. A.	516	63	12660	200	27.94	16	68	1	68.00	1/31	—
Livsey W. H.	443	131	4818	110*	15.44	2					
Llewellyn C. B.	341	23	8772	216	27.58	15	17538	711	24.66	8/72	55
Lodge L. V.	4	0	6	4	1.50	—	6	0	—	—	—
Longcroft O. B.	4	0	28	12	7.00	—	75	8	9.37	3/15	—
Longman G. H.	50	1	856	78	17.46	—	163	3	54.33	1/1	—
Lord J. C.	2	1	15	11	15.00	—					
Love R. H. A. D.	3	1	15	13*	7.50	—	6	0	—	—	—
Lowe H. F.	1	0	0	0	0.00	—					
Lowndes W. G. L. F.	72	1	1558	143	21.94	4	1503	40	37.57	3/22	—
Luard A. J. H.	8	0	60	18	7.50	—					
Lucas C. F.	26	1	502	135	20.08	1					
Luckin V. V.	14	7	17	8*	2.42	—	513	13	39.46	3/39	—

Name	Inns	NO	Runs	HS	Avge	100s	Runs	Wkts	Avge	Best	5wI
Lushington A. H.	6	0	48	21	8.00	—	98	3	32.66	2/48	—
Lynn J.	2	1	4	4*	4.00	—	34	2	17.00	2/25	—
Lyon G. H. D'o	4	0	41	29	10.25	—	42	2	21.00	1/5	—
Maartensz											
S. G. A.	17	2	283	60	18.86	—					
McBride W. N.	44	15	405	35	13.96	—	901	24	37.54	3/36	—
McCorkell N. T.	675	63	15834	203	25.87	17	117	1	117.00	1/73	—
McDonell H. C.	120	12	1747	76	16.17	—	5901	263	22.43	7/47	11
McGibbon C. E.	2	1	1	1*	1.00	—	10	0	—	—	—
McIlwaine R. J.	3	1	29	17	14.50	—	273	4	68.25	2/40	—
McIntyre A. S.	45	2	493	55	11.46	—	36	0	—	—	—
Mackenzie P. A.	36	3	652	76	19.75	—	605	17	35.58	4/34	—
McLaren F. A.	3	0	4	4	1.33	—	114	4	28.50	2/30	—
McLeod A.	18	0	271	87	15.05	—					
Malone S. J.	40	14	178	23	6.84	—	3481	103	33.79	7/55	2
Manners J. E.	11	0	355	121	32.27	1	16	0	—	—	—
Mannings G.	2	0	7	5	3.50	—					
Manser R. M.	2	0	1	1	0.50	—					
Mariner E. C.	2	0	0	0	0.00	—	20	0	—	—	—
Marshall M. D.	183	22	3447	116*	21.40	3	10746	613	17.53	8/71	35
Marshall R. E.	890	49	30303	228*	36.03	60	2403	99	24.27	6/36	5
Martin C.	8	1	9	3	1.28	—	168	9	18.66	3/38	—
Martin G.	7	5	19	6*	9.50	—	321	8	40.12	3/64	—
Martin J.	2	0	66	39	33.00	—	166	5	33.20	4/100	—
Martin W.	2	0	2	1	1.00	—					
Maru R. J.	63	22	681	62	16.60	—	6984	239	29.22	7/79	9
Maturin H.	14	0	136	28	9.71	—	180	6	30.00	4/68	—
Maundrell W. H.	1	0	0	0	0.00	—					
May J.	8	2	71	28	11.83	—	165	6	27.50	4/80	—
Mead C. P.	1171	170	48892	280*	48.84	138	9252	266	34.78	7/18	5
Meaden H. J. B.	6	1	200	9*	4.00	—					
Melle											
B. G. von B.	45	4	1207	110	29.43	1	1074	25	42.96	5/70	2
Michell E. J.	1	0	7	7	7.00	—					
Middleton T. C.	17	3	338	68*	24.14	—	39	1	39.00	1/13	—
Mildmay											
H. P. St J.	13	1	137	26	11.41	—	51	1	51.00	1/26	—
Misselbrook H.	2	0	3	3	1.50	—	39	6	6.50	4/18	—
Moberly J. C.	2	0	31	27	15.50	—					
Moorcroft W.	did not bat						68	0	—	—	—
Moore J. W.	25	6	256	30	13.47	—	72	0	—	—	—
Moore R. H.	225	7	5885	316	26.99	10	978	25	39.12	3/46	—
Mordaunt H. J.	1	0	0	0	0.00	—					
Mornement R. H.	5	0	41	19	8.20	—	171	6	28.50	3/62	—

Name	Inns	NO	Runs	HS	Avge	100s	Runs	Wkts	Avge	Best	5wI
Mottram T. J.	35	18	95	15*	5.58	—	2677	111	24.11	6/63	4
Murgatroyd H.	2	1	2	1*	2.00	—	7	0	—	—	—
Murtagh A. J.	46	5	631	65	15.39	—	434	6	72.33	2/46	—
Newman J. A.	786	121	13904	166*	20.90	9	48305	1946	24.82	9/131	128
Newton E.	32	1	568	69	18.32	—					
Nicholas M. C. J.	314	39	8836	206*	32.13	18	1962	45	43.60	5/45	1
Norbury D. V.	19	2	179	35	10.52	—	530	7	75.71	2/48	—
Nugent F. H.	2	0	0	0	0.00	—					
Olivier E.	12	4	87	43	10.87	—	359	7	51.28	4/30	—
Olivier S. R.	1	0	0	0	0.00	—					
Orr H. J.	12	2	59	11*	5.90	—	360	11	32.72	3/34	—
O'Sullivan D. R.	31	9	347	48	15.77	—	2001	84	23.82	6/26	5
Page T. H.	4	1	77	61*	25.66	—	198	4	49.50	4/115	—
Palmer C. H.	16	1	264	64	17.60	—					
Palmer R. H.	2	0	0	0	0.00	—	187	6	31.16	5/93	1
Paris C. G. A.	169	9	3660	134*	22.87	2	216	4	54.00	1/10	—
Paris W.	11	1	81	51*	8.10	52	5	10.40	3/28	—	
Parker F. A. V.	4	0	22	11	5.50	—					
Parker J. P.	66	7	1094	156	18.54	1	258	6	43.00	2/14	—
Parks R. J.	187	49	2704	89	19.59	—	166	0	—	—	—
Parsons W. D.	4	2	31	12*	15.50	—	72	1	72.00	1/23	—
Parvin A. W.	2	0	11	11	5.50	—					
Passmore G.	1	0	0	0	0.00	—					
Paver K. E.	4	0	52	26	13.00	—					
Pearce S. H. H.	2	0	18	18	9.00	—					
Pearce W. K.	10	3	127	63	18.14	—					
Pember F. W.	4	0	49	30	12.25	—					
Perse H. W.	84	8	889	71	11.69	—	3813	127	30.02	6/64	3
Phillips H. W.	9	0	53	40	5.88	—	102	0	—	—	—
Piachaud J. D.	12	6	37	13	6.16	—	850	29	29.31	4/62	—
Pillans A. A.	6	2	82	32*	20.50	—	151	6	25.16	2/31	—
Pink A.	2	0	54	39	27.00	—	15	1	15.00	1/15	—
Pitman R. W. C.	76	8	926	77	13.61	—	68	1	68.00	1/4	—
Plowden H. M.	2	0	37	34	18.50	—	46	2	23.00	2/46	—
Pocock N. E. J.	186	22	3790	164	23.10	2	396	4	99.00	1/4	—
Poore R. M.	66	7	2819	304	47.77	10	100	3	33.33	1/9	—
Porter A. L.	1	0	7	7	7.00	—					
Pothecary A. E.	445	39	9477	130	23.34	9	2140	52	41.15	4/47	—
Pothecary S. G.	16	6	103	22*	10.30	—	257	4	64.25	3/43	—
Powell E. O.	21	2	759	140	39.94	1					
Powys W. N.	3	1	8	5*	4.00	—	84	2	42.00	1/26	—
Prothero R. E.	6	1	57	24	11.40	—	96	2	48.00	1/27	—
Proud R. B.	12	1	183	38*	16.63	—					
Prouton R. O.	79	11	982	90	14.44	—					

Name	Inns	NO	Runs	HS	Avge	100s	Runs	Wkts	Avge	Best	5wI
Quinton F. W. D.	84	7	2178	178	28.28	2	855	30	28.50	5/93	1
Quinton J. M.	6	1	47	22	9.40	—	36	1	36.00	1/14	—
Raikes G. B.	17	2	409	77	27.26	—	756	25	30.24	4/30	—
Ransom V. J.	50	8	419	58	9.97	—	3071	88	34.89	5/50	3
Rawlence J. R.	2	0	42	38	21.00	—					
Rayment											
A. W. H.	339	28	6333	126	20.36	4	756	19	39.78	4/75	—
Raynbird R.	2	0	0	0	0.00	—	15	0	—	—	—
Raynbird W.	4	1	25	13	8.33	—	14	0	—	—	—
Read E. G.	6	0	37	24	6.16	—					
Redhouse —	2	0	4	4	2.00	—	13	0	—	—	—
Reed B. L.	213	11	4910	138	24.30	2	0	0	—	—	—
Reifer E. L.	26	8	357	47	19.83	—	1761	49	35.93	4/43	—
Remnant E. R.	196	32	2843	115*	17.33	1	4652	170	27.36	8/61	7
Rice J. M.	271	22	5091	161*	20.44	2	7707	230	33.50	7/48	3
Richards A. C.	6	0	104	47	17.33	—	112	3	37.33	3/45	—
Richards B. A.	342	33	15607	240	50.50	38	1675	46	36.41	7/63	1
Richards C. J. R.	2	0	48	43	24.00	—					
Ridding C. H.	4	0	33	13	8.25	—					
Ridley A. B.	4	0	43	41	10.75	—	35	2	17.50	2/30	—
Ridley A. W.	19	0	558	104	29.36	1	902	68	13.69	7/46	10
Rimell A. G. J.	4	1	82	42*	27.33	—	65	1	65.00	1/52	—
Roberts A. M. E.	65	23	583	39	13.88	—	4076	244	16.70	8/47	13
Robson C.	230	14	3299	101	15.27	1	143	1	143.00	1/40	—
Rock D. J.	65	1	1227	114	19.17	3	0	0	—	—	—
Rogers H. J.	12	0	69	18	5.75	—	62	1	62.00	1/26	—
Rogers N. H.	506	25	15292	186	31.79	26	37	0	—	—	—
Roper C.	1	0	7	7	7.00	—					
Roper D. G. B.	2	0	30	30	15.00	—					
Russell H.	2	0	11	10	5.50	—					
Russell W. C.	2	0	7	5	3.50	—					
Rutherford A. P.	1	0	18	18	18.00	—	27	0	—	—	—
Rutherford J. S.	15	1	128	33*	9.14	—	110	3	36.66	1/4	—
Ryan F. P.	33	10	138	23	6.00	—	1644	63	26.09	7/60	5
Sainsbury P. J.	913	189	19576	163	27.03	7	30060	1245	24.14	8/76	35
Sandeman											
G. A. C.	6	3	9	5*	3.00	—	124	3	41.33	2/73	—
Scott W. E. N.	7	2	102	35	20.40	—	131	4	32.75	2/66	—
Seymour A.	2	0	2	2	1.00	—					
Seymour C. R.	29	3	481	77*	18.50	—					
Shackleton D.	773	177	8602	87*	14.43	—	48674	2669	18.23	9/30	190
Sheldrake E. F. T.	5	0	52	20	10.40	—	78	1	78.00	1/41	—
Sheppard T. W.	1	0	17	17	17.00	—					
Shield I. N. R.	5	1	16	6	4.00	—	274	4	68.50	2/91	—

Name	Inns	NO	Runs	HS	Avge	100s	Runs	Wkts	Avge	Best	5wI
Shirley											
W. R. de la C.	69	10	1035	90	17.54	—	1426	52	27.42	4/51	—
Shirreff A. C.	21	3	387	77*	21.50	—	731	13	56.23	3/48	—
Shutt H.	5	3	7	6	3.50	—	231	8	28.87	4/29	—
Simpson V.	2	0	10	7	5.00	—					
Smith C. L.	242	31	9182	217	43.51	26	1962	32	61.31	3/35	—
Smith H. A. H.	41	10	327	43*	10.54	—	574	14	41.00	3/95	—
Smith R. A.	134	29	4565	209*	43.47	10	380	9	42.22	2/11	—
Smith T. M.	11	1	89	18	8.90	—					
Smoker G.	4	1	17	13	5.66	—					
Smoker H. G.	50	15	334	39*	9.54	—	733	33	22.21	7/35	2
Soames H.	2	0	54	52	27.00	—					
Soar T.	173	29	1927	95	13.38	—	7697	323	23.82	8/38	23
Southern J. W.	179	71	1653	61*	15.30	—	12283	412	29.81	6/46	17
Southerton J.	23	3	200	44	10.00	—	892	63	14.15	7/45	9
Sparrow A. J.	1	0	1	1	1.00	—					
Spencer-Smith											
G. J.	2	0	20	11	10.00	—					
Spencer-Smith O.	2	0	53	39	26.50	—					
Spens J.	20	1	546	118*	28.73	1	16	0	—	—	—
Sprinks H. R. J.	27	9	167	40	9.27	—	1338	29	46.13	4/56	—
Sprot E. M.	452	28	12212	147	28.80	13	1856	54	34.37	5/28	1
Steele D. A.	278	32	3418	80	13.89	—	4628	135	34.28	5/32	4
Steele J. W. J.	26	2	406	44	16.91	—	1519	57	26.64	6/62	3
Stephenson G. R.	343	66	4566	100*	16.48	1	39	0	—	—	—
Stevenson K.	107	39	672	31	9.88	—	7539	257	29.33	7/22	12
Stewart H.	2	0	1	1	0.50	—					
Stewart W. A.	4	1	10	6	3.33	—					
Stone J.	468	57	9167	174	22.30	5	104	1	104.00	1/77	—
Studd H. W.	7	0	217	60	31.00	—	26	0	—	—	—
Studd R. A.	6	0	169	93	28.16	—					
Style W. H. M.	2	0	1	1	0.50	—					
Sutcliffe J. F.	2	0	·24	16	12.00	—					
Sutherland T.	14	9	74	21	14.80	—	446	11	40.54	6/111	1
Sykes E. C.	2	2	5	5*	—	—					
Tate E.	51	15	256	34*	7.11	—	1738	56	31.03	8/51	2
Tate F.	8	3	50	18*	10.00	—	147	13	11.30	6/63	2
Tate H. W.	54	9	499	61*	11.08	—	1744	96	18.16	6/51	6
Tayler R. F.	4	0	68	42	17.00	—					
Taylor G. R.	37	4	306	41	9.27	—	21	1	21.00	1/8	—
Taylor J. D.	8	3	76	27*	15.20	—	24	0	—	—	—
Taylor M. N. S.	198	39	3646	103*	22.93	2	7458	308	24.21	7/23	12
Tennyson											
Hon L. H.	553	20	12626	217	23.68	15	2374	43	55.20	3/50	—

Name	Inns	NO	Runs	HS	Avge	100s	Runs	Wkts	Avge	Best	5wI
Terry V. P.	201	24	6219	175★	35.13	12	39	0	—	—	—
Thompson											
H. R. P.	1	0	16	16	16.00	—	259	2	129.50	2/106	—
Thorne R.	4	0	9	6	2.25	—					
Thresher P.	9	1	93	47★	11.62	—	19	1	19.00	1/19	—
Timms B. S. V.	273	67	3236	120	15.70	1					
Tolfree E.	8	2	53	22★	8.83	—	185	2	92.50	2/13	—
Toynbee G. P. R.	1	0	14	14	14.00	—					
Toyne S. M.	2	0	10	9	5.00	—					
Tremlett T. M.	220	56	3449	102★	21.03	1	9321	404	23.07	6/53	11
Tubb S.	19	5	170	24★	12.14	—	746	37	20.16	7/32	2
Tuck J. J.	17	2	166	32★	11.06	—	36	2	18.00	1/11	—
Tulk D. T.	2	2	8	8★	—	—	70	0	—	—	—
Turner D. R.	621	63	17115	184★	30.67	25	338	9	37.55	2/7	—
Turner F. G.	1	0	14	14	14.00	—					
Ubsdell G.	29	4	179	29	6.80	—					
Underdown G.	16	0	227	63	14.18	—	80	1	80.00	1/15	—
Utley R. P. H.	34	9	164	27	6.56	—	2080	79	26.32	6/43	4
Waldron A. N. E.	3	0	74	52	24.66	—	131	3	43.66	2/66	—
Walker C.	215	32	4990	150★	27.25	8	2544	51	49.88	5/40	2
Walker D. F.	126	11	3004	147	26.12	22	0	—	—	—	—
Walkinshaw F.	5	0	15	11	3.00	—					
Wallace N. W.	4	0	57	25	14.25	—					
Walton F.	6	1	55	16	11.00	—	165	6	27.50	3/48	—
Ward A. P.	2	1	11	6	11.00	—	57	1	57.00	1/28	—
Ward C. G.	23	0	186	30	8.08	—	135	2	67.50	1/17	—
Ward H. F.	61	0	1344	113	22.03	2	553	19	29.10	4/17	—
Ward J.	2	0	14	11	7.00	—	77	0	—	—	—
Ward M. de S. C.	10	1	141	48	15.66	—	135	0	—	—	—
Wassell A. R.	158	25	1207	61	9.07	—	8573	317	27.04	7/87	11
Watson A. L.	2	0	22	22	11.00	—					
Watson I. R.	2	0	6	5	3.00	—					
Watts A. W.	3	0	26	11	8.66	—	42	2	21.00	1/9	—
Weaver P. H. P.	3	0	55	37	18.33	—					
Webb A. S.	268	16	5475	162★	21.72	2	1023	22	46.50	2/18	—
Webb H. E.	2	0	27	16	13.50	—					
Whalley-Tooker E.	4	0	14	7	3.50	—					
Wheatley K. J.	110	14	1781	79★	18.55	—	1954	69	28.31	4/1	—
Wheeler W. C.	6	1	35	15	7.00	—	186	6	31.00	6/133	1
Whitcher W.	4	2	27	17★	13.50	—	30	0	—	—	—
White D. W.	374	101	2967	58★	10.86	—	25630	1097	23.36	9/44	56
White W. N.	107	4	2827	160★	27.44	2	15	0	—	—	—
Wild T.	3	0	40	25	13.33	—					
Wild W.	2	1	10	8	10.00	—	11	0	—	—	—

Name	Inns	NO	Runs	HS	Avge	100s	Runs	Wkts	Avge	Best	5wI
Wilder G.	2	0	13	13	6.50	—	25	3	8.33	3/14	—
Willes E. H. L.	2	1	1	1*	1.00	—	7	0	—	—	—
Williams G. E.	2	0	16	15	8.00	—					
Willoughby F. G.	15	3	60	19	5.00	—	564	25	22.56	4/39	—
Wilson T. H.	4	0	15	9	3.75	—					
Wood Alfred H.	2	0	22	11	11.00	—					
Wood Arthur H.	49	3	849	82	18.45	—	17	0	—	—	—
Wood M.	2	0	0	0	0.00	—					
Wood M. D. F.	2	0	9	5	4.50	—					
Woodroffe K. H. C.	2	1	27	18*	27.00	—	216	8	27.00	5/33	1
Wootton J.	41	10	391	53	12.61	—	1867	69	27.05	5/37	5
Worrell L. R.	42	17	289	50	11.56	—	2116	65	32.55	5/67	1
Wright H. W.	2	0	12	12	6.00	—	70	1	70.00	1/70	—
Wyatt F. J. C.	16	3	73	14*	5.61	—	935	44	21.25	6/31	4
Wynyard E. G.	129	4	4322	268	34.57	7	1549	49	31.61	6/63	1
Yaldren C. H.	1	0	8	8	8.00	—	60	1	60.00	1/52	—
Yates H. W. M.	19	3	242	65*	15.12	—	23	0	—	—	—
Young C. R.	67	7	717	48	11.95	—	3258	149	21.86	7/19	8

All first-class career records are up to and including the 1987 season. Once match v MCC at Southampton Antelope in 1880 was 12-a-side, and in the match v Nottinghamshire at Nottingham in 1914, J. Stone was allowed to replace B. G. von B. Melle, therefore the 2,251 Hampshire matches × 11 plus 2 players gives a Hampshire match total of 24,763.

The following 15 matches were 'abandoned without a ball bowled' and are therefore not included in any of the Hampshire figures shown: v Surrey at The Oval, 1903; v Somerset at Bath, 1903; v Essex at Leyton, 1903; v Worcestershire at Worcester, 1927; v Lancashire at Manchester, 1931; v Glamorgan at Swansea, 1957; v Worcestershire at Southampton, 1960; v Warwickshire at Bournemouth, 1963; v Middlesex at Lord's, 1966; v Yorkshire at Bournemouth, 1974; v Australians at Southampton, 1977; v Middlesex at Lord's, 1978; v Leicestershire at Leicester, 1979; v Surrey at The Oval, 1981 and v Lancashire at Southampton, 1986.

RESULTS OF ALL INTER-COUNTY FIRST-CLASS MATCHES 1864–1987

Year	DY	EX	GM	GS	KT	LA	LE	MX	NR	NT	SM	SY	SX	WA	WO	YO
1864							LL						LL			
1865							L					LW				
1866												LW				
1867			LLD													
1870					LL											
1875					LL								LW			
1876	LW				WW											
1877	LL				LL											
1878	DL				LL											
1880													LL			
1881													LL			
1882											WL		WL			
1883											WL	DL	LW			
1884					LW						WL	LL	LL			
1885	LL				LL						LW	LL	LW			
1895	WL	LW				WW					WL	LL	DL	LL		LW
1896	LL	WW				LW					DL	LL	WW	DL		DL
1897	DW	LD			LL	WW					WD	DL	LD	DD		LL
1898	LD	LL			DD	WD					DW	LD	LL	DD		LL
1899	LW	LD			DL	DD					DW	WL	LL	DL	DW	LD
1900	LD	DL		LL	LL	DL					LL	LL	LD	DL	DL	LL
1901	WW				WL	LD	DW				WW	DD	DL		LD	LL
1902	LD				LL	DL					LW	LW	DL	LL	DL	
1903	WL	AD			LL	DD					AL	AL	LL	DL	LL	
1904	DW				LL	LL					LD	LD	LD	LW	LL	LL
1905	WD				LL	LL	DL				DD	LL	LL	DL	DL	LD
1906	WW				LL	DW	WW				LW	LL	DL	LD	DW	LL
1907	WL		LL		WL	LD	DW	DL			WW	LL	LD	LW	DL	DD
1908	LL		WL		LW	WD	DD	WW			WL	LL	WD	LD	LD	
1909	DW		DD		LL	WD	DD	LL			WD	LL	DL	WW	WW	
1910	WW		WW	LD	LL	LL			LL	WL	WW	LW	LD	DW	LW	DL
1911	WW		WD	DD	LL	WD	LL				DL	LD	WL	LD	WL	LW
1912	DW	DD		LD	DD		LW	DW			WD	DD	DD	DW	WW	DL
1913	LW	DD		LW	LL		DD	LD		DD	WW	LL	LW	LL	WW	LD
1914	WW	DW		DW	WW	LD	WW	LD		DD	WW	DD	WD	LW	DW	DD
1919		DW		DW	DL		LD				LW	WD	WD			LD
1920		WD		WL	LL	LL	LD	LL		LL	WL	LD	DL	DW	WW	WL
1921		WL	WW	WW	WL	LL	WW	LL		LD	WW	DL	DW	DW	WW	DL
1922		DD	WW	WW	LD	DW	DD	DL		DL	WW	LD	LW	WW	WW	WL
1923		LL	WD	DD	LL	DD	LD	DW		LW	WW	DD	WL	WW	WW	DL
1924		DD		DD	LL	DD	LL	LL	DW	LW	LD	WD	DD	DD	WW	DL
1925		LD		DD	WL	LL	WW	DD	LW	DD	WD	LL	LD	WL	DL	LD
1926		WD		WW	LL	LL	WD	DD	WW	LD	DD	DD	WW	DW	WD	DD

Year	DY	EX	GM	GS	KT	LA	LE	MX	NR	NT	SM	SY	SX	WA	WO	YO
1927		LL		DL	WL	LL	DD	LD	DD	DD	WL	DW	LD	DW	WA	DD
1928		DW		LD	LL	LL	LD	DW	DW	DD	LD	DD	DW	WD	DD	DD
1929	LL	DW	WW	LL	DD	LL	WW	LD			LD	DW	DL	DW	DW	LD
1930		LD	DW	WL	LD	DD	DL	DW	LW	WD	DD		DD	LD	DD	LL
1931	LL	LL	DW	WL	DL	DA	LW		DD	LD	DW	DD	WD	DD		DL
1932	WW	WW	DW	DD	LD	DD	DD	DL	WL	LL	LL	LL			WD	WL
1933	DD	LD		DL	WD	LD	DD	LW		LD	LD	DD	LD	LL	DD	DD
1934	WL	DL		DD	DD	LD	DD	DW	WL	LD	LD	LD	LL		LD	LD
1935	LL	WD	LD	WW	LW	DD	LL	DL	DW	LL	DD	LL	DL		LL	LL
1936	DD	WD	WW	DD	DD	DW	DD	DL	WD	DL	WL	DD	WL		DD	DL
1937	LD	LL	LL	LL	WL	DD	DL		WW		WL	WL	DL	LW	WL	LL
1938	WL	LW	LL	WL	WL	LL	DD	LD	DW	DL	WW	LL	WL	LW	LD	DL
1939		LL	DD	LL	LW	LL	LW	LL	DW	DL	DL	DD	DL	DD	LL	LL
1946	WL	WL	L	LL	DL	WL	W	LL	DD	L	LL	LD	WW	L	W	LW
1947	WL	DL	L	LD	LL	LT	L	LL	DD	D	DL	W	WW	D	D	DD
1948	D	W	LL	WW	WD	D	WD	L	W	LW	WL	DL	DW	LD	DD	L
1949	W	D	DD	DD	LL	D	WW	L	L	WL	LL	LW	LW	DL	LL	L
1950	DW	D	DD	WL	TD	DL	WL	WW	L	DD	LD	D	WW	L	LL	DL
1951	DL	D	DD	DD	WD	WL	DD	WD	D	WL	LD	D	LD	D	DW	LL
1952	D	DD	WD	LW	WD	L	LL	LW	LL	DW	WD	LL	WL	DD	D	L
1953	L	WD	WD	DD	WD	L	WD	LL	DD	WL	WD	LL	LL	DL	D	L
1954	WD	D	DD	WD	LD	DD	WD	LL	D	LD	DW	L	LL	D	DL	LL
1955	LW	W	WW	DW	DW	DW	LW	LW	W	LD	WW	W	TW	D	DW	WL
1956	D	DL	LL	DD	DD	L	WD	WL	WD	DD	WW	WL	WW	WD	D	D
1957	D	LL	DA	LW	DL	L	WW	WL	DL	DW	WL	LL	DL	DW	D	L
1958	LL	W	WW	WD	WW	LW	DW	LD	D	LW	WW	D	WL	D	WD	DL
1959	LD	D	WD	WL	LW	LW	LW	WL	W	WL	WL	D	WD	L	DD	LW
1960	DL	WD	WD	WL	WD	LL	DD	LW	DD	DW	DD	LD	DL	WW	DA	LD
1961	WW	WL	WL	WW	LD	WL	WW	LD	DW	WW	WW	WW	LW	DW	DW	DLD
1962	WD	DD	WD	DL	WD	WD	WD	WD	LL	DW	DD	DD	DD	DD	DL	LD
1963	L	LD	DL	WD	DD	D	WW	WL	LW	DD	DL	WD	LD	LA	D	W
1964	D	LD	DD	WD	DD	D	LW	DD	WL	DD	DL	DL	LD	LW	W	L
1965	DD	D	DD	DL	DD	WD	LW	DD	D	DW	DL	D	WD	D	DL	WD
1966	DD	D	LD	WW	DL	LD	DD	WA	D	DL	DD	D	WD	W	DD	DD
1967	D	WD	DD	WD	DL	L	LD	DT	LD	DD	WD	WD	LD	DL	D	W
1968	DD	WW	LL	WD	DL	D	WD	DD	DL	WD	DW	DD	DW	DW	L	D
1969	D	L	DD	DL	WW	D	LW	DD	L	DL	LW	D	LW	D	W	D
1970	D	D	DD	WD	DL	D	DD	DW	L	DD	WL	L	LD	W	D	L
1971	DD	L	DD	DD	DL	DL	D	L	LW	D	W	DW	DD	L	D	W
1972	D	D	DL	DL	DL	D	L	W	W	D	D	L	WD	L	W	D
1973	W	D	WD	DW	D	W	D	D	W	W	D	D	WD	W	WW	W
1974	D	W	LD	WD	WW	D	W	L	W	W	D	D	WL	W	W	A
1975	D	W	WL	WW	DD	W	L	L	L	W	W	L	WD	W	W	L
1976	D	L	W	LL	DW	D	L	W	L	D	DL	L	WL	L	L	D
1977	D	W	LD	LW	DD	D	L	D	W	W	DL	LD	DD	D	W	W
1978	D	L	DW	LD	LW	L	L	A	D	D	DD	WD	WD	L	D	D

Year	DY	EX	GM	GS	KT	LA	LE	MX	NR	NT	SM	SY	SX	WA	WO	YO
1979	W	L	WD	LL	DL	D	A	D	D	L	DD	LL	LL	W	D	D
1980	L	D	DD	DL	LD	L	L	L	L	L	DD	DL	DD	L	W	D
1981	W	W	WD	DL	LL	W	D	D	D	W	DL	AL	LL	D	W	D
1982	D	D	WW	LW	LW	W	D	L	D	L	DW	WL	DD	W	L	D
1983	DW	W	D	WD	DW	DD	D	L	D	WD	WD	D	DW	W	WW	L
1984	L	LL	D	DD	LL	W	L	LL	L	L	WD	L	DW	LD	L	DD
1985	W	W	WL	DW	DD	W	DW	D	DL	D	WD	DD	DD	D	D	D
1986	WW	W	D	LL	LD	DA	D	D	W	WD	DD	W	DD	W	LD	D
1987	L	DD	D	DW	WW	D	D	WD	L	D	DW	D	DD	WD	W	LD

Note: All matches are County Championship matches except all those up to and including 1885, the second match with Surrey in 1946 and the third match with Yorkshire in 1961.

RESULTS OF ALL SUNDAY LEAGUE
MATCHES 1969–1987

Year	DY	EX	GM	GS	KT	LA	LE	MX	NR	NT	SM	SY	SX	WA	WO	YO
1969	W	L	L	W	L	W	W	W	W	W	W	W	W	L	W	W
1970	L	L	W	L	W	L	W	L	L	L	L	W	W	W	L	W
1971	W	W	W	L	L	W	L	W	L	W	L	L	W	W	L	W
1972	L	L	A	T	A	W	W	A	L	W	L	W	L	W	W	W
1973	A	W	A	A	W	W	L	W	W	W	W	L	W	L	W	L
1974	A	L	W	W	L	W	L	W	L	W	A	L	W	W	W	W
1975	W	W	W	W	W	L	W	W	W	W	W	W	W	L	L	W
1976	W	W	L	L	W	W	L	W	L	L	L	W	W	L	W	L
1977	A	A	W	L	W	W	L	W	A	L	W	W	W	L	L	W
1978	L	W	W	W	W	W	A	W	L	W	A	L	W	W	W	W
1979	A	W	W	W	L	L	L	L	W	L	L	L	W	W	L	W
1980	W	W	A	W	W	L	W	L	W	L	W	L	A	L	L	L
1981	L	W	W	W	L	W	W	A	W	W	L	W	L	L	L	L
1982	W	W	W	L	W	T	L	L	L	W	W	T	L	W	L	W
1983	L	W	W	L	L	W	W	A	W	W	L	W	W	L	W	L
1984	W	L	W	W	L	L	L	L	W	L	W	L	L	W	L	W
1985	L	W	A	W	A	W	A	W	L	W	A	W	W	L	W	L
1986	W	W	W	A	W	W	W	L	W	L	W	W	L	W	W	W
1987	T	W	L	T	W	L	W	W	A	L	L	W	L	W	L	A

RESULTS OF ALL NATWEST TROPHY/ GILLETTE CUP MATCHES 1963–1987

1963 *1st Round*: lost to Derby.

1964 *1st Round*: beat Wilts; *2nd Round*: lost to Warwks.

1965 *1st Round*: beat Norfolk; *2nd Round*: beat Kent; *Q/Final*: lost to Warwks.

1966 *1st Round*: beat Lincs; *2nd Round*: beat Kent; *Q/Final*: beat Surrey; *S/Final*: lost to Worcs.

1967 *1st Round*: beat Lincs; *2nd Round*: beat Glam; *Q/Final*: lost to Sussex.

1968 *1st Round*: beat Bedford; *2nd Round*: lost to Warwks.

1969 *1st Round*: bye; *2nd Round*: lost to Surrey.

1970 *1st Round*: beat Bucks; *2nd Round*: lost to Lancs.

1971 *1st Round*: bye; *2nd Round*: beat Notts; *Q/Final*: lost to Warwks.

1972 *1st Round*: beat Wilts; *2nd Round*: beat Notts; *Q/Final*: lost to Lancs.

1973 *1st Round*: beat Wilts; *2nd Round*: lost to Kent.

1974 *1st Round*: beat Derbys; *2nd Round*: lost to Yorks.

1975 *1st Round*: bye; *2nd Round*: beat Glam; *Q/Final*: lost to Lancs.

1976 *1st Round*: bye; *2nd Round*: beat Leics; *Q/Final*: beat Derbys; *S/Final*: lost to Northants

1977 *1st Round*: beat Notts; *2nd Round*: beat Yorks; *Q/Final*: lost to Middx.

1978 *1st Round*: bye; *2nd Round*: lost to Leics.

1979 *1st Round*: beat Gloucs; *2nd Round*: lost to Middx.

1980 *1st Round*: bye; *2nd Round*: beat Derbys; *Q/Final*: lost to Yorks.

1981 *1st Round*: beat Cheshire; *2nd Round*: beat Glam; *Q/Final*: lost to Lancs.

1982 *1st Round*: bye; *2nd Round*: beat Derbys; *Q/Final*: lost to Surrey.

1983 *1st Round*: beat Herts; *2nd Round*: beat Glam; *Q/Final*: beat Gloucs; *S/Final*: lost to Kent.

1984 *1st Round*: beat Norfolk; *2nd Round*: lost to Kent.

1985 *1st Round*: beat Berks; *2nd Round*: beat Leics; *Q/Final*: beat Somerset; *S/Final*: lost to Essex.

1986 *1st Round*: beat Herts; *2nd Round*: lost to Worcs.

1987 *1st Round*: beat Dorset; *2nd Round*: lost to Leics.

RESULTS IN BENSON & HEDGES CUP COMPETITION 1972–1987

1972 Fourth in Group West.
1973 First in Group West; *Q/Final*: lost to Kent.
1974 First in Group West; *Q/Final*: lost to Somerset.
1975 First in Group West; *Q/Final*: beat Somerset; *S/Final*: lost to Leics.
1976 Fifth in Group A.
1977 Second in Group A; *Q/Final*: beat Glamorgan; *S/Final*: lost to Gloucs.
1978 Third in Group B.
1979 Fifth in Group B.
1980 Fifth in Group D.
1981 Third in Group D.
1982 Fifth in Group C.
1983 Second in Group C; *Q/Final*: lost to Kent.
1984 Third in Group D.
1985 First in Group D; *Q/Final*: lost to Leics.
1986 Third in Group D.
1987 Second in Group C; *Q/Final*: lost to Yorks.

GROUNDS USED BY HAMPSHIRE 1864–1987

Ground	First	Last	First-Class Record				
			P	W	L	D	
Officers Club, Aldershot	1905	1948	5	2	2	1	
Municipal Ground, Alton	1904	1904	1	–	1	–	
Mays Bounty, Basingstoke	1906	1987	30	10	9	11	
Dean Park, Bournemouth	1897	1987	324	89	111	121	(1 tied)
J. Samuel Whites, Cowes, I.O.W.	1956	1962	7	3	1	3	
Newport, I.O.W.	1938	1939	2	1	1	–	
United Services Ground, Portsmouth	1895	1987	291	96	79	115	(1 tied)
Green Jackets, St Cross, Winchester	1875	1875	1	–	1	–	
Antelope Ground, Southampton	1864	1884	27	11	14	2	
County Ground, Southampton	1885	1987	482	131	159	188	(1 tied)
Winchester College, Winchester	1875	1875	1	–	1	–	

TEAM RECORDS

(1) HIGHEST AND LOWEST SCORE FOR HAMPSHIRE AGAINST EACH COUNTY

Opponents	Highest	Year	Lowest	Year
Derbyshire	481 *at* Portsmouth	1934	23 *at* Burton-on Trent	1958
Essex	534-7 dec *at* Leyton	1913	54 *at* Southampton	1931
Glamorgan	495 *at* Bournemouth	1976	52 *at* Cardiff	1968
Gloucestershire	594-6 dec *at* Southampton	1911	36 *at* Clifton	1920
Kent	599 *at* Southampton	1912	31 *at* Maidstone	1967
Lancashire	487 *at* Liverpool	1901	37 *at* Manchester	1900
Leicestershire	548-6 dec *at* Southampton	1927	58 *at* Leicester	1907
Middlesex	578 *at* Southampton	1925	35 *at* Portsmouth	1932
Northamptonshire	500-9 dec *at* Northampton	1939	60 *at* Northampton	1930
			60 *at* Peterborough	1932
Nottinghamshire	507 *at* Southampton	1921	30 *at* Southampton	1932
Somerset	672-7 dec *at* Taunton	1899	44 *at* Bath	1911
Surrey	454-6 *at* The Oval	1928	32 *at* The Oval	1885
Sussex	517-8 dec *at* Hastings	1924	51 *at* Portsmouth	1903
Warwickshire	616-7 dec *at* Portsmouth	1920	15 *at* Birmingham	1922
Worcestershire	481-7 dec *at* Worcester	1923	30 *at* Worcester	1903
Yorkshire	521-8 dec *at* Portsmouth	1927	36 *at* Southampton	1898

(2) HIGHEST AND LOWEST SCORE AGAINST HAMPSHIRE BY EACH COUNTY

Opponents	Highest	Year	Lowest	Year
Derbyshire	645 *at* Derby	1898	47 *at* Portsmouth	1933
Essex	584-9 dec *at* Southampton	1927	69 *at* Colchester	1931
Glamorgan	488-8 dec *at* Cardiff	1938	36 *at* Swansea	1922
Gloucestershire	489 *at* Portsmouth	1949	34 *at* Bristol	1914
Kent	610 *at* Bournemouth	1906	32 *at* Southampton	1952
Lancashire	676-7 dec *at* Manchester	1911	54 *at* Portsmouth	1937
Leicestershire	535-8 dec *at* Leicester	1938	52 *at* Bournemouth	1931
Middlesex	642-3 dec *at* Southampton	1923	59 *at* Lord's	1956
Northamptonshire	497-5 *at* Northampton	1976	50 *at* Northampton	1926
Nottinghamshire	511-8 dec *at* Nottingham	1930	42 *at* Southampton	1932
Somerset	675-9 dec *at* Bath	1924	37 *at* Weston-super-Mare	1955

Surrey	742 *at* The Oval	1909	64 *at* Basingstoke	1986
Sussex	552-7 dec *at* Portsmouth	1904	38 *at* Eastbourne	1950
Warwickshire	657-6 dec *at*			
	Birmingham	1899	36 *at* Portsmouth	1927
Worcestershire	547 *at* Southampton	1903	68 *at* Dudley	1961
Yorkshire	585-3 dec *at* Portsmouth	1920	23 *at* Middlesbrough	1965

(3) HIGHEST AND LOWEST SCORES IN LIMITED-OVERS MATCHES

	Competition	*Score*	*Opponents and Venue*	*Year*
HIGHEST:	Sunday League (John Player/ Refuge Assurance)	292-1 (40 overs)	Surrey *at* Portsmouth	1983
	Benson & Hedges Cup	321-1 (55 overs)	Minor Counties South *at* Amersham	1973
	Nat West/Gillete	371-4 (60 overs)	Glamorgan *at* Southampton	1975
LOWEST:	Sunday League (John Player/ Refuge Assurance)	43 (24.1 overs)	Essex *at* Basingstoke	1972
	Benson & Hedges Cup	94 (37.4 overs)	Glamorgan *at* Swansea	1973
	Nat West/Gillette	98 (43.1 overs)	Lancashire *at* Manchester	1975

INDIVIDUAL BATTING RECORDS

(1) DOUBLE-CENTURIES IN FIRST-CLASS MATCHES

Score	Batsman	Opponents	Venue	Year
316	R. H. Moore	Warwickshire	Bournemouth	1937
304	R. M. Poore	Somerset	Taunton	1899
280*	C. P. Mead	Nottinghamshire	Southampton	1921
268	E. G. Wynyard	Yorkshire	Southampton	1896
259	C. G. Greenidge	Sussex	Southampton	1975
258*	C. B. Fry	Gloucestershire	Southampton	1911
249*	J. G. Greig	Lancashire	Liverpool	1901
248	T. E. Jesty	Cambridge University	Cambridge	1984
241	W. L. C. Creese	Northamptonshire	Northampton	1939
240	B. A. Richards	Warwickshire	Coventry	1973
235	C. P. Mead	Worcestershire	Worcester	1922
232*	G. Brown	Yorkshire	Leeds	1920
230	G. Brown	Essex	Bournemouth	1920
228*	R. E. Marshall	Pakistanis	Bournemouth	1962
227	J. Arnold	Glamorgan	Cardiff	1932
227	C. P. Mead	Derbyshire	Ilkeston	1933
225	E. G. Wynyard	Somerset	Taunton	1899
225*	B. A. Richards	Nottinghamshire	Nottingham	1974
224	C. P. Mead	Sussex	Horsham	1921
223*	R. M. C. Gilliat	Warwickshire	Southampton	1969
222	C. P. Mead	Warwickshire	Birmingham	1923
222	C. G. Greenidge	Northamptonshire	Northampton	1986
217	Hon L. H. Tennyson	West Indians	Southampton	1928
217	C. L. Smith	Warwickshire	Birmingham	1987
216	C. B. Llewellyn	South Africans	Southampton	1901
215	E. I. M. Barrett	Gloucestershire	Southampton	1920
213*	C. P. Mead	Worcestershire	Bournemouth	1925
213*	J. R. Gray	Derbyshire	Portsmouth	1962
213	C. P. Mead	Yorkshire	Southampton	1914
212	R. E. Marshall	Somerset	Bournemouth	1961
211*	C. P. Mead	Warwickshire	Southampton	1922
211	F. E. Lacey	Kent	Southampton Ant.	1884
211	C. G. Greenidge	Sussex	Hove	1978
209*	R. A. Smith	Essex	Southend	1987
208	C. G. Greenidge	Yorkshire	Leeds	1977
207*	C. P. Mead	Warwickshire	Southampton	1911
207	C. P. Mead	Essex	Leyton	1919
206	B. A. Richards	Nottinghamshire	Portsmouth	1968
206*	M. C. J. Nicholas	Oxford University	Oxford	1982

205	V. A. Barton	Sussex	Hove	1900
204	H. A. W. Bowell	Lancashire	Bournemouth	1914
204	G. Brown	Yorkshire	Portsmouth	1927
204	C. G. Greenidge	Warwickshire	Birmingham	1985
203★	C. B. Fry	Oxford University	Southampton	1912
203	N. T. McCorkell	Gloucestershire	Gloucester	1951
203	R. E. Marshall	Derbyshire	Derby	1972
200★	C. P. Mead	Essex	Southampton	1927
200	D. A. Livingstone	Surrey	Southampton	1962
200★	C. G. Greenidge	Surrey	Guildford	1977

(2) CENTURIES IN LIMITED-OVERS MATCHES
(a) Sunday League (John Player/Refuge Assurance)

Score	Batsman	Opponents	Venue	Year
172	C. G. Greenidge	Surrey	Southampton	1987
166★	T. E. Jesty	Surrey	Portsmouth	1983
163★	C. G. Greenidge	Warwickshire	Birmingham	1979
162★	C. G. Greenidge	Lancashire	Manchester	1983
155★	B. A. Richards	Yorkshire	Hull	1970
142	V. P. Terry	Leicestershire	Southampton	1986
132★	B. A. Richards	Kent	Bournemouth	1970
125★	C. G. Greenidge	Yorkshire	Bournemouth	1986
124★	C. G. Greenidge	Sussex	Hove	1985
123	B. A. Richards	Glamorgan	Basingstoke	1974
122	C. G. Greenidge	Middlesex	Bournemouth	1978
122	C. G. Greenidge	Nottinghamshire	Nottingham	1985
116	C. G. Greenidge	Yorkshire	Portsmouth	1978
114	D. R. Turner	Essex	Colchester	1984
112	B. A. Richards	Leicestershire	Bournemouth	1975
110★	T. E. Jesty	Yorkshire	Southampton	1982
110	V. P. Terry	Nottinghamshire	Southampton	1984
109	D. R. Turner	Surrey	The Oval	1980
108★	C. G. Greenidge	Surrey	Portsmouth	1983
108	M. C. J. Nicholas	Gloucestershire	Bristol	1984
107	T. E. Jesty	Surrey	Southampton	1977
105	B. A. Richards	Leicestershire	Leicester	1972
104	B. A. Richards	Glamorgan	Southampton	1970
104	R. A. Smith	Glamorgan	Cardiff	1984
104	R. A. Smith	Surrey	Southampton	1985
102	C. G. Greenidge	Sussex	Hove	1974
102	C. G. Greenidge	Somerset	Weston-super-Mare	1975
102	B. A. Richards	Middlesex	Lord's	1977
101	B. A. Richards	Worcestershire	Worcester	1972
101	B. A. Richards	Essex	Southampton	1976

100*	V. P. Terry	Leicestershire	Basingstoke	1983
100	T. E. Jesty	Essex	Southampton	1983

(b) Benson & Hedges Cup

Score	Batsman	Opponents	Venue	Year
173*	C. G. Greenidge	Minor Counties (S)	Amersham	1973
133	C. G. Greenidge	Combined Universities	Oxford	1987
129	B. A. Richards	Gloucestershire	Bristol	1974
123*	D. R. Turner	Minor Counties (S)	Amersham	1973
123	C. G. Greenidge	MCCA	Reading	1985
111	C. G. Greenidge	Leicestershire	Leicester	1975
105	T. E. Jesty	Glamorgan	Swansea	1977
103	C. G. Greenidge	Gloucestershire	Bristol	1977

(c) NatWest Trophy/Gillette Cup

Score	Batsman	Opponents	Venue	Year
177	C. G. Greenidge	Glamorgan	Southampton	1975
165*	V. P. Terry	Berkshire	Southampton	1985
143*	B. L. Reed	Buckinghamshire	Chesham	1970
140	R. E. Marshall	Bedfordshire	Goldington	1968
140*	C. L. Smith	Dorset	Southampton	1987
129	B. A. Richards	Lancashire	Bournemouth	1972
129	B. A. Richards	Glamorgan	Southampton	1975
118	T. E. Jesty	Derbyshire	Derby	1980
112	B. L. Reed	Bedfordshire	Goldington	1968
110	R. A. Smith	Somerset	Taunton	1985
108	C. G. Greenidge	Glamorgan	Swansea	1983
106*	C. G. Greenidge	Nottinghamshire	Southampton	1977
105	V. P. Terry	Somerset	Taunton	1985
102	R. E. Marshall	Lincolnshire	Basingstoke	1967
101*	B. A. Richards	Nottinghamshire	Southampton	1977
101*	C. L. Smith	Gloucestershire	Bristol	1983
100	C. G. Greenidge	Kent	Canterbury	1973
100*	D. R. Turner	Dorset	Southampton	1987

(3) Carrying bat through a completed First-class innings

The following opening batsmen have batted throughout a completed innings in which all ten of their partners have been dismissed.

Batsman	Score	Total	Opponents	Venue	Year
C. R. Seymour	77*	(154)	Surrey	Southampton Ant.	1883
F. E. Lacey	61*	(135)	Derbyshire	Southampton	1885
R. M. Poore	49*	(97)	Somerset	Bath	1898
J. G. Greig	249*	(487)	Lancashire	Liverpool	1901
C. P. Mead	88*	(223)	Warwickshire	Leamington Spa	1909

C. P. Mead	120*	(234)	Yorkshire	Huddersfield	1911
A. S. Kennedy	152*	(344)	Nottinghamshire	Nottingham	1921
G. Brown	103*	(188)	Middlesex	Bournemouth	1926
G. Brown	150*	(294)	Surrey	The Oval	1933
C. P. Mead	117*	(221)	Nottinghamshire	Nottingham	1935
J. Bailey	70*	(139)	West Indians	Bournemouth	1939
N. H. Rogers	32*	(68)†	Leicestershire	Loughborough	1953
N. H. Rogers	172*	(327)	Gloucestershire	Bristol	1954
N. H. Rogers	125*	(221)	Somerset	Glastonbury	1954
J. R. Gray	118*	(208)	Essex	Portsmouth	1956
J. R. Gray	118*	(214)	Somerset	Bournemouth	1964
B. A. Richards	127*	(192)†	Northamptonshire	Bournemouth	1969
C. G. Greenidge	196*	(341)	Yorkshire	Leeds	1973
B. A. Richards	225*	(344)	Nottinghamshire	Nottingham	1974
B. A. Richards	71*	(179)	Middlesex	Southampton	1975
T. M. Tremlett	70*	(182)	Leicestershire	Southampton	1980
C. G. Greenidge	157*	(270)	Glamorgan	Cardiff	1982

†Denotes completed innings in which ten wickets did not fall, one or more batsmen being retired/absent hurt/ill.

(4) CARRYING BAT THROUGH A COMPLETED LIMITED-OVERS INNINGS

(a) Sunday League (John Player/Refuge Assurance)

Batsman	Score	Total	Opponents	Venue	Year
B. A. Richards	155*	(215)	Yorkshire	Hull	1970
C. G. Greenidge	163*	(250)	Warwickshire	Birmingham	1979
C. G. Greenidge	162*	(268)	Lancashire	Manchester	1983
C. G. Greenidge	108*	(292)	Surrey	Portsmouth	1983

(b) Benson & Hedges Cup

Batsman	Score	Total	Opponents	Venue	Year
C. G. Greenidge	173*	(321)	Minor Counties (S)	Amersham	1973

(c) NatWest Trophy/Gillette Cup

Batsman	Score	Total	Opponents	Venue	Year
B. L. Reed	143*	(278)	Buckinghamshire	Chesham	1970
V. P. Terry	165*	(239)	Berkshire	Southampton	1985
C. L. Smith	140*	(304)	Dorset	Southampton	1987

(5) CENTURY IN EACH INNINGS OF A FIRST-CLASS MATCH

Scores	Batsman	Opponents	Venue	Year
104 and 119*	R. M. Poore	Somerset	Portsmouth	1899
115 and 130	J. G. Greig	Worcestershire	Worcester	1905

124 and 118*	A. J. L. Hill	Somerset	Southampton	1905
102 and 100	C. B. Llewellyn	Derbyshire	Derby	1905
130 and 101*	C. B. Llewellyn	Sussex	Hove	1909
123 and 112	C. B. Fry	Kent	Canterbury	1911
109 and 100*	C. P. Mead	Leicestershire	Leicester	1911
175 and 100*	A. C. Johnston	Warwickshire	Coventry	1912
102 and 113*	C. P. Mead	Leicestershire	Southampton	1913
113 and 224	C. P. Mead	Sussex	Horsham	1921
102 and 102*	J. A. Newman	Surrey	The Oval	1927
117 and 105*	D. A. Livingstone	Kent	Canterbury	1964
130 and 104*	B. A. Richards	Northamptonshire	Northampton	1968
159 and 108	B. A. Richards	Kent	Southampton	1976
136 and 120	C. G. Greenidge	Kent	Bournemouth	1978
104 and 100*	C. G. Greenidge	Lancashire	Liverpool	1983
143* and 141	T. E. Jesty	Worcestershire	Worcester	1984
110 and 100	C. L. Smith	Oxford Univ.	Oxford	1985
103 and 180*	C. G. Greenidge	Derbyshire	Derby	1986

(6) CENTURY ON FIRST-CLASS DEBUT FOR HAMPSHIRE

Score	Batsman	Opponents	Venue	Year
126	C. H. Abercrombie	Oxford University	Southampton	1913
151	D. O. Baldry	Glamorgan	Portsmouth	1959
101*	R. E. Hayward	Sri Lankans	Bournemouth	1981

(7) 2,000 FIRST-CLASS RUNS IN A SEASON FOR HAMPSHIRE

Batsman	Total	Year	Batsman	Total	Year
C. P. Mead	2,854	1928	R. E. Marshall	2,279	1959
C. P. Mead	2,671	1921	C. P. Mead	2,270	1922
R. E. Marshall	2,607	1961	R. E. Marshall	2,262	1960
C. P. Mead	2,576	1933	J. R. Gray	2,224	1962
C. P. Mead	2,495	1913	H. Horton	2,166	1960
H. Horton	2,428	1959	J. Arnold	2,136	1934
C. P. Mead	2,406	1923	J. R. Gray	2,121	1959
C. P. Mead	2,374	1914	R. E. Marshall	2,095	1962
C. P. Mead	2,231	1927	C. G. Greenidge	2,035	1986
H. Horton	2,329	1961	J. R. Gray	2,034	1961
C. P. Mead	2,326	1926	N. H. Rogers	2,020	1952
B. A. Richards	2,314	1968	C. P. Mead	2,011	1934
			C. L. Smith	2,000	1985

INDIVIDUAL BOWLING RECORDS

(1) HAT-TRICKS IN FIRST-CLASS MATCHES

Bowler	Opponents	Venue	Year
A. W. Ridley	Sussex	Hove	1875
J. A. Newman	Australians	Southampton	1909
A. S. Kennedy	Gloucestershire	Southampton	1920
A. S. Kennedy	Somerset	Bournemouth	1920
A. S. Kennedy	Gloucestershire	Southampton	1924
G. S. Boyes	Surrey	Portsmouth	1925
G. S. Boyes	Warwickshire	Birmingham	1926
O. W. Herman	Glamorgan	Portsmouth	1938
T. A. Dean	Worcestershire	Bournemouth	1939
D. W. White	Sussex	Portsmouth	1961
D. W. White	Sussex	Hove	1962
J. W. Holder	Kent	Southampton	1972
M. D. Marshall	Somerset	Taunton	1983

(2) NINE WICKETS IN AN INNINGS FOR HAMPSHIRE

Analysis	Bowler	Opponents	Venue	Year
9-25	R. M. H. Cottam	Lancashire	Manchester	1965
9-26	A. E. G. Baring	Essex	Colchester	1931
9-30	D. Shackleton	Warwickshire	Portsmouth	1960
9-33	A. S. Kennedy	Lancashire	Liverpool	1920
9-44	D. W. White	Leicestershire	Portsmouth	1966
9-46	A. S. Kennedy	Derbyshire	Portsmouth	1929
9-57	G. S. Boyes	Somerset	Yeovil	1938
9-59	D. Shackleton	Gloucestershire	Bristol	1958
9-77	D. Shackleton	Glamorgan	Newport	1953
9-81	D. Shackleton	Gloucestershire	Bristol	1959
9-131	J. A. Newman	Essex	Bournemouth	1921

(3) 15 WICKETS IN A MATCH FOR HAMPSHIRE

Analysis	Bowler	Opponents	Venue	Year
16-88	J. A. Newman	Somerset	Weston-super-Mare	1927
15-116	A. S. Kennedy	Somerset	Bath	1922
15-142	H. Baldwin	Sussex	Hove	1898

(4) SIX WICKETS IN A LIMITED-OVERS MATCH

(a) Sunday League (John Player/Refuge Assurance)

Analysis	Bowler	Opponents	Venue	Year
6-20	T. E. Jesty	Glamorgan	Cardiff	1975

(b) Benson & Hedges Cup

None

(c) NatWest Trophy/Gillette Cup

Analysis	Bowler	Opponents	Venue	Year
7-30	P. J. Sainsbury	Norfolk	Southampton	1965
6-46	T. E. Jesty	Gloucestershire	Bristol	1979

(4) 125 WICKETS IN A SEASON (100 SINCE 1969)

Total	Bowler	Year	Total	Bowler	Year
133	C. B. Llewellyn	1910	128	D. Shackleton	1952
156	J. A. Newman	1910	143	D. Shackleton	1953
139	A. S. Kennedy	1912	157	D. Shackleton	1955
160	A. S. Kennedy	1914	134	D. Shackleton	1956
164	A. S. Kennedy	1920	154	D. Shackleton	1957
170	A. S. Kennedy	1921	126	M. Heath	1958
177	J. A. Newman	1921	163	D. Shackleton	1958
190	A. S. Kennedy	1922	140	D. Shackleton	1959
174	A. S. Kennedy	1923	130	D. Shackleton	1960
148	J. A. Newman	1923	158	D. Shackleton	1961
132	A. S. Kennedy	1925	161	D. Shackleton	1962
145	J. A. Newman	1926	142	D. Shackleton	1964
143	A. S. Kennedy	1929	144	D. Shackleton	1965
126	A. S. Kennedy	1931	128	R. M. H. Cottam	1968
140	A. S. Kennedy	1932	119	A. M. E. Roberts	1974
142	O. W. Herman	1937	134	M. D. Marshall	1982
			100	M. D. Marshall	1986

RECORD WICKET PARTNERSHIPS

(1) IN FIRST-CLASS MATCHES

FIRST WICKET (Qualification 250)

347	V. P. Terry and C. L. Smith v Warwickshire at Birmingham	1987

SECOND WICKET (Qualification 250)

321	G. Brown and E. I. M. Barrett v Gloucestershire at Southampton	1920
302	V. P. Terry and T. E. Jesty v Cambridge University at Cambridge	1984
290	D. R. Turner and M. C. J. Nicholas v Oxford University at Oxford	1983
280	G. Brown and E. I. M. Barrett v Warwickshire at Portsmouth	1920
250	A. C. Johnston and C. P. Mead v Warwickshire at Coventry	1912

THIRD WICKET (Qualification 250)

344	G. Brown and C. P. Mead v Yorkshire at Portsmouth	1927
321	C. L. Smith and T. E. Jesty v Derbyshire at Derby	1983
311	C. G. Greenidge and D. R. Turner v Gloucestershire at Gloucester	1987
292	A. C. Johnston and C. P. Mead v Warwickshire at Southampton	1911
272	D. A. Livingstone and H. Horton v Middlesex at Bournemouth	1966
269	G. Brown and C. P. Mead v Yorkshire at Leeds	1920
267★	R. E. Marshall and D. A. Livingstone v Pakistanis at Bournemouth	1962
266	R. Aird and C. P. Mead v Sussex at Hastings	1924
264★	C. B. Fry and E. I. M. Barrett v Oxford University at Southampton	1912
259	J Arnold and C. P. Mead v Derbyshire at Portsmouth	1934
251★	C. G. Greenidge and T. E. Jesty v Glamorgan at Portsmouth	1982

FOURTH WICKET (Qualification 250)

263	R. E. Marshall and D. A. Livingstone v Middlesex at Lord's	1970
259	C. P. Mead and Hon L. H. Tennyson v Leicestershire at Portsmouth	1921
259	M. C. J. Nicholas and R. A. Smith v Leicestershire at Bournemouth	1985

FIFTH WICKET (Qualification 200)

235	G. Hill and D. F. Walker v Sussex at Portsmouth	1937
231	C. B. Llewellyn and E. I. M. Barrett v Derbyshire at Southampton	1903
219	C. B. Llewellyn and J. G. Greig v South Africans at Southampton	1901
219	C. P. Mead and H. L. V. Day v Kent at Southampton	1922
209	J. Bailey and N. H. Rogers v Worcestershire at Southampton	1946

SIXTH WICKET (Qualification 200)

411	R. M. Poore and E. G. Wynyard v Somerset at Taunton	1899
313	J. A. Newman and Hon L. H. Tennyson v West Indies at Southampton	1928
251	C. P. Mead and J. A. Newman v Warwickshire at Bournemouth	1928
202	J. R. Gray and G. Hill v Essex at Southampton	1952

SEVENTH WICKET (Qualification 150)

325	G. Brown and C. H. Abercrombie v Essex at Leyton	1913

270	C. P. Mead and J. P. Parker v Kent at Canterbury	1926
202	B. A. Richards and M. N. S. Taylor v Nottinghamshire at Nottingham	1974
161	C. Walker and R. O. Prouton v Leicestershire at Portsmouth	1953
159	C. B. Fry and E. M. Sprot v Worcestershire at Bournemouth	1910
154	P. J. Sainsbury and L. Harrison v Worcestershire at Worcester	1957
153	A. L. Hosie and W. H. Livsey v Middlesex at Portsmouth	1928
153*	P. J. Sainsbury and B. S. V. Timms v Northamptonshire at Southampton	1964
150	J. A. Newman and P. E. Lawrie v Glamorgan at Southampton	1921
150	G. Brown and J. A. Newman v Kent at Canterbury	1923

EIGHTH WICKET (Qualification 150)

227	K. D. James and T. M. Tremlett v Somerset at Taunton	1985
178	C. P. Mead and C. P. Brutton v Worcestershire at Bournemouth	1925
168	M. N. S. Taylor and G. R. Stephenson v Glamorgan at Southampton	1978
162	C. P. Mead and W. K. Pearce v Glamorgan at Southampton	1923
152*	K. D. James and R. J. Parks v Nottinghamshire at Bournemouth	1987

NINTH WICKET (Qualification 150)

230	D. A. Livingstone and A. T. Castell v Surrey at Southampton	1962
197	C. P. Mead and W. R. de la C. Shirley v Warwickshire at Birmingham	1923
177	G. Brown and W. H. Livsey v Warwickshire at Birmingham	1922
157	C. P. Mead and W. H. Livsey v Nottinghamshire at Southampton	1921

TENTH WICKET (Qualification 100)

192	H. A. W. Bowell and W. H. Livsey v Worcestershire at Bournemouth	1921
147	E. M. Sprot and A. E. Fielder v Gloucestershire at Bristol	1911
127	C. P. Mead and G. S. Boyes v Worcestershire at Worcester	1922
125	A. L. Hosie and W. L. Budd v Glamorgan at Bournemouth	1935
118	C. H. Abercrombie and H. A. H. Smith v Worcestershire at Dudley	1913
117*	R. Dare and R. O. Prouton v Worcestershire at Bournemouth	1952
113	J. G. Greig and C. Robson v Lancashire at Liverpool	1901
107	W. H. Livsey and A. Jaques v Worcestershire at Southampton	1914
106	G. Brown and A. S. Kennedy v Yorkshire at Bournemouth	1913

(2) IN LIMITED-OVERS MATCHES
(a) Sunday League (John Player/Refuge Assurance)
FIRST WICKET (Qualification 150)

221	C. G. Greenidge and V. P. Terry v Sussex at Hove	1985
164	B. A. Richards and C. G. Greenidge v Leicestershire at Leicester	1972
163	C. G. Greenidge and V. P. Terry v Leicestershire at Southampton	1986

SECOND WICKET (Qualification 150)

| 269* | C. G. Greenidge and T. E. Jesty v Surrey at Portsmouth | 1983 |

THIRD WICKET (Qualification 125)

| 132* | R. M. C. Gilliat and D. A. Livingstone v Yorkshire at Southampton | 1969 |
| 127 | C. G. Greenidge and V. P. Terry v Lancashire at Manchester | 1983 |

FOURTH WICKET (Qualification 125)

219	C. G. Greenidge *and* C. L. Smith *v* Surrey *at* Southampton	1987
148	M. C. J. Nicholas *and* C. L. Smith *v* Gloucestershire *at* Bristol	1984
144	T. E. Jesty *and* M. C. J. Nicholas *v* Yorkshire *at* Southampton	1982
134	R. A. Smith *and* C. L. Smith *v* Worcestershire *at* Portsmouth	1985

FIFTH WICKET (Qualification 100)

120*	N. G. Cowley *and* D. R. Turner *v* Northamptonshire *at* Southampton	1981
105	M. C. J. Nicholas *and* C. L. Smith *v* Gloucestershire *at* Southampton	1987
104	C. L. Smith *and* M. C. J. Nicholas *v* Essex *at* Ilford	1986
100	C. L. Smith *and* J. J. E. Hardy *v* Northamptonshire *at* Southampton	1984

SIXTH WICKET

83	N. E. J. Pocock *and* V. P. Terry *v* Gloucestershire *at* Basingstoke	1979

SEVENTH WICKET

75*	M. D. Marshall *and* R. J. Parks *v* Essex *at* Portsmouth	1987

EIGHTH WICKET

53	N. E. J. Pocock *and* G. R. Stephenson *v* Northamptonshire *at* Northampton	1978

NINTH WICKET

51	M. D. Marshall *and* R. J. Parks *v* Worcestershire *at* Southampton	1982

TENTH WICKET

30*	M. N. S. Taylor *and* A. M. E. Roberts *v* Middlesex *at* Southampton	1974

(b) Benson & Hedges Cup

FIRST WICKET (Qualification 150)

194	C. G. Greenidge *and* V. P. Terry *v* Combined Universities *at* Oxford	1987
164*	B. A. Richards *and* C. G. Greenidge *v* Gloucestershire *at* Bristol	1974

SECOND WICKET (Qualification 150)

285*	C. G. Greenidge *and* D. R. Turner *v* Minor Counties (S) *at* Amersham	1973

THIRD WICKET (Qualification 125)

157	D. R. Turner *and* T. E. Jesty *v* Glamorgan *at* Swansea	1977
134	C. L. Smith *and* T. E. Jesty *v* Kent *at* Canterbury	1980

FOURTH WICKET (Qualification 125)

107*	R. A. Smith *and* D. R. Turner *v* Somerset *at* Southampton	1985

FIFTH WICKET (Qualification 100)

109	D. R. Turner *and* N. G. Cowley *v* Gloucestershire *at* Southampton	1977

SIXTH WICKET

54	T. E. Jesty *and* P. J. Sainsbury *v* Somerset *at* Bournemouth	1973

STATISTICAL SECTION

SEVENTH WICKET
64   M. D. Marshall *and* N. G. Cowley *v* Essex *at* Chelmsford   1987

EIGHTH WICKET
61   N. G. Cowley *and* S. F. Graf *v* Surrey *at* The Oval   1980

NINTH WICKET
33   T. M. Tremlett *and* E. L. Reifer *v* Gloucestershire *at* Bristol 1984

TENTH WICKET
61   J. M. Rice *and* A. M. E. Roberts *v* Gloucestershire *at* Bristol 1975

(c) NatWest Trophy/Gillette Cup
FIRST WICKET (Qualification 150)
227   R. E. Marshall *and* B. L. Reed *v* Bedfordshire *at* Goldington   1968
220* C. G. Greenidge *and* B. A. Richards *v* Nottingham *at* Southampton   1977
210   B. A. Richards *and* C. G. Greenidge *v* Glamorgan *at* Southampton   1975
152   C. G. Greenidge *and* V. P. Terry *v* Berkshire *at* Southampton   1985

SECOND WICKET
112   R. E. Marshall *and* H. Horton *v* Lincolnshire *at* Basingstoke   1967

THIRD WICKET
194* C. L. Smith *and* D. R. Turner *v* Dorset *at* Southampton   1987

FOURTH WICKET
144   V. P. Terry *and* R. A. Smith *v* Somerset *at* Taunton   1985

FIFTH WICKET
141   T. E. Jesty *and* N. E. J. Pocock *v* Derbyshire *at* Derby   1980

SIXTH WICKET
66   P. J. Sainsbury *and* A. J. Murtagh *v* Derbyshire *at* Southampton   1976

SEVENTH WICKET
59   T. E. Jesty *and* G. R. Stephenson *v* Nottinghamshire *at* Nottingham   1972

EIGHTH WICKET
55   B. S. V. Timms *and* A. T. Castell *v* Sussex *at* Hove   1967

NINTH WICKET
57   A. C. D. Ingleby-Mackenzie *and* D. Shackleton *v* Kent *at* Southampton 1966

TENTH WICKET
45   A. T. Castell *and* D. W. White *v* Lancashire *at* Manchester   1970

WICKET-KEEPING RECORDS

(1) SIX DISMISSALS IN AN INNINGS

Ct	St	Keeper	Opponents and Venue	Year
1	5	G. Ubsdell	Surrey *at* Southampton Antelope	1865
4	2	B. S. V. Timms	Leicestershire *at* Portsmouth	1964
5	1	G. R. Stephenson	Middlesex *at* Lord's	1976
6	0	R. J. Parks	Derbyshire *at* Portsmouth	1981
6	0	R. J. Parks	Essex *at* Colchester	1984
5	1	R. J. Parks	Nottinghamshire *at* Southampton	1986

(2) EIGHT DISMISSALS IN A MATCH

Total	Ct	St	Keeper	Opponents and Venue	Year
10	10	0	R. J. Parks	Derbyshire *at* Portsmouth	1981
9	4	5	W. H. Livsey	Warwickshire *at* Portsmouth	1914

(3) SEVENTY DISMISSALS IN A SEASON

Keeper	Year	Total	Ct	St	Matches
L. Harrison	1959	83	76	7	29
R. J. Parks	1986	81	73	8	25
G. R. Stephenson	1970	80	73	7	24
W. H. Livsey	1921	80	48	32	29
B. S. V. Timms	1965	79	73	6	31
B. S. V. Timms	1964	77	58	19	30
R. J. Parks	1982	76	70	6	25
W. H. Livsey	1929	74	44	30	29
R. J. Parks	1984	71	61	10	25
B. S. V. Timms	1963	70	57	13	30

(4) 400 DISMISSALS IN A CAREER

Keeper	Career	Total	Ct	St
N. T. McCorkell	1932–1951	688	512	176
L. Harrison	1939–1966	666	567	99
G. R. Stephenson	1969–1980	645	570	75
W. H. Livsey	1913–1929	629	375	254
G. Brown	1908–1933	535	484	51
R. J. Parks	1980–1987	480	430	50
J. Stone	1900–1914	474	361	113
B. S. V. Timms	1959–1968	462	402	60

Note: These figures include some catches taken in the field

FIELDING RECORDS

(1) FIVE CATCHES IN AN INNINGS

Fielder	Opponents	Venue	Year
F. W. D. Quinton	Yorkshire	Harrogate	1896
C. P. Mead	Middlesex	Portsmouth	1912
G. Brown	Somerset	Bath	1914
G. Brown	Kent	Portsmouth	1932
B. A. Richards	Gloucestershire	Gloucester	1972
N. E. J. Pocock	Oxford University	Oxford	1979

(2) SEVEN CATCHES IN A MATCH

Fielder	Opponents	Venue	Year
T. A. Dean	Essex	Colchester	1947

(3) 40 CATCHES IN A SEASON

Total	Fielder	Year
56	P. J. Sainsbury	1957
46	P. J. Sainsbury	1961
43	P. J. Sainsbury	1958
41	C. P. Mead	1914
41	C. P. Mead	1923

(4) 300 CATCHES FOR HAMPSHIRE

Total	Fielder	Career
629	C. P. Mead	1905–1936
601	P. J. Sainsbury	1954–1976
484	G. Brown	1908–1933
482	A. S. Kennedy	1907–1936
474	G. S. Boyes	1921–1939
350	J. R. Gray	1948–1966
323	E. D. R. Eagar	1946–1957
315	C. G. Greenidge	1970–1987
313	H. M. Barnard	1952–1966

HAMPSHIRE PLAYERS' TEST RECORDS

Name	Country	Tests	M	Runs	Avge	Wkts	Avge
J. Arnold	England	1931	1	34	17.00		
G. Brown	England	1921–1922	7	299	29.90		
R. M. H. Cottam	England	1968–1972	2	8	8.00	9	20.00
C. B. Fry	England	1909–1912	9	340	28.33		
C. G. Greenidge	West Indies	1974–1986	71	5033	48.39	0	—
C. Heseltine	England	1895	2	18	9.00	5	16.80
A. J. L. Hill	England	1895	3	251	62.75	4	2.00
A. S. Kennedy	England	1922	5	93	15.90	31	19.32
C. B. Llewellyn	South Africa	1895–1912	8	311	22.31	39	25.82
M. D. Marshall	West Indies	1978–1986	45	953	19.44	249	23.28
R. E. Marshall	West Indies	1951	4	143	20.42	0	—
C. P. Mead	England	1911–1922	17	1185	49.37		
B. A. Richards	South Africa	1969	4	508	72.57	1	26.00
A. M. E. Roberts	West Indies	1973–1983	71	762	14.94	202	25.61
D. Shackleton	England	1950–1963	7	113	18.83	18	43.66
C. L. Smith	England	1983–1986	8	392	30.15	3	13.00
Hon L. H. Tennyson	England	1913–1921	9	345	31.36	0	—
V. P. Terry	England	1984	2	16	5.33		
D. W. White	England	1961	2	0	0.00	4	29.75
E. G. Wynyard	England	1896–1905	3	72	12.00	0	—

HAMPSHIRE CAPTAINS

1864–1869	G. M. Ede	1936–1937	R. H. Moore
1870	A. H. Wood	1938	C. G. A. Paris
1875–1878	C. Booth	1939	G. R. Taylor
1880–1882	H. W. R. Bencraft	1946–1957	E. D. R. Eagar
1883–1885	A. H. Wood	1958–1965	A. C. D. Ingleby-
1895	H. W. R. Bencraft		Mackenzie
1896–1899	E. G. Wynyard	1966–1970	R. E. Marshall
1900–1902	C. Robson	1971–1978	R. M. C. Gilliat
1903–1914	E. M. Sprot	1979	G. R. Stephenson
1919–1933	Lord (Hon) L. H.	1980–1984	N. E. J. Pocock
	Tennyson	1985–1987	M. C. J. Nicholas
1934–1935	W. G. L. F. Lowndes		

HAMPSHIRE CRICKETERS TO BE AWARDED A BLUE AT OXFORD

H. S. Altham 1911, 1912
F. H. H. Bathurst 1948
E. H. Buckland 1884, 1885, 1886, 1887
E. D. R. Eagar 1939
J. D. Eggar 1938
A. H. Evans 1878, 1879, 1880, 1881
A. J. Evans 1909, 1910, 1911, 1912
W. H. B. Evans 1902, 1903, 1904, 1905
H. W. Forster 1887, 1888, 1889
J. St J. Frederick 1864, 1867
C. A. Fry 1959, 1960, 1961
C. B. Fry 1892, 1893, 1894, 1895
T. P. Garnier 1861, 1862, 1863
R. M. C. Gilliat 1964, 1965, 1966, 1967
F. G. G. Jellicoe 1877, 1879

E. C. Lee 1898
W. H. Lipscomb 1868
W. G. L. F. Lowndes 1921
W. N. McBride 1926
B. G. von B. Melle 1913, 1914
J. D. Piachaud 1958, 1959, 1960, 1961
R. B. Proud 1939
G. B. Raikes 1894, 1895
C. H. Ridding 1845, 1846, 1847, 1848, 1849
W. Ridding 1849, 1850, 1852, 1853
A. W. Ridley 1872, 1873, 1874, 1875
O. Spencer-Smith 1866
W. A. Stewart 1869, 1870
H. E. Webb 1948
E. H. L. Willes 1852, 1853, 1854

AT CAMBRIDGE

R. Aird 1923
A. C. P. Arnold 1914
J. P. Blake 1939
C. Booth 1862, 1863, 1864, 1865
L. Burry 1877
A. G. Cowie 1910
L. H. Gay 1892, 1893
C. F. E. Goldie 1981, 1982
A. J. L. Hill 1890, 1891, 1892, 1893
A. K. Judd 1927
F. E. Lacey 1882

G. H. Longman 1872, 1873, 1874, 1875
H. C. McDonnell 1903, 1904, 1905
H. J. Mordaunt 1888, 1889
E. Olivier 1908, 1909
H. M. Plowden 1860, 1861, 1862, 1863
W. N. Powys 1871, 1872, 1874
A. G. J. Rimell 1949, 1950
W. R. de la C. Shirley 1924
A. C. Shirreff 1939
R. A. Studd 1895
K. H. C. Woodroffe 1913, 1914

BROTHERS WHO HAVE REPRESENTED HAMPSHIRE

F. T. A. H. Bathurst, L. H. Bathurst
G. N. Bignell, H. G. Bignell
D. E. Blake, J. P. Blake
A. C. Cecil, E. D. C. Cecil
A. J. Duncan, D. W. J. Duncan
E. L. Ede, G. M. Ede (twins)
A. E. Evans, D. M. Evans
A. J. Evans, R. du B. Evans
E. E. Light, W. F. Light
F. W. D. Quinton, J. M. Quinton

A. B. Ridley, A. W. Ridley
J. S. Rutherford, A. P. Rutherford
C. L. Smith, R. A. Smith
G. J. spencer-Smith, O. Spencer-Smith
(twins)
Sir H. Stewart, W. A. Stewart
H. W. Studd, R. A. Studd
F. Tate, H. W. Tate
C. G. Ward, H. F. Ward

FATHERS AND SONS WHO HAVE REPRESENTED HAMPSHIRE

Father	Sons(s)	Father	Sons(s)
E. Barrett	E. I. M. Barrett	A. H. Evans	A. J. Evans
Sir F. H. H. Bathurst	F. T. A. H. Bathurst		R. du B. Evans
	L. H. Bathurst	C. B. Fry	S. Fry
H. A. W. Bowell	N. H. Bowell	S. Fry	C. A. Fry
S. Brutton	C. P. Brutton	C. R. Gunner	J. H. Gunner
E. L. Ede	E. M. C. Ede	O. S. Herman	R. S. Herman
		A. J. L. Hill	A. E. L. Hill

HAMPSHIRE CRICKETERS EDUCATED AT WINCHESTER COLLEGE

C. E. Briggs
E. H. Cadogan
E. S. Crofts
H. G. S. Davies
A. J. Evans
D. M. Evans
R. du B. Evans
T. P. Garnier
D. R. Guard

J. C. Moberly
F. H. Nugent
F. A. V. Parker
S. H. H. Pearce
R. B. Proud
B. L. Reed
C. H. Ridding
W. Ridding
Sir H. Stewart

G. G. Gutteres
P. M. Hall
A. C. Johnston
J. L. Kaye
A. M. Lee
E. C. Lee
F. A. G. Leveson-
Gower
H. C. McDonell

W. A. Stewart
P. Thresher
G. P. R. Toynbee
A. L. Watson
H. E. Webb
E. H. L. Willes

Sir M. Wood
H. W. M. Yates

CRICKETERS WHO PLAYED FOR THE TEAM RAISED BY THE HAMBLEDON CLUB

Edward Aburrow 1772–82
James Aylward 1773–93
– Baker 1777
William Barber 1769–77
James Bayley 1773–83
William Beldham 1787–93
Henry Bonham 1778
George Boult 1786–89
Thomas Brett 1769–78
– Clay 1791
– Colchin 1774
– Cole 1784
– Collins 1791
Rev Reynell Cotton 1773
T. Davis 1773–76
William Fennex 1786
F. Foster 1791
George Foster 1791
– Francis 1775
Richard Francis 1774–84
Andrew Freemantle 1791–93
John Freemantle 1780–82
John Goldsmith 1791
E. Hale 1791
W. Hall 1782
David Harris 1782–93
– Hawkins 1786
William Hogflesh 1769–75
– Horne 1773
Edward Hussey 1786
– Lawrence 1773

George Leer 1769–82
M. Lewis 1773
George Louch 1789
Noah Mann 1777–89
John Nyren 1783–91?
Richard Nyren 1768–86
(owing to lack of initials it is not possible to separate Richard and John Nyren's matches in every case)
Richard Purchase 1773–93
Thomas Ridge 1769–75
Thomas Scott 1791–93
– Skinner 1781
John Small 1768–96
John Small jun 1787–96
Thos Assheton Smith 1789
Henry Stewart 1798
James Stewart 1791
John Stewart 1791
Peter Stewart 1769–79
– Stone 1778
Thomas Sueter 1769–91
4th Earl of Tankerville 1777–80
Thomas Taylor 1775–91
Richard Aubrey Veck 1776–84
– Vincent 1789–91
Harry Walker 1784–93
Thomas Walker 1786–93
James Wells 1783–89
John Wells 1787–93
8th Earl of Winchelsea 1786–89

BIBLIOGRAPHY

H. S. Altham, John Arlott, E. D. R. Eagar and Roy Webber: *The Official History of Hampshire County Cricket Club* (Phoenix House, London, 1957)

F. S. Ashley-Cooper: *Hampshire County Cricket* (G. W. May, 1924)

F. S. Ashley-Cooper: *The Hambledon Cricket Chronicle* (Herbert Jenkins, London, 1924)

P. Bailey, P. Thorn, P. Wynne-Thomas: *Who's Who of Cricketers* (Newnes, Feltham, 1984)

H. Doggart: *The Heart of Cricket* (Hutchinson, London, 1967)

C. B. Fry: *Life Worth Living* (Eyre & Spottiswoode, London, 1939)

G. Greenidge: *The Man in the Middle* (David & Charles, Newton Abbot, 1980)

John May: *Cricket in North Hants* (Warren, Basingstoke, 1906)

John Nyren: *The Young Cricketer's Tutor* (Effingham Wilson, 1833)

Association of Cricket Statisticians: *Hampshire Cricketers 1861–1982*

ACKNOWLEDGEMENTS

The records and statistics were most kindly provided by Victor Isaacs, whose research into the 'figures' of Hampshire cricket has made him the authority on this complex subject. The biographical details of the players were the work of members of the Association of Cricket Statisticians, co-ordinated by Philip Thorn.

References to 'first-class' records conform to the various Guides to First-Class Cricket published by the Association of Cricket Statisticians.

Photographs have been kindly supplied by the following sources:
Patrick Eagar
Hampshire CCC
Nottinghamshire CCC
Victor Isaacs
Bill Smith
The Mansell Collection

The author and publishers would also like to thank the Hampshire County Cricket Club and its officials for their assistance in the gathering of information for this book; and the Chief Executive of the County Club for providing a preview of Hampshire's future prospects.

INDEX

Magick Unveiled

ALEX POLAK